A special issue of
Cognition and Emotion

Basic Emotions

Edited by

Nancy L. Stein

Department of Psychology, University of Chicago, U.S.A.

and

Keith Oatley

*Centre of Applied Cognitive Science, Ontario Institute for
Studies in Education, and Department of Psychology,
University of Toronto, Canada*

LEA LAWRENCE ERLBAUM ASSOCIATES, PUBLISHERS LEA
Hove (UK)   Hillsdale (USA)

Lawrence Erlbaum Associates Ltd., Publishers
27 Palmeira Mansions
Church Road
Hove
East Sussex, BN3 2FA
U.K.

British Library Cataloguing in Publication Data

Basic Emotions. – (Cognition & Emotion Series; v.6)
    I. Stein, Nancy L.   II. Oatley, Keith
    III. Series
    152.4

    ISBN 0–86377–905–0
    ISSN 0269–9931

Cover design by Joyce Chester
Index by Sue Ramsey
Typeset by Acorn Bookwork, Salisbury, U.K.
Printed and bound in the U.K. by BPCC Wheatons, Exeter

Contents

[*]This book is also a special double issue of the journal *Cognition and Emotion* which forms issues 3 and 4 of Volume 6 (1992). The page numbers used here are taken from the journal and so begin with p. 161.

COGNITION AND EMOTION, 1992, 6 (3/4), 161–168

Basic Emotions: Theory and Measurement

Nancy L. Stein

Department of Psychology, University of Chicago, U.S.A.

Keith Oatley

Centre of Applied Cognitive Science, Ontario Institute for Studies in Education, and Department of Psychology, University of Toronto, Canada

There have been new conceptualisations and new evidence bearing on the question of whether or not some emotions are basic. There has been innovation in work on cognitive appraisals of emotions, in cross-cultural research, and in developmental psychology. We introduce some of these ideas, and in introducing the contributors to this volume, we lay out four considerations that affect understanding of whether or not some emotions are basic. These considerations are the separability of components of emotion, the differences of definitions, and indicators used by different theorists of basic emotions, questions about whether some emotions are derived from others, and mappings between elicitors, accompaniments, and consequences of emotions.

INTRODUCTION

The question of whether some emotions are basic or fundamental is not new. What is new is an interest in the question from the perspective of cognitive psychology. Until recently, adherents to theories of basic emotions have approached the issue primarily from an evolutionary perspective (e.g. Plutchik, 1980). Although the demands of adaptation by means of evolution are still considered central, for cognitive theorists the focus has shifted to functions and effects of emotions in cognitive processing. Moreover, researchers in the cognitive tradition, those who work biologically and those whose research is cross-cultural are finding that the question of whether some emotions are or are not basic has united some of their

Requests for reprints should be sent to Nancy L. Stein, Department of Psychology, University of Chicago, 5848 University Avenue, Chicago, IL 60637, U.S.A.

concerns. The focus on basicness is critical because the stance each researcher takes on the issue is directly related to conceptions of how mental processes are organised.

Although there are variations, common elements of proposals that some emotions are basic have included the following: Emotions are real psychological entities, and some finite number of them are human universals. As Darwin (1872/1965) proposed, similarities of emotional expression and behaviour occur in many animal species including humans. Similarities also occur within the human species, both between infancy and adulthood, and across cultures. Therefore, generation and recognition of the facial expressions of certain specific emotions should occur in all cultures (Ekman, 1982; Ekman & Friesen, 1975). Perhaps also classification of emotion terms in human languages are based on universal dimensions (Russell, 1991; Russell, Lewicka, & Niit, 1989). If certain emotions are spoken of in some societies but not in others, the implication is that such emotions are elaborations or combinations of basic emotions. To those who believe that there are some basic emotions, this kind of formulation is a starting point, much like accepting the notion that humans have opposable thumbs, even though activities carried out with hands vary both individually and cross-culturally.

Those who argue against the idea of basic emotions have done so for different reasons. James (1890) argued that emotions named in ordinary language are too heterogeneous for scientific study. He also said that sorting emotions thus named into conceptual categories was a scientifically useless activity, because the categories would vary with the predispositions of the person making the distinctions—and his stricture would hold for categories of basic and non-basic emotions. In support of the Jamesian position, Mandler (1984) has shown how the lists of emotions taken to be basic by different theorists indicate a substantial disagreement, and this implies that the notion of basic emotions is not to be taken seriously. James believed that folk-theoretical categories and ideas of emotion will be replaced by scientific accounts.

Another criticism levelled at basic emotion theories comes from social constructionists and linguists. Some (e.g. Harré, 1986; Lutz, 1988; Wierzbicka, this volume) argue that cultures differentially influence the construction of emotion categories. Therefore, no one set of emotions can be seen as basic. Instead, socialisation will result in the construction of different categories, different manifestations, and different experiences of emotions in different cultures. For Lutz and Wierzbicka there are human universals, but these are not the categories that appear as terms for emotions in any one human language.

At present we in the field of emotion research are in the fruitful position of being able to compare several theories that have been formulated with sufficient specificity to enable tests to be carried out. At the same time empirical evidence is accumulating. Thus, we can bring to bear evidence on the competing positions that have been advanced about whether or not some emotions are basic.

A central motivation for organising this Special Issue was to discuss different approaches to the idea of basic emotions. Contributors were asked to specify their theories and the kinds of data that would put us in a better position to understand whether or not the notion of basic emotions is viable. A second motivation was to discuss the validity of the claim that emotions are elicited primarily by cognitive appraisals of the environment (environment, here, includes both external and internal dimensions). Here, distinctively cognitive research has been the driving force. It has led both to new conceptions both of what basic emotions might be, and to strong arguments against the idea of basic emotions.

THE DEVELOPMENT OF APPRAISAL THEORY

The importance of cognitive appraisals in the elicitation of emotion dates back at least to the work of Arnold (1945) and Arnold and Gasson (1954). They set forth a theory of how different cognitive appraisals could give rise to different emotions. Moreover, they laid out an explicit model of how appraisals occur. For example, Arnold and Gasson argued that the first type of appraisal is a categorisation of an event or object as positive or negative.

Depending upon this, a tendency (e.g. decision) to move towards or away from the object is activated. Thus, on the one hand emotions like love and hope arise, involving a positive tendency of moving toward the object, and on the other hand emotions like hatred and despair arise, involving a negative tendency of moving away. Arnold and Gasson go on to argue for further appraisals of eliciting events (e.g. whether the object is actually present, the degree of difficulty in attaining or avoiding it, etc.). In their theory, the elicitation of each emotion, as it is referred to in ordinary language, is made up of a number of components, where each component of the appraisal pattern requires a specific cognitive judgement (e.g. is the object wanted or unwanted, are the circumstances favourable or unfavourable, etc.). Moreover, each judgement in the appraisal has some distinctive outcome (e.g. an urge towards or away from an object, a physiological change that directs attention to favourable or unfavourable conditions, etc.).

According to this kind of theory, if the specific appraisals about an object or event were known, then the resultant emotion could be predicted. A substantial amount of research on the viability of mapping patterns of appraisal to the elicitation of specific emotions has been completed (e.g. Ellsworth, 1991; Frijda, 1986, 1987; Stein & Levine, 1987, 1989). As well as contributing to the basic research others, notably Roseman, Spindel, and Jose (1990), Roseman (1991), and Scherer (1988), have made detailed comparisons of the different theories.

The question of whether or not a set of basic emotions exists rests not so much on whether each emotion label, as used in any particular natural language, maps on to a distinctive appraisal pattern. Rather, the question of basicness resides in further implications that can be derived—for instance, of a universal biological basis of the emotion programmes elicited by appraisals, and of developmental priorities in which certain categories of emotion emerge before others.

Within the paradigm of appraisal research Smith (1989) provided evidence that has stimulated the debate about basic emotions yet further. Following the less formal observations of Darwin (1872/1965), Smith provided evidence linking specific experimental manipulations of appraisal to specific components of emotional expression and physiology that he measured. Using a directed imagery task, he asked his subjects to relive emotions in response to scenarios written to vary different aspects of appraisal. Among his findings were that increased heart rate was associated with appraisals of high effortfulness, and that eyebrow frowns were associated with perception of goal obstacles. He interpreted his results as indicating that each kind of appraisal caused a distinctive behavioural and physiological resultant.

Ortony and Turner (1990) suggested that components of the kind that Smith proposed (appraisal-resultant pairings) might be prewired, and independent of each other. They inferred that there are no basic emotions. Rather, each appraisal may elicit a specific physiological, behavioural, and mental resultant. If some appraisal-resultant pairings tend to occur in groups each of which can be referred to in some language as an emotion, this is because the conditions that tend to elicit them often occur together in the environment, and perhaps in the specific environments of a particular culture.

This line of argument is clearly a challenge to theorists of basic emotions. It has been partly responsible for stimulating us to organise this Special Issue of *Cognition and Emotion*. It has also been responsible for stimulating theorists of basic emotions to define their positions more closely. Part of this debate has occurred in *Psychological Review*, with the paper of Ortony and Turner (1990), and replies by Izard (in press) and Panksepp (in press). Ellsworth (1991) has also recently argued that the componential structure of the appraisal process might necessitate a revision of current theories of basic emotions.

CONTRIBUTORS TO THE SPECIAL ISSUE

What we have done for this Special Issue of *Cognition and Emotion* is to ask some researchers who have new developments of theory relevant to the issue of basic emotions, or new pieces of evidence relevant to this issue, to contribute. Attention has been given to examining the different assumptions used to support a theory of basic emotions. Several investigators have arguments to support or refute the notion of basic emotions. In this volume, Ekman, Johnson-Laird and Oatley, and Stein and Trabasso advance claims and evidence that would support a theory of basic emotions. Camras and Davidson take issue with some aspects of current theories of basic emotions, bringing evidence to bear that does not neatly fit into current models of basic emotions. Wierzbicka, although not denying universality in this domain, and indeed proposing a new basis for it, shows how variation in the languages of different cultures leads to variation in emotion categories.

We will not summarise each of these contributions here—we will let the contributors speak for themselves. We believe that each contribution represents a substantial step towards clarifying the questions surrounding basic emotions, and that together they enable us to reach new and more satisfying understanding of emotions.

FOUR ISSUES IN DECIDING WHETHER OR NOT BASIC EMOTIONS EXIST

In attempting to understand the requirements for theories of basic emotions, and for theories denying basic emotions, we believe four issues need to be addressed. The first concerns the separability and independence of components that comprise the appraisal process and lead to emotional responses. Can individual components in the process of appraisal occur alone and function independently of one another? Or are certain portions of the appraisal process more like a patterned motor neuronal network, in which a group of components function in synchrony to create a patterned output when a certain set of conditions activates it? The answer to this question does not directly predict whether or not a basic emotions theory will be supported. What the answers would tell us, however, is how different investigators conceive of the primitives of emotion categories. For example, in Ortony and Turner's (1990) argument against basic emotions, the components of the appraisal process are taken to be independent of one another. Oatley and Johnson Laird (1987), and Johnson-Laird and Oatley (this volume), argue that, on the contrary, each basic emotion is elicited as one psychological piece, as a psychological primitive that cannot be further decomposed. Moreover, according to them, basic emotion categories can be defined by these primitive components. Stein and Trabasso (this volume) also support a theory of basic emotions, but they argue that although the components of the appraisal process can be decomposed into individual components (e.g. do I like this event, do I want to maintain its existence, have the conditions for its maintenance changed?, etc.), the elicitation of any basic emotion is dependent upon a specific pattern of components being activated. They argue that activating any single component will not in and of itself elicit any of the basic emotions. Their argument is similar to that of Ekman (this volume).

A second issue concerns the fact that different theorists list different numbers and kinds of basic emotions. If emotion categories were universal, then why should this be? What needs to be clarified here, we believe, is whether the same or different definitions of emotion, and same or different indicators of emotions are being used. The definition of emotion affects which emotions are thought to be basic. For example, in some systems (Mandler, 1984; Stein & Levine, 1987) surprise is not an emotion even though it has a corresponding facial expression. Although surprise signals an unexpected change in the environment, the change can be either good or bad. Thus, if a theory requires that each basic emotion specify information about the direction of an unexpected change, surprise will not be a basic emotion. For investigators who do not include this constraint in their definition of emotion categories, then surprise may be included among basic emotions because it has a unique facial expression (Ekman, this volume; Ekman & Friesen, 1975), and the indicator of facial expression is the one for which some of the best evidence has been gathered.

A third issue concerning the notion of basicness is which emotion categories are considered to be basic and which are considered to be variants or developments of the basic categories. An example of the problem can be seen by comparing theories such as Stein and Levine's (1987), and Roseman's (1991). In Roseman's scheme, a distinction is made between the category of happiness (getting something that was wanted) and the category of relief (not having to continue to tolerate an aversive state). In Stein and Levine's theory (1987), although these two combinations are different (one focused on attaining a positive state, the other focused on avoiding an aversive state), these two combinations are treated as equivalent because both result in the promotion of a positive state of well-being. Both lead to the maintenance of important goals. The question remains: Are both happiness and relief basic categories of emotion? Or, is relief part of the larger category of happiness from which it can be derived? More radically, no decompositions based on English emotion terms may be satisfactory: Instead as Wierzbicka (this volume) argues we should hypothesise universals that are not bound to any single human language.

She postulates some universals of this kind that could underlie the semantics of emotion terms.

Fourth, there is an issue of whether each emotion needs to have a corresponding unique precipitating event, an associated state of the autonomic nervous system, an expression, and a behavioural response. Some theories of basic emotions imply that there are such unique elicitors, accompaniments, and resultants. Camras (this volume), however, provides data to show that elicitation of emotion in infants can be quite different from elicitation in adults. Some of the expressions that in adults are taken to indicate discrete emotions, such as anger and sadness, might indicate different degrees of distress. Stein and Trabasso (this volume) contend that no one set of precipitating events can be shown always to elicit the same emotion. Rather, it is in the inferences brought to bear on constructing the meaning of the precipitating event that a pattern of appraisals will define each basic emotion.

Davidson raises similar issues with respect to whether or not unique behavioural actions follow from the experience of different emotions. For example, some theorists believe that anger should always involve an approach toward an object whereas fear should involve withdrawal. Moreover, unique patterns of autonomic activity should be found with each emotion. According to Davidson, however, these unique mapping relations do not exist for all instances of a particular emotion. Ekman (this volume) argues that a specific one-to-one correspondence between the experience of an emotion and its expression does not need to occur as emotions can be inhibited, and there can be competition among the different emotions. However, when components of the expressive systems are not being inhibited, each emotion will carry unique behavioural characteristics that can be used to distinguish one emotion from another. Investigators are now having to reckon with the absence of simple one-to-one mappings between elicitors, accompaniments, and consequences of emotion, at least in some situations. Such mappings, and the circumstances that affect them, then become a central issue.

The overall contribution of this volume is part of an effort to delineate what it means to support or oppose a theory of basic emotions. This Special Issue includes papers that press towards more specificity of theory, and hence towards more discriminability among the different approaches. Moreover, contributors present new evidence and suggest ways of actively testing working hypotheses. The reader will not find definitive answers to all the questions that can be raised about basic emotions. Each article does, however, advance our understanding of whether or not there are basic emotions, and of the implications of the new ideas and findings.

Manuscript received 26 November 1991

REFERENCES

Arnold, M.B. (1945). Physiological differentiation of emotional states. *Psychological Review*, 52, 35–48.

Arnold, M.B. & Gasson, J.A. (1954). Feelings and emotions as dynamic factors in personality integration. In M.B. Arnold and J.A. Gasson (Eds), *The human person*. New York: Ronald.

Darwin, C. (1872). *The expression of the emotions in man and animals*. [Reprinted, 1965.] University of Chicago Press.

Ekman, P. (1982). *Emotion in the human face*. Cambridge University Press.

Ekman, P. & Friesen, W.V. (1975). *Unmasking the face: A guide to recognizing emotions from clues*. New Jersey: Prentice Hall.

Ellsworth, P. (1991). Some implications of cognitive appraisal theories of emotion. In K.T. Strongman (Ed.), *International review of studies on emotion*. Chichester: Wiley.

Frijda, N.H. (1986). *The emotions*. Cambridge University Press.

Frijda, N.H. (1987). Emotion, cognitive structure, and action tendency. *Cognition and Emotion*, 1, 115–143.

Harré, R. (Ed.) (1986). *The social construction of emotions*. Oxford: Blackwell.

Izard, C.E. (In press). Basic emotions, relations among emotions, and emotion-cognition relationships. *Psychological Review*.

James, W. (1890). *The principles of psychology*. New York: Holt.

Lutz, C. (1988). *Unnatural emotions: Everyday sentiments on a Micronesia atoll and their challenge to Western theory*. University of Chicago Press.

Mandler, G. (1984). *Mind and body: Psychology of emotions and stress*. New York: Norton.

Oatley, K. & Johnson-Laird, P. (1987). Toward a cognitive theory of emotion. *Cognition and Emotion*, 1, 29–50.

Ortony, A. & Turner, T.J. (1990). What's basic about basic emotions? *Psychological Review*, 97, 313–331.

Panksepp, J. (In press). A critical role for "affective neuroscience" in resolving what is basic about basic emotions: Response to Ortony and Turner. *Psychological Review*.

Plutchik, R. (1980). A general psychoevolutionary theory of emotion. In R. Plutchik & H. Kellerman (Eds), *Emotion: Theory, research and experience*, Vol. 1, *Theories of emotion*. New York: Academic Press.

Roseman, I.J. (1991). Appraisal determinants of discrete emotions. *Cognition and Emotion*, 5, 161–200.

Roseman, I.J., Spindel, M.S., & Jose, P.E. (1989). Appraisals of emotion-eliciting events: Testing a theory of discrete emotions. *Journal of Personality and Social Psychology*, 59, 899–915.

Russell, J.A. (1991). Culture and the categorization of emotion. *Psychological Bulletin*, 110, 426–450.

Russell, J.A., Lewicka, M., & Niit, T. (1989). A cross cultural study of a circumplex model of affect. *Journal of Personality and Social Psychology*, 57, 848–856.

Scherer, K.R. (1988). Criteria for emotion antecedent appraisal: A review. In V. Hamilton, G.H. Bower, & N.H. Frijda (Eds), *Cognitive perspectives on emotion and motivation*. Kluwer: Dordrecht.

Smith, C.A. (1989). Dimensions of appraisal and physiological response in emotion. *Journal of Personality and Social Psychology*, 56, 339–353.

Stein, N.L. & Levine, L.J. (1987). Thinking about feelings: The development and organization of emotion knowledge. In R.E. Snow & M. Farr (Eds), *Aptitude, learning, and instruction: Cognition, conation, and affect*, Vol. 3. Hillsdale NJ: Lawrence Erlbaum Associates Inc, pp. 165–198.

Stein, N.L. & Levine, L.J. (1989). The causal organisation of emotion knowledge. A developmental study. *Cognition and Emotion*, 3, 343–378.

COGNITION AND EMOTION, 1992, 6 (3/4), 169–200

An Argument for Basic Emotions

Paul Ekman
University of California, San Francisco, U.S.A.

Emotions are viewed as having evolved through their adaptive value in dealing with fundamental life-tasks. Each emotion has unique features: signal, physiology, and antecedent events. Each emotion also has character-istics in common with other emotions: rapid onset, short duration, unbidden occurrence, automatic appraisal, and coherence among responses. These shared and unique characteristics are the product of our evolution, and distinguish emotions from other affective phenomena.

INTRODUCTION

In this article I reach beyond what is empirically known, to consider what the evidence suggests is likely to be found. What I present is more of a research agenda than a theory about emotion, although theory is involved. I will indicate where I think the evidence is clear, where it is tentative, where it is merely anecdotal but seems persuasive, and where I am simply extrapolating or guessing.

The logic which underlies this effort is my attempt to answer questions which arose when I and others found evidence, more than 20 years ago, that certain facial expressions of emotion appeared to be universal (for a recent review of that work see Ekman, 1989). These findings forced me to reject my previous beliefs that: (1) a pleasant-unpleasant scale was suf-ficient to capture the differences among emotions; and (2) the relationship between a facial configuration and what it signified is socially learned and culturally variable. I found in Darwin (1872/1965) and Tomkins (1962) an

---

Requests for reprints should be sent to Paul Ekman, University of California – San Francisco, 401 Parnassus, San Francisco, CA 94143–0984, U.S.A.

I thank Richard Davidson, Phoebe Ellsworth, Wallace V. Friesen, Dacher Keltner, Richard Lazarus, Robert Levenson, Harriet Oster, and Erika Rosenberg for their helpful criticisms and suggestions on earlier versions of this paper. I also thank the Editors of this Special Issue, Nancy Stein and Keith Oatley, for their encouragement and helpful criticisms. Preparation was supported by a Research Scientist Award from the National Institute of Mental Health (MH06091).

alternative framework which better fit my data, although I do not accept in total what either said.

There are two key issues, which I use the adjective *basic* to convey about the position I have adopted and will explain here. (1) There are a number of separate emotions which differ one from another in important ways. (2) Evolution played an important role in shaping both the unique and the common features which these emotions display as well as their current function.[1] Let me explain each of these ideas in more detail.

A number of separate, discrete, emotional states, such as fear, anger, and enjoyment, can be identified which differ not only in expression but probably in other important aspects, such as appraisal, antecedent events, probable behavioural response, physiology, etc. This basic emotions perspective is in contrast to those who treat emotions as fundamentally similar in most respects, differing only in terms of one or more dimensions, the most common ones being arousal, pleasantness, and activity; or those who carve emotions into just a positive and a negative state.[2]

Those who describe separate emotions differ in terms of how many different basic emotions they recognise (although there is considerable overlap, far more than Ortony and Turner, 1990, acknowledge), and what specific characteristics they posit such emotions share. Most of my presentation will describe nine characteristics of the emotions of anger, fear, sadness, enjoyment, disgust, and surprise. I will also raise the possibility that contempt, shame, guilt, embarrassment, and awe may also be found to share these nine characteristics.

To identify separate discrete emotions does not necessarily require that one also take an evolutionary view of emotions. A social constructionist could allow for separate emotions without embracing the second meaning of the adjective "basic". Even the discovery of universals in expression or in antecedent events does not require giving a major role to evolution. Instead, one can attribute universals to species-constant learning—social

---

[1]A third usage of the term "basic" is to postulate that other non-basic emotions are combinations of the basic emotions, which may be called blends or mixed emotional states (Ekman & Friesen, 1975; Plutchik, 1962; Tomkins, 1963; Tomkins & McCarter, 1964). I will not deal with this usage of the phrase basic emotions. Instead, my focus will be upon the first two meanings of basic emotions—that there are separate discrete emotions, which have evolved to prepare us to deal with fundamental life-tasks. I am grateful to K. Oatley for suggesting that I make clear these different ways in which the term basic has been used.

[2]In earlier writings (Ekman, Friesen, & Ellsworth, 1972) we made this same distinction in terms of those who studied the recognition of emotion from the face in terms of emotion *categories* or emotion *dimensions*.

learning which will usually occur for all members of the species regardless of culture (cf. Allport, 1924). In this view, it is ontogeny not phylogeny which is responsible for any commonalities in emotion, universals in expression are due to what ethologists call conventionalisation not ritualisation (see Ekman, 1979, for a discussion of these distinctions as applied to emotion).

The second meaning of the adjective "basic" is to indicate instead the view that emotions evolved for their adaptive value in dealing with *fundamental life-tasks*. Innate factors play a role in accounting for the characteristics they share, not species-constant or species-variable learning. There are a number of ways to describe these fundamental life-tasks. Johnson-Laird and Oatley (this issue) say they are "universal human predicaments, such as achievements, losses, frustrations, etc. . . . [E]ach emotion thus prompts us in a direction which in the course of evolution has done better than other solutions in recurring circumstances that are relevant to goals". Lazarus talks of "common adaptational tasks as these are appraised and configured into core relational themes" (1991, p. 202) and gives examples of facing an immediate danger, experiencing an irrevocable loss, progressing towards the realisation of a goal, etc. Stein and Trabasso (this issue) say that in happiness a goal is attained or maintained, in sadness there is a failure to attain or maintain a goal, in anger an agent causes a loss of a goal, and in fear there is an expectation of failure to achieve a goal. Toobey and Cosmides tell us that emotions impose ". . . on the present world an interpretative landscape derived from the covariant structure of the past . . ." Emotions they say (1990, pp. 407–408) deal with recurrent ". . . adaptive situations[,] [f]ighting, falling in love, escaping predators, confronting sexual infidelity, and so on, each [of which] recurred innumerable times in evolutionary history . . ." Toobey and Cosmides emphasise what I consider the crucial element which distinguishes the emotions: Our appraisal of a current event is influenced by our ancestral past.

These different descriptions are quite compatible, each emphasising another aspect of the phenomenon. Common to all these views is the presumption that emotions are designed to deal with inter-organismic encounters, between people or between people and other animals. Nevertheless, it is important to note that emotions can and do occur when we are not in the presence of others, and are not imagining other people. We can have emotional reactions to thunder, music, loss of physical support, auto-erotic activity, etc. Yet I believe the primary function of emotion is to mobilise the organism to deal quickly with important interpersonal encounters, prepared to do so in part, at least, by what types of activity have been adaptive in the past. The past refers in part to what has been adaptive in the past history of our species, and the past refers also to what has been adaptive in our own life history.[3]

Before saying more about the characteristics which distinguish emotions from other affective states, I must first explain the concept of emotion families, containing both a distinguishing theme and a number of variations around that theme.

EMOTION FAMILIES

Each of the basic emotions is not a single affective state but a *family* of related states (Ekman & Friesen, 1975). In using the term family I do not mean to imply the structure of a human family, but more generally to refer to "a group of things related by common characteristics" (*Webster's ninth new collegiate dictionary*, 1987). Each member of an emotion family shares certain characteristics, for example, commonalities in expression, in physiological activity, in nature of the antecedent events which call them forth, and perhaps also in the appraisal processes. These shared characteristics within a family differ between emotion families, distinguishing one family from another.

My use of the term "family" can be illustrated by Ekman and Friesen's (1975, 1978) description of the family of anger expressions. They specified not one anger expression but more than 60 anger expressions. Each of the anger expressions share certain configurational (muscular patterns) features, by which they recognisably differ from the family of fear expressions, disgust expressions, etc. For example, in all members of the anger family the brows are lowered and drawn together, the upper eyelid is raised and the muscle in the lips is tightened. Other muscular actions may or may not be evident in anger expressions, such as a tightened lower eyelid, lips pressed together tightly or tightly open in a square shape, tightening of the lip corners, pushing the lower lip upwards, etc. Variations in the family of anger facial expressions are hypothesised to reflect whether or not the anger is controlled, whether the anger is simulated or spontaneous, and the specifics of the event which provoked anger. There is also

---

[3]Fridlund (1991) created a false dichotomy between those who consider facial expressions to have solely an interpersonal signalling function and those who consider such expressions to be emotional responses linked to other aspects of emotional experience. Obviously they are both, and in no way unrelated. Fridlund also claims that facial expressions do not occur unless another person is present and dismisses any evidence to the contrary as being due to one imagining another person to be present. Ekman and Friesen (1969) took a more complex position, proposing that the presence or absence of others can act to amplify or de-amplify expressions, depending upon the social context and their role relationships.

evidence that the strength of the muscular contractions are related to intensity of a reported emotion (Ekman, Friesen, & Ancoli, 1980).

Each emotion family can be considered to constitute a *theme* and *variations*. The theme is composed of the characteristics unique to that family. The variations on that theme are the product of various influences: individual differences in biological constitution; different learning experiences; and differences specific to and reflecting the nature of the particular occasion in which an emotion occurs. Ohman's (1986) description of a multiple-level evolutionary perspective suggests that the themes may be largely the product of our evolution and given genetically, while the variations reflect learning, both species constant and species variable learning experiences. This learning, he maintains (p. 127) is "...constrained and shaped by evolution".

There are some resemblances to the way I am using the term family, with theme and variations and Rosch's (1973) discussion of categories and prototypes. I am proposing that the themes are not simply the most common feature of a basic emotion category, but are the core elements, the product of our evolution, to be found in all instances of an emotion. Also, I do not propose that the boundaries between basic emotion families are fuzzy.[4]

There is some evidence about which are the themes and which are the variations in regards to facial expression, but it is far from conclusive. Presumably, there should be greater cross-cultural consensus about theme expressions than about the expressions which represent the variations within a family, but no one has yet done such research. One of the major empirical tasks ahead is to isolate the theme and variations for each emotion family, considering not just expression, but also physiology, subjective experience, appraisal, and other cognitive activities. (On identification of the themes for cognitive appraisal see Johnson-Laird and Oatley, this issue; Roseman, 1991; Stein and Trabasso, this issue.)

The confusion which has plagued the field of emotion research about what are the emotions, has been due, I believe to two problems. The first has been the failure to recognise that many of the emotion terms refer to variations within a family. Shaver, Schwartz, Kirson, and O'Connor (1987, p. 1072) analysing their subjects similarity rating of emotion words, came to a similar conclusion although they did not utilise the term emotion family.

---

[4]I am grateful to the editors for urging that I make some mention of how this part of my discussion relates to Rosch. Space does not allow a full discussion of how my use of family, basic, and theme differs from Rosch.

It seems possible, given the results, that all of the terms in the emotion lexicon—at least the hundred or so that are most prototypical of the category *emotion*—refer in one way or another to a mere handful of basic-level emotions. Each term seems to specify either the intensity of the basic emotion in question . . . or the antecedent context in which the emotion arises . . .[5]

Johnson-Laird and Oatley's (1989) analysis of emotion words supported their contention that there are five basic emotions: happiness; sadness; anger; fear; and disgust. Their list is exactly the same as the group of emotions which share the nine characteristics I will describe. The names we use to refer to the basic emotions should attempt to denote the family theme. There should be many other emotion names within a family for lexically marked variations. But, there is no reason to expect that our usual use of language will perfectly represent this matter.

The confusion about what are the emotions has been due not just to a failure, by some, to organise emotions into families, with themes and variations, but also to a failure to distinguish emotions from other affective phenomena, such as moods, emotional traits and attitudes, and emotional disorders. At the conclusion of this paper I will briefly describe these other affective phenomena which differ from the emotions.

THE NINE CHARACTERISTICS WHICH DISTINGUISH BASIC EMOTIONS

Table 1 lists these characteristics which I will separately consider. Some distinguish one emotion from another (1, 3, and 4). The other characteristics I propose are useful in distinguishing emotions from other affective states, such as moods, emotional traits, emotional attitudes, etc. I have not included three characteristics which some might expect to be on such a list—ontogeny, thought processes, and subjective experience.

I acknowledge that the first appearance of each emotion is an important matter, and how emotion is socialised and changes over the life course is central to our understanding of emotion. But I do *not* maintain that if biology has played an important role in emotion then emotions must appear, fully differentiated, at birth or early in life before much opportun-

---

[5]Shaver et al.'s list of basic emotions and the emotion families listed at the beginning of this paper only partially overlap, but that may be because Shaver considered only the lexicon, examined subjects who were not experiencing an emotion, and asked for abstract ratings of words rather than how people talk about emotion. There is no reason to expect that the lexicon, particularly what emerges from rating scales, will map perfectly with what is found by analysing spontaneous emotional behaviour, focusing on expression, physiology, and actual emotion talk.

TABLE 1
Characteristics which Distinguish Basic Emotions from One Another
and from Other Affective Phenomena

	Basic with regard to:	
	Distinctive States	Biological Contribution
1. Distinctive universal signals	x	x
2. Presence in other primates		x
3. Distinctive physiology	x	x
4. Distinctive universals in antecedent events	x	x
5. Coherence among emotional response		x
6. Quick onset		x
7. Brief duration		x
8. Automatic appraisal		x
9. Unbidden occurrence		x

ity for learning has occurred. Izard (1977) disagrees and has reported evidence which he believes shows the early appearance of each emotion. His position and evidence has been convincingly challenged by Camras (this issue) and also by Oster, Hegley, and Nagel (in press). When this matter is settled, regularities in the first appearance of each emotion may be useful in differentiating one emotion from another, and thus usefully added to Table 1.

I expect that specific emotions regulate the way in which we think, and that this will be evident in memories, imagery, and expectations. I suspect that the relationship between emotions and thoughts are not solely a function of social learning because of biological constraints put on the thought system as well as the emotion system. I have not included this in my list of characteristics because it is not yet clear how thought processes are related to other characteristics of emotional behaviour.

The subjective experience of emotion, how each emotion feels, is for some at the centre of what an emotion is. This presumably includes physical sensations, and other feelings which are the consequence of feedback from the various response changes which occur uniquely for each emotion. Again this is excluded because too little is known about how subjectivity maps on to other aspects of an emotional experience.

Distinctive Universal Signals

The strongest evidence for distinguishing one emotion from another comes from research on facial expressions. There is robust, consistent evidence of a distinctive, universal facial expression for anger, fear, enjoyment, sadness, and disgust. This evidence is based not just on high agreement across literate and preliterate cultures in the labelling of what these expressions signal, but also from studies of the actual expression of emotions, both deliberate and spontaneous, and the association of expressions with social interactive contexts (see Ekman, 1989, for a recent overview).

It should be noted, however, that for each emotion more than one universal expression has been identified, but their description here would take me further afield (see Ekman & Friesen, 1975, 1978). Although the study has not been done in other cultures Etcoff's (1990) novel study of the judgement of faces, which found few confusions exist at the boundaries between emotions, also provides strong evidence in support of the view that there are a number of separate emotions. (See Johnson-Laird and Oatley, this issue, for a description of Etcoff's study.)

The evidence for a unique facial expression for surprise and contempt is not as firm. Surprise expressions were recognised across literate cultures, and in the two studies of preliterate cultures (reported in Ekman, 1972) surprise was distinguished from anger, disgust, and happiness, but the surprise faces were distinguished from fear faces in only one of the two preliterate cultures studied. Etcoff and Magee (in press) found evidence that surprise is perceived differently than other emotions, not defining an exclusive category. It would be important to know if her findings on surprise and on other emotions would replicate in other languages.

Contempt expressions were not included in preliterate culture studies, and the current evidence on literate cultures is contradictory (Ekman & Friesen, 1986, 1988; Ekman & Heider, 1988; Izard & Haynes, 1988; Russell, in press; Ricci-Bitti, Brighetti, Garotti, & Boggi-Cavallo, 1988). There are a number of new studies again confirming that contempt expressions are recognised across cultures (Ekman, O'Sullivan, & Matsumoto, in press; Matsumoto & Kudoh, submitted).

Izard (1971) reported cross-cultural evidence for an interest expression, but it is not clear whether he isolated an expression which was different from simple visual attention. Also, in Izard's cross-cultural studies the observers may have chosen interest by exclusion. There are similar problems with the stimulus Izard used for shame in his cross-cultural studies, in which the person is looking away from the camera.

Facial muscle movement is only one form of expression. Tomkins (1962) postulated a distinct vocal expression for each of the emotions which have distinctive facial expressions. Although there is as yet no empirical evidence across Western and non-Western cultures to determine whether this is so, I expect that when that work is done Tomkins will be proven correct.

It is not possible to be certain that there are no other emotions which have a universal facial expression, but none have been suggested. Friesen and I inspected hundreds of hours of motion picture films of spontaneous behaviour in two preliterate cultures (taken by Carleton Gajdusek in the 1960s), and saw no other expressions than the ones I have discussed. But that is only an impression, and those who believe there are other universal expressions should obtain the evidence.

I believe that emotional expressions provide information to conspecifics, as well as to other animals, about antecedent events, concomitant responses, and probable next behaviour. For example, when you see a person with a disgust expression, you know that the person is responding to something offensive to taste or smell, literally or metaphorically, that the person is likely to make sounds such as "yuck" rather than "yum", and is likely to turn away from the source of stimulation. We still lack systematic cross-cultural data to support my claim about what an expression signals. It requires obtaining open-ended responses from subjects who are shown expressions out of context and asked to describe what they can infer. Stein, Trabasso, and their colleagues have done some of that work with children, but to date on only some emotions, and only in our own culture.

Emotional expressions are crucial to the development and regulation of interpersonal relationships. To mention just three examples, facial expressions should be involved in the formation of attachments (in infancy as well as in courtship), and in the regulation, acceleration, or deceleration of aggression. People I have studied who have congenital facial paralysis (Mobius syndrome) report great difficulty in developing and maintaining even causal relationships if there is no capability for facial expressiveness.[6] Ross (1981) also found that stroke patients who can not properly identify the prosody that accompanies speech or who cannot generate the prosody that accompanies emotion utterances have severe interpersonal difficulties.

Basic emotions can occur without any evident signal. This may be due to deliberate or habitual attempts to inhibit the appearance of a signal. Also, a threshold may need to be crossed to bring about an expressive signal, and that threshold may vary across individuals. If we could measure the brain areas which send information to the facial nucleus during spontaneous emotional experience, I expect we would find that there is some distinctive activity even in low threshold states or when an individual is attempting to inhibit emotion. This remains an empirical question.

Should we consider an affective state to be a basic emotion if there never is a distinctive signal? I will return to that question after describing the other eight characteristics of basic emotions.

The evidence of universality in expression is consistent with the view, espoused by Darwin (1872/1965), that these expressions, and the emotions they signal, are the product of evolution. Ortony and Turner (1990) and

---

[6]See a report by a Mobius patient (Goldblatt & Williams, 1986).

Ellsworth (1991) have offered a different interpretation of this evidence, proposing that it is the single muscle actions which have universal meaning, not their combination into full face emotional expressions. I (Ekman, in press) have shown how their proposal is not supported by much systematic research and contradicts known facts about the muscular basis of facial expressions.[7]

The finding of universal facial expressions is consistent with an evolutionary explanation of emotion, but does not rule out alternative explanations. Allport (1924) explained how learning experiences common to all humans could account for the origin of the disgust expression. All that is innate is the muscle movements that are required to eject matter from the oral cavity. All infants will make those movements when they regurgitate food which tastes or smells bad. Over time all members of the species will associate those facial muscle movements with anything which is metaphorically related, producing this disgust expression to social events which are distasteful. I (Ekman, 1979) offered a similar explanation for the origin of the raised brows in surprise. All biology contributes, from this viewpoint, is that raising the brows increases the superior visual field allowing more to be seen and more light to enter the retina. All members of the species might learn to use this muscular action in expressions like surprise which metaphorically involve taking in more or unexpected input. It is much harder to explain the smile in enjoyment, or the sad facial expression on the basis of species-constant learning.

This explanation would be compelling if it were shown that congenitally blind children never raise the brow in surprise. Unfortunately there is no definitive data relevant to this or to any other crucial test of the species-constant learning explanation of universal facial expressions. The evolutionary explanation is strengthened by data, albeit not very strong or systematic, on the presence of some emotional expressions in other primates.

Comparable Expressions in other Animals

Darwin considered such evidence crucial, for it was his interest in demonstrating the power of evolutionary theory which led him to write *The expression of emotion in man and animals* (1872/1965). In modern times,

---

[7]There is no evidence to support their claim that the four muscle actions they describe have universal signal value. Even if some elemental muscle movements were to be shown to have universal signal value, that would not prove that the meaning of the complex facial expressions is derived from the meanings of the muscular elements. It might just as well be the reverse. Ortony and Turner's view also implies that all facial expressions of emotion are composed of more than one element, which is not the case for disgust.

Plutchik (1962) was the first to make this characteristic the organising principle of his theory of emotion.

There is some evidence for similar facial expressions in other primates for fear and anger, possibly also for sadness and happiness (Chevalier-Skolnikoff, 1973; Redican, 1982). Unfortunately, the work they cite is old, and based on casual rather than systematic study of this question. No primatologist has specifically attempted to identify the universe of facial expressions in another species to compare them to what is known about human expressions. The techniques for measuring human expression in muscular terms (Ekman & Friesen, 1976, 1978; Izard, 1979), could be modified for use with other primates, allowing very precise comparisons of the muscular displays.

Although the more systematic primate studies have yet to be completed, researchers have observed that other primates generate facial expressions similar to those observed in humans. These observations are also consistent with an evolutionary explanation of the origin of expression, and more generally with the position that biology plays an important role in these emotions. There is no necessary reason why every emotion must appear in other animals, some emotions might have emerged only in humans. Lazarus (1991) suggests this is so for pride, shame, and gratitude. I do not know of convincing evidence that these states are not evident in other animals. Furthermore, I do not believe that there has been sufficient study of these states mentioned by Lazarus to determine which of the nine characteristics found in basic emotions they share. So the issue remains an open one.

If basic emotions evolved to deal with fundamental life-tasks, they should not only provide information through expressions to conspecifics about what is occurring, but there should also be physiological changes preparing the organism to respond differently in different emotional states.

Emotion-specific physiology

There is evidence (Ekman, Levenson, & Friesen, 1983; Levenson, Ekman, & Friesen, 1990) for distinctive patterns of autonomic nervous system (ANS) activity for anger, fear, and disgust, and it appears that there may also be a distinctive pattern for sadness (Levenson, Carstensen, Friesen, & Ekman, 1991). These findings have now been replicated in four separate experiments, in two different age groups. Although there are some inconsistencies between the ANS patterns they found and the findings of other investigators, we should not ignore the many consistencies with the results of Schwartz, Weinberger, and Singer (1981); Ax (1953); Roberts and Weerts (1982); and Graham (1962). Levenson (1988) has reviewed this and earlier work explaining why methodological problems in the latter may be responsible for the some failures to find emotion-specific ANS activity.

The only recent challenge to our findings was Stemmler's (1989) report that ANS patterning was specific to how the emotion was elicited. However, this may be due to a number of methodological problems including measuring physiology a considerable period after the induction was over, and studying very low emotional intensities, and including a substantial number of subjects who reported not experiencing the emotion.[8] We have preliminary evidence in two different studies (Levenson et al., 1990; Ekman & Davidson, submitted) of the same emotion-specific pattern when emotion was elicited in very different ways. Clearly, the matter is far from settled. Noting that qualification, I will further consider what the implications are if further research strengthens and supports our findings to date of emotion-specific physiology.

Such evidence would be a challenge to those who view emotion as a social construction with no important biological contribution. A social constructionist might dismiss our findings by claiming that these different patterns of ANS activity were socially learned not the product of evolution. Their argument would be that people are taught to engage in different types of behaviour when experiencing different emotions. Over time this will establish different patterns of ANS activity, subserving these different action patterns. If people show the same emotion-specific ANS activity that may simply reflect common, culturally based, socialisation practices. Presumably those who advocate such a view should expect different behavioural patterns to be taught for each emotion, and therefore different patterns of ANS activity with each emotion, to be found in cultures which are known to differ in their attitudes about emotion.

Simply put, the social constructionist emphasises the past history of the individual, whereas the evolutionary theorist emphasises the past history of the species in explaining why there is emotion-specific ANS activity. If it is only ontogeny, than to the extent to which different people learn different ways of behaving when experiencing one or another emotion, there should be different patterns of ANS activity observed for the emotions we have studied. Levenson, Ekman, Heider, and Friesen (in press) recently repeated their experiments in a non-Western culture. They studied the Minangkabau of Western Sumatra, a fundamentalist Moslim, matrilineal society. They replicated Ekman et al.'s (1983) original findings of emotion-

---

[8]See Levenson, Ekman, and Friesen (1990) for a fuller discussion of the problems in Stemmler's study. Tassinary, Cacioppo, and Geen (1989) report another failure to replicate our findings, but they relegate this to a footnote and do not provide enough information to know what they actually did.

specific ANS activity in this very different culture. This provides important support consistent with an evolutionary view that these are basic emotions.

Does the failure to find emotion-specific ANS activity for enjoyment and surprise mean that these are not basic emotions? Kemper (1978) would make that argument, for he views differentiated ANS activity as the *sine qua non* for basic emotions. But consider why we expect emotion-specific ANS activity in the first place. Our presumption is that these ANS patterns evolved because they subserve patterns of motor behaviour which were adaptive for each of these emotions, preparing the organism for quite different actions. For example, fighting might well have been the adaptive action in anger, which is consistent with the finding that blood goes to the hands in anger. Fleeing from a predator might well have been the adaptive action in fear, which is consistent with the finding that blood goes to large skeletal muscles (see Levenson, Ekman, & Friesen, 1990, for a more elaborate discussion of this reasoning).

Freezing in fear might seem to create a problem for this line of reasoning, but not if freezing is interpreted as a fearful state in which the organism is nevertheless still prepared, autonomically, for fast flight if the freezing action does not provide concealment. Not every fearful experience involves a threat from which one can flee. A doctor's report that more tests are necessary to confirm whether the preliminary results are correct in indicating a terminal illness, arouse fear, but the event is not one the person can flee from. The ANS pattern of activity which subserves flight might still occur in this example, if the evolved motor programme for this emotion is flight. It is a question which awaits research.

Ohman's (1986) analysis of fear is relevant to these complexities. He distinguishes fear of animals, fear of people, and fear of inanimate objects, suggesting that the evolutionarily given actions may be different for fear of a predator as compared to social fears. It is not clear whether he views predator fear as including fear of other aggressive humans, or is it strictly limited to fear of other animals? Nor is it certain from his writings whether he would consider the fear of the doctor's news about terminal illness to be a predator or social fear.

If no specific pattern of motor activity had survival value for an emotion, then there would be no reason to expect a specific pattern of ANS activity to have been established for that emotion. That is why I think we have not found an emotion-specific pattern, a pattern which differs from each of the other emotions, for either surprise or enjoyment.

Frijda (1986) should disagree for he has proposed an action readiness for every emotion. I know of no observational data (examining what people actually do rather than how they answer questionnaires), which shows that there is a universal action pattern for the emotions of sadness, amusement, relief, contentment, or the enjoyment which occurs when hearing music, watching a sunset, or receiving strokes to the body or the ego. It is not that actions never occur in any of these states, but it is not self-evident that there is any uniform, universal tendency for one or another action in each of these different positive emotions. (Stein and Trabasso, in this issue, similarly question Frijda's view.) Further, it seems likely that when any of the agreeable emotions are occurring, one's survival is not at stake, there is no urgent need to act. A slightly different argument can be made for surprise. No motor action is required or relevant, but instead processing and evaluation of the new unexpected information.

It is not just in regard to positive emotions where there is a lack of observational data to demonstrate decisively an action tendency. There is no such data for *any* emotion which shows a universal, uniform action tendency whenever that emotion occurs. Johnson-Laird and Oatley's (this issue) suggestion that there is an action plan rather than action readiness, allows more flexibility, but again it is not clear what the action plan would be for some emotions. Stein and Levine (1989) have found certain action plans for certain emotions in children, but again they have not studied all emotions, and their data are limited to one culture.

Plans are important, but they are not actions. They are not a substitute for observational data on what actions people engage in, with any regularity, during particular emotions in particular social contexts. In all likelihood there will be more variation in observed actions than in action plans, but that remains to be determined. Furthermore, similarly there may be more variation in action plans than in the evolved readiness to perform motor acts which our findings of emotion-specific ANS activity implies.

I have no argument with Davidson's (this issue) belief that approaching vs. withdrawing is a fundamental issue in terms of the action plans which may be associated with each basic emotion. However, there is no definitive evidence to show that all positive emotions always involve just approach. Certainly, anger, fear, and disgust can involve approach or withdrawal. Is Davidson arguing that for each emotion, evolution prepares us to *either* approach or avoid, and it is only social learning which may add the other action pattern? If that was so it might be possible to measure electromyographically the beginning of that tendency even when the action taken is different. For now, I propose we do not regard either an action readiness or emotion-specific ANS activity as the *sine qua non* for defining basic emotions.

However, it is necessary to posit emotion-specific central nervous system (CNS) activity in my account of basic emotions. The distinctive features of each emotion, including the changes not just in expression but in memories, imagery, expectations, and other cognitive activities, could not occur without CNS organisation and direction. There must be *unique* physiological patterns for each emotion, and these CNS patterns should be specific to these emotions not found in other mental activity. Here, I am reaching far beyond the data, but not far beyond what the new techniques for measuring brain activity may allow us to discover in this decade.

My contention is consistent with the findings of those who have used EEG measures of regional brain activity to study emotion (see Davidson, 1984, 1987, for reviews of this literature). Davidson et al.'s (1990) recent findings of different patterns of regional brain activity coincident with enjoyment and disgust facial expressions can be explained as reflecting *either* differences in approach vs. withdrawal or positive vs. negative emotions. More critical for my argument are new, not yet published findings (Ekman & Davidson, submitted), which uncovered more differentiated regional brain activity when subjects voluntarily made the facial configurations found with each of the six basic emotions. This evidence must be regarded as tentative, as it is not yet replicated, but the evidence was strong, and it is encouraging for this line of reasoning and research.

Universal Antecedent Events

If emotions are viewed as having evolved to deal with fundamental life-tasks in ways which have been adaptive phylogenetically, then it is logically consistent to expect that there will be some common elements in the contexts in which emotions are found to occur. This is not to presume that every social context which calls forth an emotion will be the same for all people within or across cultures. Clearly there must be major differences attributable to social learning experiences. Ohman (1986, pp. 128–129) describes well how both evolution and social learning contribute to the establishment of those events which call forth one or another emotion.

> [E]volutionary economy has left to environmental influences to inscribe the exact characteristics of dangerous predators . . . [L]earning is critically involved in selecting which stimuli activate the predatory defense system. But this learning is likely to be biologically primed or constrained in the sense that the responses are much more easily attached to some types of stimuli than to others. In other words, it is appropriate to speak about biologically prepared learning. Thus it is likely to require only minimal input in terms of training, and to result in very persistent responses that are not easily extinguished.

Ohman cites research by Mineka, Davidson, Cook, and Keir (1984) showing that limited exposure is sufficient for establishing snake fears in the monkey which are very difficult to extinguish. Lazarus (1991) cites this same study to argue his rather similar view. Although he emphasises what he calls "meaning analysis", Lazarus also describes common antecedent events. Johnson-Laird and Oatley's (this issue) view is also similar.

My view on this matter, which is in agreement with Ohman, Lazarus, Johnson-Laird and Oatley, and Stein and her colleagues, developed in the 1970s when I learned of the findings of Boucher and Brant, which they did not publish until some years later (1981). They found commonalities in emotion antecedents in the many non-Western cultures they examined. It was not in the specific details but on a more abstract level that universality in antecedent events was found. The loss of a significant other, they found (Boucher, 1983, p. 407), is ". . . an antecedent to sadness in many, perhaps all cultures. But who a significant other is or can be will differ from culture to culture".

On the basis of Boucher and Brant's findings, Ekman and Friesen (1975) formulated prototypic interpersonal events which would universally call forth each of this set of emotions. For example, the antecedent event for fear is physical or psychological harm. Lazarus (1991), has a similar but in some ways different account, describing what he calls the "core relational theme" unique to the appraisal of each emotion. Neither of us has evidence, but what we each have proposed is consistent with Boucher and Brant's findings, and with those of Scherer and his group (Scherer, Summerfield, & Wallbott, 1983) in their study of the antecedents of emotion in Western cultures.

Unfortunately, there is little ethological description of the commonalities in the naturally occurring antecedent events for emotions within and across cultures. There is questionnaire and also interview data in which subjects are asked to describe emotional events. However, we do not yet know the extent to which such data resembles what actually occurs during emotion, how much idealisation, and stereotyping may occur when subjects coldly describe what they think about their emotional experience.

Coherence in Response Systems

There is an extensive literature reporting contradictory findings on whether there is or is not coherence in expression and autonomic changes during emotion (see reviews by Buck, 1977; and by Fridlund, Ekman, & Oster, 1987, pp. 195–199). It is not possible as yet to determine whether the dissociations between autonomic and expressive behaviour that have been found are normative or instead reflect differences in personality, temperament, and/or differential attempts to inhibit activity. For now, I propose that when we examine individuals who have not chronically or at the moment tried to inhibit their feelings or expression, we will find that there is *some* coherence, some systematic relationship between these two response systems during emotional events (for those emotions which do have a distinctive ANS pattern). I am positing that the autonomic responses and expressive changes are not, by nature, disconnected, although there will be large individual differences, some constitutional and some based on social learning. And, I am also positing connection rather than disconnection between facial expressions of emotion and distinctive patterns of CNS activity, and not limited just to the brain areas involved in production of the facial expression. An important qualifier, is that such connections between emotion-specific CNS activity and facial expressions of emotion will only obtain when we distinguish actual, spontaneous emotional expressions from more social or deliberate expressions (cf. Ekman, Davidson, & Friesen, 1990).

I have described five characteristics shared by each of the basic emotion families: (1) distinctive universal signals; (2) presence in other primates; (3) distinctive physiology; (4) universal, distinctive antecedent events; and (5) coherence among response systems. Let me now add four other characteristics which are more interpretative, but consistent, if not dictated, with the evidence I have summarised and with other findings.

Quick Onset

It is in the nature of emotion, I believe, that emotions can begin so quickly that they can happen before one is aware that they have started. Indeed, quick onset is fundamental I believe to the adaptive value of emotions, mobilising us to respond to important events with little time required for consideration or preparation. There is some evidence from both expression and physiology to support the proposal that emotions can onset quickly. Ekman and Friesen (1978) found that facial expressions can begin in a matter of milliseconds after an emotion-provoking stimulus, although not as quickly as we found the startle reactions begins, which I consider a reflex (Ekman, Friesen, & Simons, 1985). Collaborations with Levenson on ANS activity and with Davidson on CNS activity suggest that physiological changes may also begin in fractions of a second.

Clearly, emotions do not always begin so quickly. There are occasions, when an emotion unfolds very slowly, taking a number of seconds or minutes for characteristically emotional responses to occur. I will return to this later when discussing appraisal.

Brief Duration

It is not only adaptive for emotions to be capable of mobilising the organism very quickly (onset), but for the response changes so mobilised not to last very long unless the emotion is evoked again. If one emotion-arousing event typically produced a set of response changes which endured for hours regardless of what was occurring in the external world, emotions would be less responsive than I think they are to rapidly changing circumstances. It may be that under exceptional circumstances a single emotion endures for more than seconds or minutes, but I think it more likely that close inspection would reveal that the same emotion is being repeatedly evoked. All, however, that I need to commit myself to is that emotions usually last only for seconds, not minutes, hours or days.

There is no agreement about how exactly long emotions last, and no agreement about which aspect of emotion must be considered to empirically make that determination. Motor behaviour is probably a better index of when emotions begin than when they are over. Some of the ANS changes last longer than others, and both may last longer than people subjectively believe they are experiencing the emotion, hence the observation after the near-miss car accident, "I am no longer afraid but I feel as if I am".

My proposal that emotions are typically a matter of seconds not minutes or hours, is supported by some preliminary evidence. Examining the duration of both expressive and physiological changes during spontaneous emotional events suggests a short time span. When subjects have reported experiencing an emotion for 15 or 20 minutes, and I have had access to a videotaped record of their preceding behaviour, I found that they showed multiple expressions of that emotion. My interpretation of such incidents is that people summate in their verbal report what was actually a series of repeated but discrete emotion episodes. Unfortunately, I did not have physiological data also in those cases, so I cannot be certain whether the physiological changes were as episodic as the expressions.

A final reason for proposing that emotions are brief in duration is to distinguish emotions from moods, which last for hours or days. Although moods are highly saturated with one or another emotion—irritability with anger, dysphoria with sadness, apprehensiveness with fear, euphoria with a type of enjoyment—I have explained elsewhere (Ekman, 1984, 1991) how moods differ from emotions not only in duration, but also in what brings them forth, and in their physiology.

Frijda, Mesquita, Sonnemans, and Van Goozen (in press) propose that emotions last between 5 seconds and several hours. These figures are similar to those proposed by Scherer, Wallbott, and Summerfield (1986), probably because both Scherer et al. and Frijda relied upon what subjects who were not feeling an emotion reported about how long they think emotions last. Frijda also distinguishes "acute" from not so acute emotions, the former having expressive behaviour and distinct physiology. However, Frijda says he does not know how long acute emotions last. Frijda and Scherer et al. do agree with Ekman and Friesen's (1975) proposal that some emotions are typically of shorter duration than others, and that moods last much longer than emotions. In work in progress, Stein and Trabasso have children enact emotions, and they find that the emotional responses last for seconds not minutes or hours.

Learning more about the duration of emotions requires, I believe, actually examining the occurrence of emotions in the stream of behaviour, not just asking people. Levenson and Gottman are measuring emotions during the course of marital interaction and they (personal communication) report observing many emotional events which last seconds not minutes.

Automatic Appraisal Mechanism

I (Ekman, 1977, pp. 58–59) proposed two appraisal mechanisms, one automatic and the other extended:

> There must be an appraiser mechanism which selectively attends to those stimuli (external or internal) which are the occasion for . . . [one or another emotion]. Since the interval between stimulus and emotional response is sometimes extraordinarily short, the appraisal mechanism must be capable of operating with great speed. Often the appraisal is not only quick but it happens without awareness, so I must postulate that the appraisal mechanism is able to operate automatically. It must be constructed so that it quickly attends to some stimuli, determining not only that they pertain to emotion, but to which emotion . . . Appraisal is not always automatic. Sometimes the evaluation of what is happening is slow, deliberate and conscious. With such a more extended appraisal there may be some automatic arousal, but perhaps not of a kind which is differentiated. The person could be said to be aroused or alerted, but no specific emotion is operative. Cognition plays the important role in determining what will transpire. During such extended appraisal the evaluation may match to the selective filters of the automatic appraiser . . . It need not be, however; the experience may be diffuse rather than specific to one emotion.

Similar views have since been described by Zajonc (1985); Ohman (1986); Leventhal and Scherer (1987); and Buck (1985). LeDoux's study (1991, p. 50) of the anatomy of emotion has led him also to take a view nearly identical to what I propose.

> Emotional processing systems . . . tend to use the minimal stimulus representation possible to activate emotional response control systems, which characteristically involve relatively hard-wired, species-typical behaviors and physiological reactions. Emotional reactions . . . need to be executed with speed, and the use of the highest level of stimulus processing is maladaptive when a lower level will do . . . However, not all emotional reactions can be mediated by primitive sensory events and subcortical neural circuits.

In a major shift in his own position to incorporate the evidence on basic emotions Lazarus (1991, Ch.5, p. 3) recently adopted my position on this issue: "I distinguish between two modes of appraisal: one automatic, unreflective, and unconscious or preconscious, the other deliberate and conscious." Lazarus succinctly described what he called a "psychobiological principle", which he said (pp. 191–192) "provides for universals in the emotion process. Once the appraisals have been made, the emotional response is a foregone conclusion, a consequence of biology". Here, Lazarus goes further than I do, as I believe that the responses reflect not just biology but social learning as well. Stein and Trabasso's (this issue) analysis of appraisal, although based on very different data, is very similar, as they point out, to Lazarus's position.

It is not known exactly how a biological contribution to appraisal operates, what it is that is given, which is then operated on automatically. It seems reasonable to presume that that which is biologically given must be related to the universal antecedents of emotion described above. How does this occur, by what mechanism?

Automatic appraisal does not simply and solely operate on what is given biologically, dealing only with stimulus events that exactly fit what is given. In all likelihood, not enough is given for automatic appraisal to ever operate without considerable amplification and detailing through social learning. (See especially Ohman, 1986, on this point.) An exception might be the appraisal which occurs to a sudden loss of support or when an object is perceived to be moving very quickly directly into one's visual field. But such examples are probably rare. Perhaps they act as metaphors for many other events to become associated through experience with emotion.

Automatic appraisal operates also on a variety of stimulus events that we have repeatedly encountered or with events which although rare were extraordinarily intense. Lazarus notes how differences in our experience allows for enormous variations in the specifics of what calls forth emotions which are attributable to personality, family, and culture. And yet it is not totally malleable. There are some commonalities in what calls forth an emotion for anyone (Toobey & Cosmides, 1990, pp. 418–419).

> The ancestrally recurrent structured situation that the organism categorizes itself as being in is the 'meaning' of the situation for that organism. It 'sees', i.e. is organized to respond to, previous fitness contingencies, not present ones . . . Emotions . . . lead organisms to act as if certain things were true about the present circumstances whether or not they are because they were true of past circumstances . . . In this lies their strength and their weakness . . . [The automatic appraisal] cannot detect when the invariances that held true ancestrally no longer obtain.

Often in civilised life, our emotions occur in response to words not actions, to events which are complex and indirect, and it is an extended appraisal process which operates with consciousness and deliberation. Then the person is quite aware of what Lazarus calls the "meaning analysis" which occurs. Here is another entry place for social learning to generate large differences between cultural groups, and major individual differences within a culture.

A number of theorists (see reviews by Ellsworth, 1991; Scherer, 1991) have developed models of how appraisal processes may operate. Reading their descriptions and considering most of their data sources it appears that they are considering only extended appraisal, but I think that they believe their models to characterise automatic appraisal as well. Their models are not contradictory with a basic emotions position, but they apparently do see a contradiction. Lazarus, I believe, is the only appraisal theorist who also incorporates basic emotions in his framework. Lazarus differs from the other appraisal theorists in not offering a model of how the appraisal process works. Instead he more abstractly describes the relevant principle and the prototypic events (core relational themes) for each emotion.

Unbidden Occurrence

Because emotions can occur with rapid onset, through automatic appraisal, with little awareness, and with involuntary response changes in expression and physiology, we often experience emotions as happening to, not chosen by us. One can not simply elect when to have which emotion. Psychotherapists would have less business if that was so. When emotions are the product of extended appraisal and the onset is more gradual it is more possible to interfere with or influence what emotion one is beginning to experience. But when the emotion is a result of automatic appraisal the person must struggle with forces within to control what is happening. "[A]n automatic involuntary aspect is present in the experience of all emotion" (Stein and Trabasso, this issue).

It is easier to control the skeletal muscular set than the facial expression, easier to inhibit or control the facial expressions, than the sound of the voice, and probably easier to change the voice than some of the autonomic changes (see Ekman, 1985). The robustness and quickness of emotional response are likely areas of individual difference, and hence differences also in the extent to which emotion is experienced as unbidden.

People do choose to put themselves in situations in which an emotion is likely to occur, arranging circumstances known to be likely to bring on the emotion, but that does not contradict the claim that emotions are unbidden. It is the fact that we cannot choose the emotions which we have which allows people to account for and explain their behaviour by noting they were in the grip of an emotion when the behaviour occurred.

THE PROBLEM OF POSITIVE EMOTIONS

Friesen and I (Ekman & Friesen, 1975) described a number of different *positive emotions*. I have used the term enjoyment as a gloss to cover amusement, relief, sensory pleasure, pride in achievement, the thrill of excitement, satisfaction, and contentment. (I do not claim this is an exhaustive list of the positive emotions.) The problem is that each of these positive emotions does *not* have a distinctive signal (Ekman & Friesen, 1982), although each of the basic negative emotions does have such a distinctive signal. Instead, all of the positive emotions share what I have called the Duchenne smile (Ekman, 1989; Ekman et al., 1990), which is marked by not only the smiling lips (produced by the *zygomaticus major* muscle), but also by the pulling inwards of the skin surrounding the eyes (produced by the *orbicularis oculi, pars lateralis* muscle). Now, it may be that when the voice is studied carefully, each of these positive emotions will be found to have its own distinctive vocal signature. But suppose that is not so, why might it be that emotions which differ as much as relief and the thrill of excitement, might not have their own distinctive signal?

Perhaps it has not been relevant to survival to know which positive emotion was occurring, only that it was a positive emotion rather than anger, fear, disgust, or sadness. Such an idea is implied by Darwin in his principle of antithesis. Ellsworth (personal communication, May 1991) questioned whether it would not matter in sexual selection whether one was being seduced or laughed at, but the little work done on signs of flirtation and/or sexual interest, Eibl-Eibesfeldt (1972) suggests this looks nothing like laughter. I do acknowledge that people are not always certain whether another is amused with them, or whether they are the object of another's amusement, but that underlines the problem it does not provide an answer. Lazarus (personal communication, June 1991) disagrees with me, believing that it is important and necessary to know, for example, whether one's partner or lover is happy or satisfied. We (Frank, Ekman, & Friesen, in press) have recently found that people can distinguish the enjoyment, or Duchenne smile, from a more social, fabricated smile. Perhaps differences in the timing and in accompanying vocalisation allow the other types of enjoyment to be readily distinguished from one another.

One solution to the problem of there being but one facial signal for these different positive emotions would be if they are all considered to be members of the enjoyment emotion family. The thrill of excitement, relief, contentment, might all be different variations on a common theme, just as annoyance, fury, resentment, and outrage are all members of the anger family. But this is not a decision to be made theoretically in order to deal with an inconsistency in one's theory. If these positive states are to be considered members of one family, research should find a commonality in the physiology of these positive states, a common theme albeit with variations, and a common theme in the antecedent events.

Are there Other Basic Emotions which have these Nine Characteristics?

The evidence is far from complete for anger, fear, disgust, and sadness, and I have indicated more uncertainty about the positive emotions (except in their differences from the negative emotions), and about interest, contempt, surprise, guilt, and shame. I do not think there are other emotions which share all nine characteristics, but that is an empirical matter. Let me briefly describe three more affective states about which even less is known, which are candidates to be considered as basic emotions.

Embarrassment. Most researchers have tried to diminish its impact upon the emotional state they are trying to evoke rather than focus upon embarrassment itself. A number of theorists consider embarrassment to be part of the shame or guilt family. Although arguing that embarrassment is a form of shame Izard (1977) does not explain why people do not typically blush in shame.

I expect that when the research is completed, embarrassment will be found to have all of the characteristics I have described, but with an unusual signal—the blush. I do not know if the blushing in embarrassment is very evident in dark skinned persons, and if it is not, that would make for a signal which is much more apparent in some races than in others. In embarrassment, people often want to hide, and that is consistent with a less explicit signal than what occurs in the other basic emotions. Miller and Fahey (1991) suggests that blushing can only occur in the presence of another person, not when one is alone. If this is so, it would be a second way in which embarrassment differs from the other basic emotions because they can occur when alone, although they typically occur in response to the actual or remembered actions of others. Recent work by Keltner (personal communication, October 1991) suggests that the embarrassment signal involves a sequence of facial and head movements, rather than one set of co-ordinated muscle movements which occur simultaneously. Keltner also has evidence that observers can distinguish between embarrassment and amusement.

Awe. Unlike embarrassment, it is not easy to provoke awe in a laboratory. It is rare, but I think there is a reasonable chance that it will also be found to share all nine characteristics.

Excitement. Tomkins (1962) said excitement is intense, extreme interest, a position adopted subsequently by Izard (1971). I suspect that excitement is a separate emotion, no more related to interest than it is to enjoyment or fear. Again, there has been little research on excitement itself.

GENERAL CONSIDERATIONS

Must a Basic Emotion have all Nine Characteristics?

Those who ask this question usually are specifically questioning the necessity of two of the characteristics: a unique, universal signal, and presence in other animals. I see no reason to argue that the unique signal must be facial. Vocalisation would be just as good, or a patterned, distinctive set of body or head movements with or without the face. The more difficult question is what if there is no signal of any kind? I have no way of knowing how to answer such a question other than by trying to discover whether there are actually such signal-less affective states in nature which have all of the other eight characteristics. That research has not been done. The value of the basic emotion approach is to focus our attention on such gaps in our knowledge. Our task must be to describe nature, to find out what is, not to prescribe on some a priori basis.

It would certainly be important if emotions which have the other eight characteristics but no distinct signal were discovered. Such emotions would have very different social consequences, privately experienced with no notification to conspecifics. I think it unlikely that there are such emotions, and if they are found we should be interested in how different they may function in our social life.

I also think it is unlikely that we will find an emotion that is not evident in any other animal yet has all of the other characteristics I have described. Again, this is a question to settle by research not by argument. I do not reject the possibility of emotions emerging in humans which are not shown by other animals, I just think it is improbable.

Does any One Characteristic Distinguish the Basic Emotions?

I do not think any of the nine characteristics should be regarded as the *sine qua non* for emotions, the hallmark which distinguishes emotions from other affective phenomena. What is unique is that when an emotion occurs we are dealing with current fundamental life-tasks in ways which were adaptive in our evolutionary past. This is not to deny that our own individual past experience will also influence how we deal with these fundamental life-tasks, but that is not what is unique to emotions. It is our past as a species in dealing with fundamental life-tasks and how that organises and at least initially influences how we appraise and respond to a current event which marks the emotions.

This is not much help for empiricists who want to know when we can tell—as observers—if an emotion is occurring. "An observer can infer that an emotion is likely to be occurring when:

- the response system changes are complex, when it is not just facial, or skeletal, or vocal, or [physiological], . . . but a combination;
- the changes are organised, in the sense of being inter-related and distinctive . . .;
- the changes happen quickly;
- some of the response system changes are ones common to all people; and
- some of the responses are not unique to *homo sapiens*.

This is *not* the only time emotion occurs, but when an observer's estimate is *most* likely to be safe" (Ekman, 1977, p. 62).

How to Deal with all the Other Emotions, such as Smugness, Hope, Grief, Jealousy, etc.

Although the emotions I propose to be basic include those most often considered by other theorists, certainly some affective states remain which I have not so far considered. I have nine answers to the question of what to do with these other emotion-related phenomena.

First, the concept of emotion families, which I introduced at the beginning of this paper, allows the inclusion within a family of many variations around a common theme. Thus, many different emotion terms will be found within each family.

Second, it is worth noting that the list of basic emotions and possible basic emotions is not a short one. It includes (in alphabetical order) anger, awe, contempt, disgust, embarrassment, excitement, fear, guilt, interest, sadness, shame, and surprise. And also enjoyment, which is comprised of at least amusement, contentment, relief, enjoyment from sensory sources, and enjoyment based on accomplishment. The exact number of emotions is not germane to the basic emotions approach, but it is one of the values of that approach to focus attention on trying to discover which affective phenomena share the nine characteristics I described and therefore should be designated basic emotions.

Third, a number of emotion terms can be considered as moods, e.g. apprehension, dysphoria, euphoria, irritation. Although each of these moods is highly saturated with one or another emotion, I have argued elsewhere (Ekman, 1984, in press) that they differ from emotions in what calls them forth, their time course, the appraisals involved, and the physiological substrate.

Fourth, a number of emotion terms can be considered as *emotional attitudes*, for example, love or hatred. They are more sustained, and typically involve more than one emotion.

Fifth, a number of terms can be considered as designating *emotional traits* (e.g. hostile, melancholic, timorous, Pollyannaish), and sixth, still other terms designate *emotional disorders* (e.g. major depression, anxiety disorder, mania, pathological violence). Both the traits and disorders involve emotions, typically more than one, but they differ from each other and from the emotions themselves, in terms of their time course, and in other ways as well (see Ekman, 1984, in press).

Seventh, a number of what others consider to be emotions I think are more complex, involving settings and stories in which emotions occur.[9] I have called these *emotional plots*. Grief, jealousy, and infatuation are such emotional plots which specify (Ekman, 1984, p. 329)

> ... the particular context within which specific emotions will be felt by specific persons, casting the actors and what has or is about to transpire. [Grief, for example,] ... specifies two actors, the deceased and the survivor, something about their past relationship, the survivor was attached to the deceased, the pivotal event, one of the actors died. The survivor is likely to feel distress, sadness, and perhaps fear and anger.

Grief is much more specific than sadness. We know that in grief a death has occurred, in sadness we only know that the person has suffered an important loss, but not what kind of loss. Jealousy is another example of an emotional plot. It tells us the cast of three, their roles, something about the past history, and the emotions each cast member is likely to feel. Anger may be felt by the spurned one, but sadness and fear may also be felt. We also know something about the feelings of the rival and the object of mutual attention. An emotional plot contains much more specific information, than do any of the basic emotions. Oatley and Johnson-Laird (1987) had a similar concept for what they called "complex emotions".

Eighth, is the possibility of *blends*, terms which describe the co-occurrence of two quite different emotions, as for example, scorn being a

---

[9]Tomkins (1962) should be credited for emphasising that emotions have generality rather than containing specific information, although he made this distinction to differentiate emotions from pain, not from what I am calling emotional plots.

blend of enjoyment and disgust. Although I think there is lexical evidence for blend terms (e.g. Plutchik, 1962), the evidence for the existence of blends in terms of physiology and expression is meagre. It is equally possible that blend terms are used to designate a rapid sequence of two basic emotions. Johnson-Laird and Oatley (this issue) talk of *mixed* emotions, and perhaps this would be a better term, allowing for both blends and rapidly sequential emotions. This too is an area much in need of research.

Ninth, is the possibility that there are more emotional words than there are basic emotions, terms which refer not only to the emotion but features of the eliciting situation, of differential responses to that situation, etc. Oatley and Johnson-Laird (1987) and Stein and Trabasso (this issue) elaborate how this occurs, and how such variations in emotion terms can be dealt with from a basic emotions viewpoint.

THE VALUE OF THE BASIC EMOTIONS POSITION

The basic emotions position which I have described does not dismiss the variety of affective phenomena, it attempts to organise those phenomena, highlighting possible differences between basic emotions and other affective phenomena, which can only be determined by further research. It should be clear by now that I do not allow for "non-basic" emotions. All the emotions which share the nine characteristics I have described are basic. Further research will show, I believe, that they each have unique features (signal, physiology, and antecedent events). Each emotion also has features in common with other emotions—rapid onset, short duration, unbidden occurrence, automatic appraisal, and coherence among responses—which allow us to begin to deal with fundamental life-tasks quickly without much elaborated planning, in ways that have been adaptive in our past.

If all emotions are basic, what then is the value of using that term. It underlines the differences between this and other viewpoints and approaches to emotion which do not consider emotions to be separate from one another, and/or do not take an evolutionary viewpoint. It captures what is unique about emotion, and what emotions have in common which distinguish them from other phenomena. The basic emotions framework makes sense of the nine characteristics I have described which distinguish emotions from other affective phenomena.[10] This framework serves us

---

[10]Adopting a basic emotions viewpoint does not, however, require a commitment to one or another position about how emotional behaviour is organised and regulated. In earlier writings (Ekman, 1972, 1977) I elaborated on Tomkins' (1962) concept of an "affect program", which has been criticised by Camras (this issue), Davidson (this issue), and Lazarus (1991). I am currently evaluating the advantages and disadvantages of that concept as compared to a neural network.

well in raising for empirical study a number of questions about other affective states which further research might show are also basic emotions. The adjective "basic" should not be the issue, however, but instead what questions this stance raises for research about emotion. It was this position which led myself and Friesen, and quite independently Izard, to seek evidence on the universality of facial expression. It was this position which also motivated phylogenetic comparisons (Chevalier-Skolnikoff, 1973; Redican, 1982). It also guided much of the recent research on emotion-specific physiology which I described earlier, and research on the early development of expression (see Fridlund, Ekman, & Oster's, 1987 review). Thirty years ago before Tomkins (1962) and Plutchik (1962) published their quite different theories of basic emotions, these findings did not exist, and emotion was not the popular topic it is today. When we consider what has been learned about emotional *responses* I think it is reasonable to acknowledge that the basic emotions approach provided the basis for the questions which were asked. Clearly, this has not been the case for the generation of recent research offering different models of appraisal, although perhaps the basic emotions approach was influential indirectly, for some of the appraisal model theorists reacted against this position.

The nine characteristics I have described are meant as challenges for more research. They point us to what we still need to learn about the emotions. They highlight the gaps in our knowledge. The utility of this approach will be evident 10 years from now by what research it generates to confirm or disconfirm the possibilities I have suggested, and new possibilities I have not conceived of.

Manuscript received 8 October 1990
Revised manuscript received 25 November 1991

REFERENCES

Allport, F.H. (1924). *Social psychology*. Boston: Houghton Mifflin.

Ax, A.F. (1953). The physiological differentiation between fear and anger in humans. *Psychosomatic Medicine*, 15, 433–442.

Boucher, J.D. (1983). Antecedents to emotions across cultures. In S.H. Irvine & J.W. Berry (Eds), *Human assessment and cultural factors*. New York: Plenum, pp. 407–420.

Boucher, J.D. & Brant, M.E. (1981). Judgment of emotion: American and Maylay antecedents. *Journal of Cross-Cultural Psychology*, 12, 272–283.

Buck, R. (1985). Prime theory: A integrated theory of motivation and emotion. *Psychological Review*, 92, 389–413.

Buck, R.W. (1977). Nonverbal communication of affect in preschool children: Relationships with personality and skin conductance. *Journal of Personality and Social Psychology*, 35, 225–236.

Chevalier-Skolnikoff, S. (1973). Facial expression of emotion in nonhuman primates. In P. Ekman (Ed.), *Darwin and facial expression*. New York: Academic Press, pp. 11–83.

Darwin, C. (1872). *The expression of the emotions in man and animals.* [Reprinted 1965.] University of Chicago Press.

Davidson, R.J. (1984). Affect, cognition and hemispheric specialization. In C.E. Izard, J. Kagan, & R. Zajonc (Eds), *Emotion, cognition and behavior.* Cambridge University Press, pp. 320–365.

Davidson, R.J. (1987). Cerebral asymmetry and the nature of emotion: Implications for the study of individual differences and psychopathology. In R. Takahashi, P. Flor-Henry, J. Gruzelier, & S. Niwa (Eds), *Cerebral dynamics, laterality and psychopathology.* New York: Elsevier.

Davidson, R.J., Ekman, P., Saron, C., Senulis, J., & Friesen, W.V. (1990). Emotional expression and brain physiology. I: Approach/withdrawal and cerebral asymmetry. *Journal of Personality and Social Psychology, 58,* 330–341.

Eibl-Eibesfeldt, I. (1972). Similarities and differences between cultures in expressive movements. In R.A. Hinde (Ed.), *Non-verbal communication.* Cambridge University Press, pp. 297–314.

Ekman, P. (1972). Universals and cultural differences in facial expressions of emotion. In J. Cole (Ed.), *Nebraska symposium on motivation, 1971,* Vol. 19. Lincoln, NE.: University of Nebraska Press, pp. 207–283.

Ekman, P. (1977). Biological and cultural contributions to body and facial movement. In J. Blacking (Ed.), *Anthropology of the body.* London: Academic Press, pp. 34–84.

Ekman, P. (1979). About brows: Emotional and conversational signals. In M. von Cranach, K. Foppa, W. Lepenies, & D. Ploog (Eds), *Human ethology.* Cambridge University Press, pp. 169–248.

Ekman, P. (1984). Expression and the nature of emotion. In K. Scherer & P. Ekman (Eds), *Approaches to emotion.* Hillsdale, NJ: Lawrence Erlbaum Associates Inc., pp. 319–344.

Ekman, P. (1985). *Telling lies: Clues to deceit in the marketplace, marriage, and politics.* New York: Norton. [Paperback edition, New York: Berkeley Books, 1986.]

Ekman, P. (1989). The argument and evidence about universals in facial expressions of emotion. In H. Wagner & A. Manstead (Eds), *Handbook of social psychophysiology.* Chichester: Wiley, pp. 143–164.

Ekman, P. (1991). *Distinguishing emotions from other affective states.* Unpublished manuscript.

Ekman, P. (In press). Facial expression of emotion: New findings, new questions. *Psychological Science.*

Ekman, P. & Davidson, R.J. (Submitted). *Voluntary smiling changes regional brain activity.*

Ekman, P. & Friesen, W.V. (1969). The repertoire of nonverbal behavior: Categories, origins, usage, and coding. *Semiotica, 1,* 49–98.

Ekman, P. & Friesen, W.V. (1975). *Unmasking the face: A guide to recognizing emotions from facial clues.* New Jersey: Prentice Hall. [Reprinted edition, Palo Alto, CA: Consulting Psychologists Press, 1984.]

Ekman, P. & Friesen, W.V. (1976). Measuring facial movement. *Environmental Psychology and Nonverbal Behavior, 1*(1), 56–75.

Ekman, P. & Friesen, W.V. (1978). *Facial action coding system: A technique for the measurement of facial movement.* Palo Alto, CA: Consulting Psychologists Press.

Ekman, P. & Friesen, W.V. (1982). Felt, false and miserable smiles. *Journal of Nonverbal Behavior, 6*(4), 238–252.

Ekman, P. & Friesen, W.V. (1986). A new pan cultural expression of emotion. *Motivation and Emotion, 10,* 159–168.

Ekman, P. & Friesen, W.V. (1988). Who knows what about contempt: A reply to Izard and Haynes. *Motivation and Emotion, 12,* 17–22.

Ekman, P. & Heider, K.G. (1988). The universality of a contempt expression: A replication. *Motivation and Emotion, 12*(4), 303–308.

Ekman, P., Friesen, W.V., & Ellsworth, P. (1972). *Emotion in the human face*: *Guidelines for research and an integration of findings*. New York: Pergamon.

Ekman, P., Friesen, W.V., & Ancoli, S. (1980). Facial signs of emotional experience. *Journal of Personality and Social Psychology*, *39*(6), 1125–1134.

Ekman, P., Levenson, R.W., & Friesen, W.V. (1983). Autonomic nervous system activity distinguishes between emotions. *Science*, *221*, 1208–1210.

Ekman, P., Friesen, W.V., & Simons, R.C. (1985). Is the startle reaction an emotion? *Journal of Personality and Social Psychology*, *49*(5), 1416–1426.

Ekman, P., Davidson, R.J., & Friesen, W.V. (1990). The Duchenne smile: Emotional expression and brain physiology. II. *Journal of Personality and Social Psychology*, *58*, 342–353.

Ekman, P., O'Sullivan, M., & Matsumoto, D. (In press). Confusions about contest in the judgment of facial expression: A reply to "Contempt and the Relativity Thesis". *Motivation and Emotion*.

Ellsworth, P. (1991). Some implications of cognitive appraisal theories of emotion. In K.T. Strongman (Ed.), *International review of studies on emotion*. Chichester and New York: Wiley, pp. 143–161.

Etcoff, N.L. & Magee, J.J. (In press). Categorical perception of facial expressions. *Cognition*.

Frank, M.G., Ekman, P., & Friesen, W.V. (In press). Behavioral markers of the smile of enjoyment. *Journal of Personality and Social Psychology*.

Fridlund, A.J. (1991). Evolution and facial action in reflex, social motive, and paralanguage. *Biological Psychology*, *32*, 3–100.

Fridlund, A., Ekman, P., & Oster, H. (1987). Facial expressions of emotion. In A. Siegman & S. Feldstein (Eds), *Nonverbal behavior and communication*. Hillsdale, NJ: Lawrence Erlbaum Associates Inc, pp. 143–224.

Frijda, N.H. (1986). *The emotions*. Cambridge University Press.

Frijda, N.H., Mesquita, B., Sonnemans, J., & Van Goozen, S. (In press). The duration of affective phenomena or emotions, sentiments and passions. *International review of studies on emotion*, Vol. 1. Chichester: Wiley.

Goldblatt, D. & Williams, D. (1986). "I an smiling!" Mobius' syndrome inside and out. *Journal of Child Neurology*, *1*, 71–78.

Graham, D.T. (1962). Some research on psychophysiologic specificity and its relation to psychosomatic disease. In R. Roessler & N.S. Greenfield (Eds), *Physiological correlates of psychological disorder*. Madison: University of Wisconsin Press, pp. 221–238.

Izard, C.E. (1971). *The face of emotion*. New York: Appleton-Century-Crofts.

Izard, C.E. (1977). *Human emotions*. New York: Plenum.

Izard, C.E. (1979). *The maximally discriminative facial movement coding system (MAX)*. Unpublished manuscript. Available from Instructional Resource Center, University of Delaware, Newark, Delaware.

Izard, C. & Haynes, O.M. (1988). On the form and universality of the contempt expression: A challenge to Ekman and Friesen's claim of discovery. *Motivation and Emotion*, *12*, 1–16.

Johnson-Laird, P.N. & Oatley, K. (1989). The language of emotions: An analysis of a semantic field. *Cognition and Emotion*, *3*, 81–123.

Kemper, T.D. (1978). *A social interactional theory of emotions*. New York: Wiley.

Lazarus, R.S. (1991). *Emotion and adaptation*. Oxford University Press.

LeDoux, J.E. (1991). Emotion and the brain. *The Journal of NIH Research*, *3*, 49–51.

Levenson, R.W. (1988). Emotion and the autonomic nervous system: A prospectus for research on autonomic specificity. In N.H. Wagner (Ed.), *Social psychophysiology*: *Theory and clinical applications*. London: Wiley, pp. 17–42.

Levenson, R.W., Ekman, P., & Friesen, W.V. (1990). Voluntary facial expression generates emotion-specific nervous system activity. *Psychophysiology*, *27*, 363–384.

Levenson, R.W., Carstensen, L.L., Friesen, W.V., & Ekman, P. (1991). Emotion, physiology, and expression in old age. *Psychology and Aging*, *6*, 28–35.

Levenson, R.W., Ekman, P., Heider, K., & Friesen, W.V. (In press). Emotion and autonomic nervous system activity in an Indonesian culture. *Journal of Personality and Social Psychology*.

Leventhal, H. & Scherer, K.R. (1987). The relationship of emotion to cognition: A functional approach to a semantic controversy. *Cognition and Emotion*, *1*, 3–28.

Matsumoto, D.R. & Kudoh, T. (Submitted). Cultural differences in judgments of emotion and other personal attributes: What's in a smile?

Miller, R.S. & Fahey, D.E. (1991, August). *Blushing as an appeasement gesture: Felt, displayed and observed embarrassment*. Paper presented at the meeting of the American Psychological Association, San Francisco, CA.

Mineka, S., Davidson, M., Cook, M., & Keir, R. (1984). Observational conditioning of snake fear in Rhesus monkeys. *Journal of Abnormal Psychology*, *93*, 355–372.

Oatley, K. & Johnson-Laird, P.N. (1987). Towards a cognitive theory of the emotions. *Cognition and Emotion*, *1*, 29–50.

Ohman, A. (1986). Face the beast and fear the face: Animal and social fears as prototypes for evolutionary analyses of emotion. *Psychophysiology*, *23*, 123–145.

Ortony, A. & Turner, T.J. (1990). What's basic about basic emotions? *Psychological Review*, *97*, 313–331.

Oster, H., Hegley, D., & Nagel, L. (In press). Adult judgment and fine-grained analysis of infant facial expressions: Testing the validity of *a priori* coding formulas. *Developmental Psychology*.

Plutchik, R. (1962). *The emotions: Facts, theories and a new model*. New York: Random House.

Redican, W.K. (1982). An evolutionary perspective on human facial displays. In P. Ekman (Ed.), *Emotion in the human face* (2nd edn). Elmsford, New York: Pergamon, pp. 212–280.

Ricci-Bitti, P.E., Brighetti, G., Garotti, P.L., & Boggi-Cavallo, P. (1988). *Is contempt expressed by pan-cultural facial movements?* Paper presented at the XXIV International Congress of Psychology, Sydney, Australia.

Roberts, R.J. & Weerts, T.C. (1982). Cardiovascular responding during anger and fear imagery. *Psychological Reports*, *50*, 219–230.

Rosch, E.H. (1973). Natural categories. *Cognitive Psychology*, *4*, 328–350.

Roseman, I.J. (1991). Appraisal determinants of discrete emotion. *Cognition and Emotion*, *5*(3), 161–200.

Ross, E.D. (1981). The aprosodias: functional-anatomical organization of the affective components of language in the right hemisphere. *Archives of Neurology*, *38*, 561–569.

Russell, J. (In press). Negative results on a reported facial expression of contempt. *Motivation and Emotion*.

Scherer, K.R. (1991). Criteria for emotion-antecedent appraisal: a review. In V. Hamilton, G.H. Bower, & N.H. Fridja (Eds), *Cognitive perspectives on motivation and emotion*. Kluwer: Dordrecht: pp. 89–126.

Scherer, K.R., Summerfield, W.B., & Wallbott, H.G. (1983). Cross-national research on antecedents and components of emotion: A progress report. *Social Science Information*, *22*, 355–385.

Scherer, K.R., Wallbott, H.G., & Summerfield, W.B. (Eds) (1986). *Experiencing emotion: A cross-cultural study*. Cambridge University Press.

Schwartz, G.E., Weinberger, D.A., & Singer, J.A. (1981). Cardiovascular differentiation of happiness, sadness, anger and fear following imagery and exercise. *Psychosomatic Medicine, 43*, 343–364.

Shaver, P., Schwartz, J., Kirson, D., & O'Connor, C. (1987). Emotion knowledge: Further exploration of a prototype approach. *Journal of Personality and Social Psychology, 52*, 1061–1086.

Stein, N.L. & Levine, L.J. (1989). The causal organisation of emotional knowledge: A developmental study. *Cognition and Emotion, 3*(4), 343–378.

Stemmler, G. (1989). The autonomic differentiation of emotions revisited: Convergent and discriminant validation. *Psychophysiology, 26*, 617–632.

Tassinary, L.G., Cacioppo, J.T., & Geen, T.R. (1989). A psychometric study of surface electrode placements for facial electromyographic recording. I. *Psychophysiology, 26*, 1–16.

Toobey, J. & Cosmides, L. (1990). The past explains the present: Emotional adaptations and the structure of ancestral environments. *Ethology and Sociobiology, 11*, 375–424.

Tomkins, S.S. (1962). *Affect, imagery, consciousness*. Vol. 1. *The positive affects*. New York: Springer.

Tomkins, S.S. (1963). *Affect, imagery, consciousness*. Vol. 2. *The negative affects*. New York: Springer.

Tomkins, S.S. & McCarter, R. (1964). What and where are the primary affects? Some evidence for a theory. *Perceptual and Motor Skills, 18*, 119–158.

Zajonc, R.B. (1985). Emotion and facial efference: A theory reclaimed. *Science, 228*, 15–21.

COGNITION AND EMOTION, 1992, 6 (3/4), 201–223

Basic Emotions, Rationality, and Folk Theory

P.N. Johnson-Laird

Department of Psychology, Princeton University, U.S.A.

Keith Oatley

Centre for Applied Cognitive Science, Ontario Institute for Studies in Education, Toronto, Canada

Answering the question of whether there are basic emotions requires considering the functions of emotions. We propose that just a few emotions are basic and that they have functions in managing action. When no fully rational solution is available for a problem of action, a basic emotion functions to prompt us in a direction that is better than a random choice. We contrast this kind of theory with a componential approach which we argue is either a version of the theory of basic emotions or else leads to the doctrine that emotions are mistaken tenets of folk psychology. We defend the psychological reality of the folk theory of emotions, and we argue that universal basic emotions make it possible to understand people from distant cultures, and to translate emotional terminology from one language to another. Finally, we show how theories of basic emotions can be tested, and indicate the kinds of empirical result that can bear on the issue.

INTRODUCTION

How many emotions are there? There are several possible replies to this question. One is that the question is meaningless, but this response amounts to rejecting the ordinary concept of emotion. It is akin to answering that emotions do not exist—that they are false tenets of folk theories, i.e. of the common sense theories that lay people have about mind and behaviour, which contrast with scientific and other kinds of specialist theories (D'Andrade, 1987). Another answer is that although individuals experience only a finite number of emotions in their lifetimes, there are indefinitely many possible emotions that they might experience. This view can be coupled with the claim that one never experiences the

---

Requests for reprints should be sent to Dr P.N. Johnson-Laird, Department of Psychology, Princeton University, Princeton, NJ 08544, U.S.A.

same emotion twice. If there is an indefinite number of emotions, then we can ask how they relate, if at all, to one another. Each emotion might be unique and unrelated to any other. Such a conception is metaphysically defensible but removes emotions from the domain of scientific investigation. Each wave on the seashore is unique, but the science of hydrodynamics idealises waves, and from this abstract standpoint treats waves that are, in fact, distinguishable as the same.

In this paper we will put a different view, that folk psychology and scientific psychology both have something in common. Folk psychology treats different experiences as instances of the same emotion, so in daily life, we talk of different occasions of fear, anger, happiness, and so on. Likewise, a science of emotions is bound to treat different emotional experiences as members of the same class. Hence, we can ask our question again, but slightly differently. How many sorts of emotion are there?

One answer is that there is a small finite set of distinguishable emotions that are the bases of all emotional experiences. This is the hypothesis of basic emotions as primitive unanalysable elements at the psychological level of the system. Another answer is that there are many sorts of emotion, but every distinct sort is generated from among the same finite set of components, much as, say, each chemical molecule is constructed from atoms. Hence, all emotions would be on a par—there would be no sense in which some emotions were basic whereas others were complex.

To be more specific, a theory of basic emotions might analyse embarrassment as founded on the basic emotion of fear, with some other non-emotion component such as a cognition of a particular sort, i.e. knowing that one is the object of unwelcome attention. A componential theory in which no emotions are basic might distinguish embarrassment from fear in terms of different appraisal-response elements that make up each kind of emotion. Such a theory then holds that because of its components each type of emotion has its own unique psychology and physiology, although perhaps with some components in common. Both the theory of basic emotions and the componential theory postulate that an emotional experience depends on various elements. The crucial distinction is that no components can be an emotion *per se* in the componential approach, whereas one component of any emotional experience is always a basic emotion according to the basic theory. Both theories assume that a science of emotions is possible only if there is a finite basis for emotional experience. Both assume that emotions can be taken to pieces analytically. The question is: Is there always a piece that consists in an irreducible basic emotion or are there sub-emotional elements, such as appraisal-response components, into which all emotions can be analysed?

There are various ways in principle of establishing the nature of the finite basis of emotions. In this paper, we will examine the lesson that the function of emotions can teach us with reference to limitations of human rationality. Next, we will enquire into the set of basic emotions. Once we have outlined a theory of them, we will contrast it with a componential theory, and we will show that the componential approach turns out to be a version of the theory of basic emotions or else leads to the doctrine that emotions are a false tenet of folk psychology. We will defend the psychological reality of the folk theory of the emotions, and we will counter arguments based on the difficulty of translating emotional terminology from one language to another. Finally, we will show how the theory of basic emotions can be corroborated, and describe some of these results.

THE NEGLECT OF FUNCTION

What function, if any, do emotions serve? The question has been somewhat neglected by theorists, and one can read much on the cognitive underpinnings of emotions that does not address this issue. Yet, in our view, it is the key to whether or not there is a small set of basic emotions: The hypothesis of basic emotions makes sense only if it elucidates problems faced by the cognitive system. Although elements of current theories of emotions can be traced back at least to the nineteenth century, the intellectual history of the topic has lacked cumulative coherence. Without any clear sense of the psychological function of emotions, it has been difficult to generate more than a patchwork of ideas and observations. With such a sense, perhaps the scientific understanding of emotions will become cumulative, analogously, say, to the understanding of visual perception.

One reason for the neglect of function is probably the pervasive influence of William James. Like Descartes (1649/1911) he classed emotions with perceptions (e.g. James, 1890): They are perceptions of events inside the body. Beyond his claim that not all emotions are accidental, he had little to say about what purposes they might have. Because, according to James, emotions are percepts of bodily feedback from physiological changes, or from actions that have already taken place, emotions occur too late to affect either the control of these actions or the decisions that led to them. Just as there are indefinitely many percepts of the outer world there are, in James's view, indefinitely many feelings, each reflecting a particular pattern of proprioception and physiological perturbation.

James's influence may account for the importance that many theorists place on emotions as primarily pleasant or unpleasant, that is, as "valenced" (e.g. Frijda, 1987; Ortony & Clore, 1989). If emotions are not a system for the immediate control of actions, then they are important endpoints giving colour to experience. Incidentally they can then have motivational consequences. People strive to attain them if pleasant, and to avoid them if unpleasant (Hammond, 1990).

In short, James's theory of emotion contributes to the development of a powerful tradition. His conclusions, perhaps serendipitously, resonate with the high valuation of "experience" as such in Western culture. Pleasantness and unpleasantness have become the crucial characteristics of emotions over and above their own strict individuality. Within this tradition, the possible existence of a set of basic emotions seems both unattractive theoretically and intractable empirically.

RATIONALITY AND THE FUNCTION OF EMOTIONS

Analyses of mental processes in cognitive science assume that each process has functions independently of its particular embodiment. From this perspective, emotions should have a function that could be embodied in a system based either on carbon-like humans or on silicon-like computers. As many people within cognitive science have argued, function is accordingly best thought of in terms of the design of the system. During natural selection systems are fitted to functions, although as a means of design, evolution is notoriously a "tinkerer" not a grand architect. A priori there are many possible designs to enable organisms to cope with their environment.

The simplest possible design relies on "fixed action patterns" and is found in insects. Consider, for instance, the common tick, which is a parasite of mammals. According to von Uexkull (1957), the female tick lacks eyes, but at one stage in her life cycle the photosensitivity of her skin triggers the action of climbing a bush from which she then hangs. She lets go only when a second trigger occurs: The smell of butyric acid, which is secreted by the sweat glands of all mammals. If she happens to land on a passing animal, a third trigger comes into operation: The warmth of her host's body. Propelled by this taxis, she burrows through the hair to the skin, and there she punctures the skin and fills herself with blood. Once full, she drops off the animal to lay her eggs on the earth. And the cycle continues anew.

This sort of design works well when classes of events can be mapped one-to-one on to appropriate responses. Perfect performance is impossible, e.g. a tick may drop but miss the passing mammal. Yet, the solution is rational in the following sense: All that is necessary for a reasonable chance for individuals to survive and to reproduce is built into the species-specific procedures for action. In principle, there are no uncertainties about what to do: The stimulus either unlocks the fixed action pattern, or not. Of course, this certainty can be the undoing of a species if there is a significant change in its environment.

At the other extreme in the theoretical series of designs are those that are impeccably rational. They are maximally flexible because they enable the organism to determine which goals to pursue at any point in time, and to decide at each choice point the best course of action in pursuit of those goals. No contingency is unanticipated, and performance is invariably optimal. Creators of artificial intelligences have aspired to such designs; philosophers have argued that they are realised in human thought (e.g. Dennett, 1978, p. 20; Cohen, 1981); and psychologists have claimed that apparent errors are merely failures in performance that do not impeach the underlying rationality of the system (e.g. Henle, 1978).

In designs based on fixed action patterns or on impeccable rationality, there is no occasion for anything corresponding to an emotion. There are no surprises, no misunderstandings, no irresolvable conflicts. Human beings are neither equipped with a set of responses each matched to an important stimulus, nor do they possess impeccable rationality. A fully rational system of thought is a paragon that cannot be realised by any finite device. Any set of observations is compatible with an infinitude of different valid conclusions, and so no finite organism can follow up all of them (Johnson-Laird, 1983; Cherniak, 1986; Stich, 1990). Moreover, human reasoners make genuine mistakes in reasoning—mistakes that they even acknowledge in some cases. They make invalid inferences that should not occur if their thinking were guided by valid formal rules of inference (Johnson-Laird & Byrne, 1991). In short, to paraphrase de Sousa (1987): Human beings are neither insects nor omniscient, omnipotent gods.

If impeccable rationality is impossible, what design is embodied in human beings? Johnson-Laird and Byrne (in press) argue for a significant modification of the competence-performance distinction. The original distinction hinged on the idea that rational competence is based on valid rules of inference, which, like the rules of grammar, might sometimes be inadequately reflected in actual performance. The new notion of rational competence depends instead on a meta-principle: An inference is valid provided that there is no model of the premises in which its conclusion is false. Individuals have a tacit grasp of this meta-principle, and they put it into practice by building mental models of premises, drawing useful conclusions from them, and then searching for alternative models that might refute such conclusion. But they have no grasp of any specific logical rules, and they have no comprehensive algorithm for valid thinking, i.e. for searching for models that refute conclusions. The meta-principle is defensible as a rational requirement for any system for deductive inference, although it alone does not guarantee the validity of inferences. To argue that errors arise as result of performance factors is misleading, however, because it suggests a failure to put into practice correct rules, whereas there are no rules to put into practice, only the higher-order meta-principle. This principle is compatible with the observations of deductive failure, and with the arguments against impeccable rationality.

Granted that reasoning is fallible and time-consuming, Oatley and Johnson-Laird (1987), following Simon (1967), and a tradition of cognitive theorists, proposed that the function of emotions is to fill the gap between fixed action patterns and impeccable rationality. For many species, including *homo sapiens*, the world is too complex to form perfect mental models, so events and the outcomes of actions are often unanticipated. The problem that Simon identified is that complex systems acting in the natural world, as opposed to a simplified microworld, need something equivalent to interrupt signals in computation. Such signals are necessary in systems that have limited resources, and that need to be influenced by unforeseen events demanding urgent attention. Emotions, as Simon noted, seem to be co-extensive with the occurrence of such problems. They arise particularly when individuals have many concurrent goals, including mutually incompatible ones, and their resources of time, ability, and processing power, are too limited to make a fully rational choice. Moreover, social mammals often cannot achieve their more valuable objectives alone, and so they need to interact with others. Co-operation calls for mutual plans, but it is impossible to guarantee that copies of the plan kept by each partner are identical. Competition calls for antagonistic plans, and it is impossible to determine their outcome. The biological system of emotions offers a solution to these problems, particularly those that arise from the limits of rational principles to govern or to predict complex social interactions. Emotions enable social species to co-ordinate their behaviour, to respond to emergencies, to prioritise goals, to prepare for appropriate actions, and to make progress towards goals. They do so even though individuals have only limited abilities to cogitate.

Emotions guide individual and group behaviour. Social mammals are unable to determine the best course of action at many of the junctures in their lives. Even in humans, the resources for rational thought are often too slow and too error-prone to solve this problem. The function of emotions is accordingly to bridge the gaps of rationality. We argue that this bridge is possible only if many specific junctures can be mapped into a few broad classes of reaction.

We have proposed (Oatley & Johnson-Laird, 1987) that the cognitive evaluation of a juncture in action calls into readiness a small and distinctive suite of action plans that has been selected as appropriate to it. Each basic emotion thus prompts both the individual and the group in a way that in the course of evolution has been more successful than alternative kinds of prompting in broadly defined, recurring circumstances that are relevant to goals. Thus, when the broad class of event occurs that indicates achievement of a subgoal that increases the probability of attaining a goal, then its cognitive evaluation initiates an internal emotional signal. We propose that emotion signals of this kind have no propositional content or syntactic structure: They have a control function rather than an informational function. The signal that is sent when subgoals are achieved acts to prompt the individual to continue the same line of action. When a goal is lost, a different emotion signal is sent. It prompts the individual to disengage from that goal. The internal emotional signals have causal effects within the organism, preparing it physiologically for each general class of actions. In the case of human beings, the signals can in addition be experienced subjectively as emotions. The signal caused by a successful achievement is experienced as happiness, and the signal caused by the loss of a goal as sadness. An important consequence of the ensuing actions is the communication of the individual's emotional state to others in the same social group—an example is the distinctive type of alarm signal sent by certain social mammals and birds. The receipt of such external signals has emotional consequences for these other individuals too.

If the emotional guidance of action is to be rapid, successful, and independent of reasoning which is too time-consuming, then the cognitive evaluations must be coarse and the resulting suites of actions must be broad and flexible. There are two key issues here. First, many events in the world must be mapped on to a relatively small number of categories, which each elicit a distinct set of bodily, behavioural, and (at least in the case of humans) phenomenological consequences. If there were very many categories, then the problem of deciding amongst them would re-emerge as a time-consuming matter. Secondly, the small repertoire of actions triggered by a particular emotion must be useful to a wide class of specific triggering events. For example, if there is a conflict in goals because an event threatens an individual's safety during the course of another action, then the emotion of fear prepares a small repertoire of actions, which includes stopping the current action, checking everything that has been done recently, monitoring the environment, fleeing, being prepared for fighting, physical exertion, or bodily harm. In the case of human beings, the repertoire can be supplemented with action sequences that have been practised. The purpose of fire drills, for instance, is to enable people to learn how to leave a building in the event of a fire without having to think about what to do.

Although we have not yet developed a computer simulation of this theory, it is based on computational considerations. Such considerations are called "computational" because they are at a particular level of analysis (Marr, 1982), in which knowledge of aspects of the social and physical environment is mapped on to a design for the kinds of operations that could cope with these aspects. Emotions function in real time to redistribute cognitive resources and to manage goal priorities. When an event has been detected that requires re-computing these priorities, an emotion occurs and it helps to manage either the continuation of the current course of action or the transition to another sequence of action. Emotions help to specify which goals will be actively pursued, and which abandoned, or assigned to a subsidiary or dormant status (see also Stein & Levine, 1990). Emotions have further consequences by way of external signals that co-ordinate group behaviour.

We can summarise the argument so far in three propositions:

Proposition 1. Events and their significance for goals are often unforeseen because: (a) finite organisms cannot be impeccably rational, and they have imperfect models of the world; (b) individuals with several goals are often unable to satisfy all of them simultaneously; and (c) social animals interact together in ways that cannot always be anticipated.

Proposition 2. It follows that junctures in action will occur at which an individual needs to act, but for which there is no fully rational method to select the next action.

Proposition 3. Emotions function to redistribute cognitive resources at junctures in action, particularly where neither cogitation nor reflexes (the residue of fixed action patterns) determine an appropriate course of action. Because some action is probably better than becoming lost in thought, a biologically based system makes ready a small repertoire of actions appropriate to a recognisable type of goal-relevant event. The mechanism tends to constrain the individual to choose the next action sequence from this repertoire. Such a mechanism is a result of natural selection, and the repertoires of actions include both species-specific patterns and individually acquired habits.

WHICH EMOTIONS ARE BASIC?

Many theorists have proposed sets of basic emotions. There are differences among the theories and among the sets of basic emotions that have been proposed. These differences prompt sceptics to argue that it is no longer clear what is meant by the claim that some emotions are basic, and that it has no testable content (see, for example, Ortony & Turner, 1990). Most previous theories, however, have not been based on a functional analysis. Their principal motivation has been to bring order to the disparate set of human emotions by seeking to derive them from a set of basic emotions, e.g. by postulating a set of opposites, by analogy to chemistry or to the mixing of colours (e.g. McDougall, 1926; Plutchik, 1962). Pride, for instance, has been proposed to be a combination of joy and anger; and love a combination of joy and acceptance. Some of the postulates of such theories, however, have no empirical support either subjectively or physiologically, and this again has been noted by sceptics. It is a common experience to have "mixed" feelings, but this state is characterised by an awareness of alternative and conflicting emotions (see also Ellworth & Smith, 1988; Stein & Levine, 1989). Indeed, our own research (Oatley & Duncan, in press) shows that in more than a third of episodes of happiness, sadness, anger, and fear, a person experiences simultaneously two basic emotions. The most common such mixture is sadness and anger—caused, for instance, by a loss which also frustrates some plan. Our method does not discriminate between true simultaneity and rapid alternation of underlying states. What individuals do not report, however, is the existence of a single emotion made up from phenomenally remote constituents.

According to our theory, emotions are a result of coarse cognitive evaluations that elicit internal and external signals and corresponding suites of action plans. They are emotions because they have cognitive rather than physiological causes. From an analysis of the ontology of simple social mammals, we have proposed the following set of basic emotions: happiness, sadness, anger, fear, disgust (Oatley & Johnson-Laird, 1987), and perhaps desire (Oatley & Johnson-Laird, 1990). Hence, specific emotions are typically caused by the perceptions of general categories of event: (1) happiness with perception of improving progress towards a goal; (2) sadness when a goal is lost; (3) anger when a plan is blocked; (4) fear when a goal conflict or a threat to self-preservation occurs; (5) disgust with a perception of something to reject; and (6) desire with a perception of something to approach. These emotions are indeed basic—however, depending on how the evidence points, other emotions may be basic too. The names of the basic emotions have misleading enthno- and anthropocentric connotations, but in English they come close to suggesting the emotional behaviours of social mammals.

We argue that the status of the basic emotions is corroborated in five ways. First, each of them is an emotion that appears to be universal, and to have universal concomitants, such as a corresponding facial expression (see Ekman, 1973, and Ekman, this issue). Second, each has either a bodily or phenomenological component that can be experienced without the individual knowing the cause of the emotion. Third, the semantics of the large emotional vocabulary of English can be explicated without having to appeal to any other emotions (see Johnson-Laird & Oatley, 1989). Fourth, each term denoting a basic emotion is primitive in the sense that it is semantically unanalysable. It refers to a phenomenological primitive that one needs to have experienced in order to grasp the meaning of the terms. If Mr Spock (of *Star Trek*) does not experience emotions, then it is impossible to explain to him what happiness or sadness are. We could explain what kinds of events are likely to cause these states; we could explain what physiological changes they are likely to bring about and what actions they are likely to elicit. With some perceptual training, such as experience with Ekman's Facial Action Coding System (Ekman & Friesen, 1978), he would be able to discriminate amongst facial displays of emotions. But we could not explain to him what it was like to feel happy or sad, any more than we could explain what red was like to a person who was completely colour blind. Fifth, the apparent complexity of human emotional experience comes from the diverse cognitive evaluations that can elicit and accompany the basic emotions, and that can differ from one culture to another. The accompanying cognitions are also reflected in the vocabulary of emotions. An emotion term accordingly refers to a subset of the basic emotions, typically just a single basic emotion, perhaps with an indication of the intensity of the emotion, as in the series: "contentedness", "happiness", "joy", "ecstasy". A term can also convey that the state has a known cause or object. For example, to use the term, "glad", properly, is to imply a conscious propositional knowledge of what caused the happiness: That one is glad that something has, or has not, happened.

Basic Emotions vs. Components of Emotions

Our theory of basic emotions contrasts with a recent componential proposal made by Ortony and Turner (1990), which is also computationally motivated (see Ortony, Clore, & Collins, 1988). Ortony and Turner reject the hypothesis of basic emotions, and instead they consider it more profitable to analyse emotional expressions and responses in terms of dissociable components that are innate. Their theory is akin to the notion that the underlying components of facial expressions, and other emotional responses, are governed by a system of production rules of the form:

If an Event E1 occurs, then do Action A1
If an Event E2 occurs, then do Action A2
. . . and so on.

As an example, Ortony and Turner (p. 332) consider the apparently universal facial expression of anger, which they analyse in terms of separate and dissociable components. We can capture the essence of their claims in the following production rules:

If you become conscious of being unable to attain a goal, then furrow your brow.
If you desire to be aggressive towards the agent responsible for the blockage, then form an open, square mouth that shows your teeth.
If you are determined to remove the source of the goal blockage, then compress your lips.
If you devote considerable attention to the visual environment, then raise your upper eyelids.

These dissociable elements of the prototypical facial expression of anger are invoked by an event in relation to a goal: a goal blockage. This event, however, has attributes such as the "existence of an identifiable agent responsible for the blockage", which may, or may not, be present in any given episode. Ortony and Turner go on to make a case for dissociable physiological components underlying emotional experiences. "Our view", they write (p. 322) "is that such differences in physiological responses are usually better interpreted as indicating not so much the presence of specific emotions as the presence of dissociable components of emotions, namely specific appraisals and their corresponding responses".

We see several problems with a componential analysis of this sort. First, Ortony and Turner allow only "external causes of co-occurrences of sub-components" (p. 323). So, although their system is like a set of production rules, because the independence of sub-components is so fundamental to them, anything that might bind rules together internally is excluded. In contrast to computational production systems which have the power of universal Turing machines, no logical operations between rules are described. Moreover, although alternative environmental events may trigger a single rule, there is no indication that the same event might trigger alternative rules. Hence, there is no indication that their mechanism might generate default operations for states of uncertainty. The system they discuss, therefore, does not address the functional issue of filling the gap between fixed action patterns and impeccable rationality that we have discussed in the previous section. It is hard, indeed, to see how the system differs in principle from the fixed action patterns of insects. Secondly, their account takes a critical step towards treating emotions as a myth of folk psychology. As Ortony and Turner make clear, the dissociable actions that they propose are not caused or linked by anger. On the contrary, the theory dismantles anger into a set of components, which can differ from one case to another. There need be nothing in common to all occasions of anger. How is it possible then for individuals to refer to anger in so many diverse situations? One possible answer is that there is a prototypical set of components underlying all experiences of anger (cf. Fehr & Russell, 1984). Granted a certain number of the characteristic components of anger, then individuals experience the emotion. Such an approach has some plausibility as an account of the concept of an emotion such as anger. However, Ortony and Turner (p. 323) specifically argue against it as an analysis of the emotion itself.

In our view anger typically corresponds to the following sequence:

- an individual's goal is frustrated, often but not necessarily by another agent;
- the individual perceives the blockage;

- a basic anger signal propagates through the cognitive system which the individual experiences as feeling angry;
- as a result of this signal, physiological mechanisms prepare the body for aggression, the face assumes an expression in which the brows are furrowed, etc; and
- plans are made ready for removing the blockage.

The important component in this sequence is the third one: a specific signal propagates which the individual experiences as feeling angry. This component alone is sufficient for an individual to be angry. One can be angry for no known reason, that is, without any awareness of a goal-blockage and without betraying one's feelings by facial expressions or bodily behaviours. If an individual feels angry in such circumstances, then, according to our theory of basic emotions, the feeling is mediated by a primitive unanalysable signal of anger that impinges on consciousness, but without knowing anything else about the state. For a componential analysis, however, a feeling of anger must be mediated by a set of dissociable components that can differ from one such experience to another. Ortony and Turner make this point with great clarity in their discussion of fear (p. 327): "There are various kinds of fear, each consisting of somewhat different components."

It is hard to see what these components of a feeling could be. One putative view is that emotions are valenced experiences, anger is a negative experience, and so the subjective experience is composed of the following components:

$$Emotion + Negative\ valence + X$$

where X is a set of subjective components that distinguish anger from other negative emotions, such as fear. There is a striking dilemma for such a view, however. Either X includes a set of components common to all subjective experiences of anger, or else it does not. If it does contain a common set of components, then we are back once again at a theory of basic emotions: underlying any experience of anger is a common set of components. Hence, on this side of the dilemma, the componential theory is entirely compatible with the theory of basic emotions.

We suspect that Ortony and Turner prefer the other side of the dilemma in which subjective experiences of anger do not contain common elements. In this case, there really is nothing in common to all occasions of anger other than:

$$Emotion + Negative\ valence$$

But these two components fail to distinguish anger from other negative emotions. Hence, this view leads ineluctably to the conclusion that emotions as distinct subjective experiences, such as anger, fear, and sadness, have no real existence. To reject common components is to reject, not just basic emotions, but all the everyday categories of emotion: One is indeed forced to treat them as a myth of folk psychology.

FOLK THEORIES AND SCIENTIFIC THEORIES OF EMOTIONS

We argued in the previous section that the rejection of basic emotions leads to a rejection of the naïve everyday categories of emotion too. This sceptical view of emotion has always attracted adherents, who regard folk psychology as based on errors that are as egregious as those that underlie naïve physics. Ultimately, according to this form of reductionism, the ideas and terms of folk theory will be replaced by proper scientific explanations. Once again, William James anticipated the critique of folk psychology. Here he is on the pointlessness of studying emotion terms of ordinary language, and of trying to sort them into categories, such as basic and non-basic (James, 1890, p. 485):

> If one should seek to name each particular one of them [emotions] of which the human heart is the seat, it is plain that the limit to their number would lie in the introspective vocabulary of the seeker, each race of men having found names for some shade of feeling which other races have left undiscriminated. If we should seek to break the emotions, thus enumerated, into groups, according to their affinities, it is again plain that all sorts of groupings would be possible, according as we chose this character or that as a basis, and that all groupings would be equally real and true.

In more recent times, the argument from this side has gone somewhat as follows: Accounts which include intentional terms, such as "desiring that something", or "believing that something", are folk theories that seek to explain and predict individual's actions. Just as naïve physics depends on the misleading idea of impetus, so folk psychology depends on the misleading idea that beliefs and desires cause behaviour. Newton replaced impetus by coherent laws of motion; so, too, the psychology of belief and desire will be replaced by a proper scientific account of behaviour that will be based, not on such "intentional" concepts, but on the neurophysiology of the nervous system (see, for example, Stich, 1983; Churchland, 1984).

The view implicit in our theory of emotions is that folk psychology is not a myth. It embodies important truths: that individuals have beliefs and desires and needs, that they use their beliefs to decide what to do to attain their goals and then try to carry out these actions—and that emotions have effects on behaviour. An achievement of cognitive science is to rehabilitate mental terms following their banishment during "Behaviourism", and to show how the psychology of "belief and desire" can be modelled computationally. There is no warrant for the generalisation from naïve physics to the conclusion that all folk theories are mistaken. In particular, psychological phenomena and physical phenomena are different. A putative account of, say, physical motion is corrigible. But the subjective experience of an emotion is incorrigible in the sense that it is not a hypothesis that could be falsified by evidence in the way that hypotheses about the physical world may be. If you feel definitely happy, you will not be mistaken that you are happy, because, according to us, the feeling of happiness is a direct phenomenological result of a certain kind of signal in the cognitive system. The (folk theoretical) concept which in English is called happiness indicates just such a feeling. It indicates something real. Like sleepiness, or pain, or thirst, it is subjective, not open to consensual validation or evidential refutation.

When an emotion signal does impinge on consciousness it does not have to be interpreted to determine which emotion it represents. It does not represent an emotional state. A conscious emotion is the experience of an emotion signal. Such an experience leaves room for various kinds of doubt, for instance about its cause, about the interpretation of the emotion-eliciting event, about whether the feeling is strong enough to be sure that an emotion really is occurring, or about what kind of emotion it is—particularly if for some reason the emotion is suppressed, or if two emotions occur as a mixture. But, we argue, in straightforward cases where the emotion is felt strongly, e.g. feeling happy at seeing a good friend, feeling angry if someone lets you down, feeling afraid at a traffic accident, there is no doubt about the nature of the emotion itself. So, in the structured diaries of 30 patients attending a gastrointestinal clinic, each asked to record four episodes of emotion of any kind, half of their emotion episodes were experienced in this way. For each episode subjects were asked: "Would you call it a type of any of the following?—happiness/joy, sadness/grief, anger/irritation, fear/anxiety or disgust/hatred." They were then asked to rate how sure they were about this choice on an 11 point scale from 0 (not at all sure) to 10 (completely sure), (Duncan & Oatley, in prep.). All episodes of emotion were rated as one of the five types. Subjects rated 50.4% of their categorisations as "completely sure", and only 14% of episodes at 5 or below on the scale of certainty of categorisation. Our claim is also supported by the ready ability of children to learn and to understand the causal sequence of events underlying emotions—the chain from the perception of a goal-related event, to the emotion, and then to a change in action (Stein & Levine, 1989). The cause of the emotion is typically obvious; and this defence of folk psychology is consistent with the existence of basic emotions.

Subjective experiences, of having beliefs, desires, emotions, lie at the heart of folk psychology. As a theory, however, the folk theory of emotions provides little account of psychological mechanisms, or their physiological bases. The goal of a cognitive science of emotions is thus to spell out a mechanism that is at least consistent with common observations of the causes and consequences of emotions. The persistence over time of these observations does not indicate a stagnation of explanation as a result of isolation from evidence. The evidence is the set of observations of the causes and consequences of emotions to which people are continuously open.

Sceptics might imagine that this hypothesis of a convergence between folk theory and scientific theory is a quirk peculiar to us. But other researchers too, with quite different theories from ours, have come to the same conclusion. Ortony and his colleagues argue that individuals can be usefully consulted about what terms refer to emotions, and that these everyday intuitions map on to the scientific theory of emotions (Ortony et al., 1988). Similarly, Fehr and Russell (1984) and Shaver, Schwartz, Kirson, & O'Connor (1987), have consulted people in a range of ways about their categorisations of emotion terms. These investigators also assume that people know that emotions are caused by certain types of events related to goals. They postulate a correspondence between the results of their studies and scientific categories, and, in the case of Shaver et al., their results support basic categories of emotions, which correspond to some degree to those that we have postulated.

Our hypothesis of a convergence between folk theories of emotions and scientific theories of emotions is, like any other scientific claim, open to refutation. There are indeed several ways to challenge it. One is to argue that self-reports are neither reliable nor valid, and only objective reports of behaviour or physiology should have any part in science. Evidence for such assertions can be derived from the work of Nisbett and Wilson (1977) and Nisbett and Ross (1980), which shows that people are often poor judges of the causes of their judgements and behaviour. The true causes include social conformity, compliance to subtle conditions of experimental designs, and attributional biases. Individuals are not conscious of these factors, and their explanations of their own behaviour ignore them. Instead, they focus on events that are salient, without weighing in any statistically appropriate manner relevant causal factors. They also display pervasive mental short-comings. They can make gross errors of judgement about the causal effects of their own or others' actions (Jenkins & Ward, 1965), they overlook falsifying evidence (Wason, 1960), and they are biased by information that is more immediately available or that appears to be more representative of the case in hand (Kahneman, Slovic, & Tversky, 1982).

Thus, the argument goes, people do not know the causes of either their behaviour or of their mental states in any way that resembles a scientific account. Not only do they lack a privileged introspective access to how events cause behaviour, but they are regularly misled by their introspec-tions. They are subject to inbuilt mental deficits in reasoning that will necessarily lead them astray. Hence, folk psychology is not merely irrele-vant to scientific theories, but to attend to it is positively misleading.

This kind of argument has encouraged many to eschew evidence based on self-reports, but we believe this is mistaken, for three inter-related reasons.

First, as many of the psychologists studying the shortcomings of the human inferential system have themselves pointed out, their studies deli-berately focus on cognitive illusions much as perceptual psychologists seek visual illusions with the goal of revealing the workings of the cognitive system. No psychologist argues from the existence of visual illusions to the claim that all vision is illusory and non-veridical. Likewise, the failures of inference in the psychological laboratory hardly justify the claim that human reasoning is intrinsically irrational (see Johnson-Laird & Byrne, in press).

Secondly, as Craik (1943) proposed, the brain models important entities, attributes, and relations in the world. If it had not converged on successful models of important sequences, we would not be able to operate in the world. Thought, behaviour, and communication, are successful more often than not—the central postulates of folk psychology are based on essen-tially correct, though radically incomplete, mental models. Actions are caused by goals in conjunction with beliefs. The reason, for example, that the engineers in charge at Chernobyl did not report the destruction of the nuclear reactor to the authorities in Moscow is because they did not believe that the reactor had been destroyed. They persisted in the view that the reactor was intact, despite much evidence to the contrary, including the reports of two young probationary engineers whom they had sent to examine it and who paid with their lives for their observations (Medvedev, 1990). Work on inferential failure may reveal causes of such pathological disbelief, but what is clear is that the belief led to a failure to report the scale of the disaster, and that this failure contributed to the appalling delay in evacuating the area.

Thirdly, emotions usually follow immediately after the events that cause them. Therefore, people will not ordinarily suffer the kinds of illusions of thinking just indicated. Such errors occur easily, for instance when causes are probabilistic and temporally distant from effects, as in the studies of Jenkins and Ward. The mechanisms of human learning have been success-fully tuned by evolution to sequences in which a causal event is regularly and closely followed by a caused event, as routinely demonstrated in both classical and instrumental conditioning experiments. People are indeed bad in intuitions and judgements made outside this range, but their judgements about emotions derive from many experiences within it. Even if, as we agree, people do not have introspective access to many kinds of mental process, they can introspect the distinctive phenomenal occurrence of an emotion and they can connect such an occurrence with a putative causal event, which in the typical case is obvious rather than hidden or subtle. Both emotions and their usual causes fall within focal attention. As Ericsson and Simon (1980) argue, it is precisely such data that can be verbalised. Data that are outside attention require inferences of the kind that are subject to the errors pointed out by Nisbett, Wilson, Ross, and others.

LANGUAGE AND THE UNIVERSALITY OF BASIC EMOTIONS

A different argument against the existence of basic emotions concerns language and cross-cultural studies. Wierzbicka (this issue), argues that theorists have assumed the universality of categories and facial expressions that correspond to English terms. This ethnocentricity is immediately revealed, the argument goes, if one takes an emotional term from some other culture and tries to apply it to an English-speaking culture. For example, the Ifaluk emotion of *fago* (translated by Lutz, 1982, as "compassion-love-sadness") seems natural and basic to the culture, but it also seems to have no counterpart in English. Likewise, Lutz describes the Ifaluk emotion called *song*, which she translates roughly as "justified anger". Wierzbicka argues that this emotion does not correspond to any basic notion of anger, and that it should not be referred to by the English word, "anger". This argument is important; and we would like to clarify our position.

When a theorist proposes that the emotion or facial expression of, say, "happiness" is a basic and thus universal emotion, the claim is that among the basic emotions, which have evolved in social mammals and which are experienced and communicated among humans, is one that in English is most closely referred to as "happiness". If we have seemed to imply that the English "happiness" is the basic emotion, we apologise. What we mean is that there is a basic emotion, for which in English "happiness" or perhaps "enjoyment" or, to use Wierzbicka's phrase "something like happy" are the nearest indicators. The underlying emotion can be communicated between people nonverbally, and its communication can be effective despite deep gulfs of language and culture. In another language, the emotional terminology will be different, and whatever term corresponds most closely to "happiness" is likely to differ in its connotations. Thus, on Ifaluk, Lutz describes a concept *ker*, which she translates as "happiness/excitement". Cultural attitudes differ: People on Ifaluk do not believe that they have a Jeffersonian right to the pursuit of *ker*. Although pleasant, it has a negative social connotation, and people are distrustful of it because it can lead to showing off, and neglect of concern for others which is highly valued on Ifaluk. Nuances of this kind thus reflect different conscious attitudes to each emotion, cultural differences in its causation, and differences in the forms of morally acceptable behaviour to which it may lead. Moreover, most emotion terms in a language have a meaning that combines reference to a basic emotion with other semantic information, such as the cause of the emotion. Thus, for example, "embarrassment" refers to a state corresponding to fear (a basic emotion) caused by finding oneself an object of unwelcome social attention—a common experience in the English-speaking world. Different languages are therefore likely to focus on different causes and objects of emotion, and so emotional terms may be difficult to translate from one language to another. As many philosophers from Quine (1960) onwards have pointed out, when you seek a translation of a word or expression from one language to another, then you must attribute a certain degree of common rationality to the other culture. You are likely to be sceptical about the accuracy of the translation if it implies total irrationality and that you should cease to treat the individuals of the alien culture as having any meaningful beliefs. Indeed, some philosophers go further and argue that complete rationality is a prerequisite if an individual is to be said to hold any meaningful beliefs (Davidson, 1975; Dennett, 1978, p. 20). If emotion terms were fundamentally untranslatable, as Wierzbicka sometimes seems to imply, then it should be impossible for native speakers of incommensurable languages ever to learn one another's terminology. The emotional life of the Ifaluk should remain forever beyond Lutz's empathic grasp. The emotion of the inhabitants of some alien planet may truly be beyond our comprehension, but no such individuals have ever been found on earth. It may be difficult to translate words denoting emotions, but it is not impossible to empathise with a culture and to learn to experience the corresponding emotions.

In short, our general theory of the semantics of emotion terms, which was applied to English terms in the first instance, should be equally applicable to other languages. It preserves the notions—common to both folk theories and scientific theories—that emotions are distinctive states, that they are caused by recognisable events of which people can be consciously aware, and that they can be directed to objects or to other people.

IS THE THEORY TESTABLE?

In this final section, we will counter the criticism that the theory of basic emotions is too vaguely defined to be susceptible of empirical test (Mandler, 1984; Ortony & Turner, 1990). We believe that this criticism is prompted not by any conceptual difficulty in testing the existence of basic emotions, but by the practical difficulty of such investigations. Indeed, few investigations have been performed that fulfil the conditions to make a compelling case.

One way of falsifying the hypothesis of basic emotions would be to show that the apparent diversity of emotions cannot be reduced to a small basic set because different varieties of, say, fear, have no underlying components in common. What is needed is a set of cumulative studies that test for the universal existence of a small set of basic emotions corresponding to folk theoretical categories. These studies should investigate whether such emotions are experienced, communicated, and recognised universally; and they should investigate whether they have common components in their underlying neurophysiology. Hence, the studies need to examine different cultures, infants on whom culture has yet to impinge, and the physiological systems of animals and human beings (see Panksepp, 1982). It is even possible that certain eliciting conditions for basic emotions will prove to be universal, or at least common to diverse cultures, although the theory does not strictly call for this condition to hold.

Studies of basic emotions are complex, difficult, and time-consuming. Yet, various researchers have begun to undertake them. Ekman and his colleagues have carried out a paradigmatic set of studies that meet the necessary conditions (see Ekman's paper in this issue). They have shown in particular that facial expressions of a basic set of emotions are common across diverse cultural groups, and that basic emotions have distinctive physiological accompaniments.

A stringent hypothesis is that basic emotions should be perceived categorically, just as, for example, the contrast between certain English consonants, has been tested by Etcoff (1990). What distinguishes "bit" from "pit" is a few milliseconds of onset in voicing, i.e. the vibrations of the larynx in the articulation of the phonemes /b/ and /p/. For equal physical differences in voicing onset time, it is difficult to discriminate between two sounds lying on one side or the other of the boundary between /b/ and /p/, but easy to discriminate between two sounds that straddle this boundary. Etcoff argued that if there are basic emotions, then the perception of facial expressions should also be categorical in the same way. Happy faces should be sorted into one category, sad ones into another, and so on. She argued that if she could create equal physical increments in scales ranging between different basic emotions, then there would be categorical boundaries. On one side of them people would see one emotion, on the other a different one, but on either side discrimination should be poorer than across the boundary. She created equal increments using Brennan's (1985) computer program for drawing faces in a way that includes details of eyebrows, eyelids, and mouth. She traced 21 photographs from Ekman and Friesen's

(1976) pictures of facial affect from three models, who each posed express-ions of a putative set of basic emotions: sadness, anger, fear, disgust, surprise, and a neutral state. She then used the program to create an incremental series of 11 faces that changed in equal physical increments from one emotion to another. For instance, in one series faces number 1 and number 11 were respectively drawings from the digitised photographs of happy and sad faces of one of the models. Face number 2 derived from the average positions of 10 sets of points from the happy face +1 set from the sad face; face number 3 derived from 9 sets from the happy face +2 sets from the sad face, and so on. With standard psychophysical methods, she then tested the hypothesis of categorical perception of these faces. She observed an abrupt shift in discriminability between the faces in all the series except the one from surprise to fear. She also observed the same effect between the emotion faces and the neutral faces, although the gradations of the neutral faces were more discriminable than those between the emotion faces.

A further corroboration of basic emotions has been obtained by Conway and Bekerian (1987). They found in studies of similarity judgements that emotion terms fell into groups corresponding to basic emotions: happiness/love/joy—misery/grief/sadness—fear/panic/terror—and   anger/jealousy/hate. They then used lexical decision tasks to investigate the representation of these concepts in memory. In one experiment, the subjects read two sentences that had previously been judged appropriate to a particular emotion, such as love. They then immediately carried out a lexical decision task in which they were shown a string of letters and had to decide whether or not it was a word. It was either another emotion word from the same basic group, e.g. "joy", an emotion word from another basic group, e.g. "sadness", or a nonword. Interspersed with emotion trials were trials with emotionally neutral filler sentences and words and nonwords. The subjects' reaction times were faster for words from the same basic emotion group than for words from a different emotion group.

These experiments corroborate basic emotions within a single culture. Because the theory postulates an innate and universal foundation for basic emotions, it predicts that the phenomena observed by Etcoff and by Conway and Bekerian should generalise in the same way across different cultures.

CONCLUSION

We have made a case for the psychological reality of emotions and for their foundation on a small set of basic emotions: happiness, sadness, anger, fear, desire, and disgust. Each basic emotion depends on an innate and universal internal mental signal, which can be elicited by rapid and coarse cognitive evaluations that may be common to diverse cultures. These evaluations concern progress towards goals. The internal signals are causal precursors of subjective experience, somatic change, and plans for action. They are also precursors to external signals, such as facial expressions, that communicate the emotion to others. The theory can be contrasted with the rival hypothesis that there are no basic emotions, but instead more fundamental components, out of which all emotional experiences are constructed (Ortony & Turner, 1990). On the one hand, if there are supposed to be components in common to all subjective experiences of, say, fear, including cases where individuals have no knowledge of the cause of the emotion and react in no outward way to it, then the theory is entirely compatible with basic emotions. On the other hand, if there are not supposed to be any components in common to all subjective experiences of an emotion such as fear, then the theory amounts to a rejection of the folk categories of emotion. Emotions are nothing more than naïve illusions. Once dispelled, they will cease to exist as useful pre-theoretical categories for cognitive science. We have argued that there are no strong grounds for rejecting folk psychology; Ortony and his colleagues have defended a similar position (Ortony et al., 1988). Yet, Ortony and Turner (1990) have questioned both the concept of the basic emotions, and what would count as empirical evidence for or against them. They say that "current uses of the notion do not permit coherent answers to be given to such questions" (p. 329). Their own componential theory, however, seems to be either a variant of the basic emotion hypothesis or else a repudiation of the folk theory. The case for basic emotions has not convinced everybody, but the tests that have been carried out appear to corroborate it.

Manuscript received 4 April 1991
Revised manuscript received 22 November 1991

REFERENCES

Brennan, S. (1985). The caricature generator. *Leonardo*, *18*, 170–178.
Cherniak, C. (1986). *Minimal rationality*. Cambridge, MA: MIT Press.
Cohen, L.J. (1981). Can human irrationality be experimentally demonstrated? *Behavioral and Brain Sciences*, *4*, 317–370.
Churchland, P.M. (1984). *Matter and consciousness*. Cambridge, MA: MIT Press.
Conway, M.A. & Bekerian, D.A. (1987). Situational knowledge and emotions. *Cognition and Emotion*, *1*, 145–191.
Craik, K.J.W. (1943). *The nature of explanation*. Cambridge University Press.
Davidson, D. (1975). *Thought and talk*. In Guttenplan, S. (Ed.), *Mind and language*. Oxford University Press.
Dennett, D.C. (1978). *Brainstorms*. Cambridge, MA: MIT Press.

Descartes, R. (1911). *Passions de l'âme*. In E.L. Haldane & G.R. Ross (Eds and Trans.), *The philosophical works of Descartes*. [Originally published 1649.] Cambridge University Press.

D'Andrade, R. (1987). A folk model of the mind. In D. Holland & N. Quinn (Eds), *Cultural models in language and thought*. Cambridge University Press.

de Sousa, R. (1987). *The rationality of emotions*. Cambridge, MA: MIT Press.

Ekman, P. (1973). Cross-cultural studies of facial expression. In P. Ekman (Ed.), *Darwin and facial expression: A century of research in review*. New York: Academic Press.

Ekman, P. & Friesen, W.V. (1976). *Pictures of facial affect*. Palo Alto, CA: Consulting Psychologists Press.

Ekman, P. & Friesen, W.V. (1978). *Facial Action Coding System (FACS): A technique of the measurement of facial action*. Palo Alto, CA: Consulting Psychologists Press.

Ellsworth, P.C. & Smith, C.A. (1988). From appraisal to emotion: Differences among unpleasant feelings. *Motivation and Emotion*, *12*, 271–302.

Ericsson, K.A. & Simon, H.A. (1980). Verbal reports as data. *Psychological Review*, *87*, 215–251.

Etcoff, N. (1990). *Categorical perception of facial expressions*. Paper presented to the Fifth Annual Meeting of the International Society for Research on Emotions, Rutgers University NJ, 25–28 July.

Fehr, B. & Russell, J.A. (1984). Concept of emotion viewed from a prototype perspective. *Journal of Experimental Psychology: General*, *113*, 464–486.

Frijda, N.H. (1987). Comment on Oatley and Johnson-Laird's 'Towards a cognitive theory of emotions'. *Cognition and Emotion*, *1*, 51–59.

Hammond, M. (1990). Affective maximization: A new macro-theory in the sociology of emotion. In T.D. Kemper (Ed.), *Research agendas in the sociology of emotions*. Albany, NY: State University of New York Press.

Henle, M. (1978). Foreword to R. Revlin & R.E. Mayer (Eds), *Human reasoning*. Washington: Winston.

James, W. (1890). *The principles of psychology*. New York: Holt.

Jenkins, H. & Ward, W. (1965). Judgements of contingency between responses and outcomes. *Psychological Monographs*, *79*, No. 594.

Johnson-Laird, P.N. (1983). *Mental models*. Cambridge, MA: Harvard University Press/ Cambridge University Press.

Johnson-Laird, P.N. & Byrne, R.M.J. (1991). *Deduction*. Hove: Lawrence Erlbaum Associates Ltd.

Johnson-Laird, P.N. & Byrne, R.M.J. (In press). Models and deductive rationality. In K. Manktelow & D. Over (Eds), *Rationality*. London: Routledge.

Johnson-Laird, P.N. & Oatley, K. (1989). The meaning of emotions: Analysis of a semantic field. *Cognition and Emotion*, *3*, 81–123.

Kahneman, D., Slovic, P., & Tversky, A. (1982). *Judgement under uncertainty: Heuristics and biases*. Cambridge University Press.

Lutz, C. (1982). The domain of emotion words on Ifaluk. *American Ethnologist*, *9*, 113–128.

Mandler, G. (1984). *Mind and body: Psychology and emotions and stress*. New York: Norton.

Marr, D. (1982). *Vision*. San Francisco, CA: Freeman.

McDougall, W. (1926). *An Introduction to social psychology*. Boston: Luce.

Medvedev, Z.A. (1990). *The legacy of Chernobyl*. New York: Norton.

Nisbett, R.E. & Ross, L. (1980). *Human inference: Strategies and shortcomings of social judgement*. Englewood Cliffs, NJ: Prentice Hall.

Nisbett, R.E. & Wilson, T.D. (1977). Telling more than we can know: Verbal reports on mental processes. *Psychological Review*, *84*, 231–259.

Oatley, K. & Duncan, E. (In press). Structured diaries for emotions in daily life. In K. Strongman (Ed.), *International review of studies of emotion*, Vol. 2. Chichester: Wiley.

Oatley, K. & Johnson-Laird, P.N. (1987). Towards a cognitive theory of emotions. *Cognition and Emotion, 1*, 29–50.

Oatley, K. & Johnson-Laird, P.N. (1990). Semantic primitives for emotions. *Cognition and Emotion, 4*, 129–143.

Ortony, A. & Clore, G.L. (1989). Emotions, moods, and conscious awareness: Comment on Johnson-Laird & Oatley's "The language of emotions: An analysis of a semantic field". *Cognition and Emotion, 3*, 125–137.

Ortony, A., Clore, G.L., & Collins, A. (1988). *The cognitive structure of emotions*. Cambridge University Press.

Ortony, A. & Turner, T.J. (1990). What's basic about basic emotions? *Psychological Review, 97*, 313–331.

Panksepp, J. (1982). Towards a general psychobiological theory of emotions. *Behavioral and Brain Sciences, 5*, 407–467.

Plutchik, R. (1962). *The emotions: Facts, theories, and a new model*. New York: Random House.

Quine, W.V.O. (1960). *Word and object*. Cambridge, MA: MIT Press.

Shaver, P., Schwartz, J., Kirson, D., & O'Connor, C. (1987). Emotion knowledge: Further exploration of a prototype approach. *Journal of Personality and Social Psychology, 52*, 1061–1086.

Simon, H.A. (1967). Motivational and emotional controls of cognition. *Psychological Review, 74*, 29–39.

Stein, N.L. & Levine, L.J. (1989). The causal organisation of emotional knowledge: A developmental study. *Cognition and Emotion, 3*, 343–378.

Stein, N.L. & Levine, L.J. (1990). Making sense out of emotion: The representation and use of goal-structured knowledge. In N.L. Stein, T. Trabasso, & B. Leventhal (Eds), *Psychological and biological approaches to emotion*. Hillsdale, NJ: Lawrence Erlbaum Associates Inc.

Stich, S. (1983). *From folk psychology to cognitive science*. Cambridge, MA: MIT Press.

Stich, S. (1990). Rationality. In D.N. Osherson & E.E. Smith (Eds), *Thinking: An invitation to cognitive science*, Vol. 3. Cambridge, MA: MIT Press.

von Uexkull, J. (1957). A stroll through the worlds of animals and men. In C.H. Schiller (Ed. and Trans.), *Instinctive behavior: The development of the modern concept*. London: Methuen.

Wason, P. (1960). On the failure to eliminate hypotheses in a conceptual task. *Quarterly Journal of Experimental Psychology, 12*, 129–140.

COGNITION AND EMOTION, 1992, 6 (3/4), 225–244

The Organisation of Emotional Experience: Creating Links among Emotion, Thinking, Language, and Intentional Action

Nancy L. Stein and Tom Trabasso

Department of Psychology, University of Chicago, U.S.A.

This paper discusses how emotional experience is interpreted, understood, and represented. Changes in the status of valued goals, and whether or not these goals can be attained or maintained are key conditions in determining the occurrence of an emotional experience. In addition, assessing the certainty with which goals can be maintained is critical as to which emotion is experienced. This small set of dimensions can be used to identify, and differentiate emotions that are considered to be basic. Basic emotion categories share features, and their elicitation is contingent on a number of components coming into conjunction with one another simultaneously. Thus, for any one basic emotion to be elicited, at least three converging components need to be activated. This view of the conditions for emotion is discussed with reference to componential theories of emotion, and to its developmental and cross-cultural implications.

INTRODUCTION

How do we represent and understand an emotional experience that unfolds over time? How is knowledge about emotion organised and how does this knowledge interact with and influence the expression of emotion? These are the central questions that guide our approach to the study of emotion. As such, we are interested in the conditions that give rise to emotional events, the thinking and reasoning processes associated with emotion, and those dimensions that lead to the construction of a durable, memory representation of the emotional experience. In representing and remembering emotional events, we believe that people's knowledge about valued

Requests for reprints should be sent to Dr Nancy Stein, Department of Psychology, University of Chicago, 5848 University Avenue, Chicago, IL 60637, U.S.A.

This research was supported by grants from the Smart Foundation on Early Learning and from the National Institute of Child Health and Human Development, Grant HD 25742 to T. Trabasso and N.L. Stein, and Grant HD 17431 to T. Trabasso.

goals and their outcomes is central to the evocation of emotion. Knowledge about emotion is constrained by both biological and psychological properties of the human organism. Many properties of emotional reactions are a function of the architecture and processing capacities of the person, and yet much knowledge about emotion is acquired through personal experiences, observation, and social interaction. We believe that an analysis of how one understands the unfolding of an emotional experience in time gives us insight, both personally and theoretically, into the relationship between cognition and emotion, the categorical nature of emotions, and how emotions are related to one another. The study of the active, online nature of appraisal and planning processes during an emotional experience, when carried out for the most frequent emotions, also sheds light on developmental and cultural issues surrounding the controversies over basic emotions.

The Meaning of Emotions

A set of dimensions that characterises the appraisal and planning processes that evoke each of the four emotions of happiness, sadness, anger, and fear have been described by the first author and her associates (Stein & Jewett, 1986; Stein & Levine, 1987, 1989, 1990). The dynamic quality of the appraisal process that leads to different emotional experiences indicates how each emotion is separate and unique from the other four emotions. The separability of these emotions is what defines, in part, their being basic categories. The conceptual analysis of these emotions can also be used to indicate how each emotion category can be characterised by a central tendency or prototype analysis.

Both of the present authors have studied how emotions can share common features and thus bear similarity to one another, how they can co-occur successively over time to the same antecedent event, and how different emotions can result in overlapping plans of action (Levine, 1991; Stein & Jewett, 1986; Stein & Levine, 1989, 1990; Stein & Trabasso, 1989; Trabasso, Stein, & Johnson, 1981). Thus, the shared and unique properties of each of the four emotion categories provide a means by which emotional experience can be described. The resulting model is dynamic in nature, describing changes in antecedent conditions, emotional reactions, goals, thoughts, plans, actions, and outcomes. In this sense, the model bears some similarity to the process descriptions called for by Ortony and Turner (1990). The assumptions underlying our process model are, however, quite different from those of Ortony and Turner.

As some of the cognitive dimensions used to evaluate a precipitating event map on to more than one emotion, the same set of objective environmental circumstances can elicit more than one emotion. For example, losing a favourite toy can elicit either or both anger and sadness. Both emotions are elicited when valued goals are blocked and not maintained. The same course of action can also be motivated by the experience of different emotions. Pulling a young child away from an electrical outlet can be motivated by either fear or anger or both. Therefore, it is not the observable antecedent events or consequential actions that define the unique characteristics of each emotion. Each emotion is unique because its meaning analysis maps on to distinctive dimensions with respect to changes in the status of important goals and values. Knowledge about goal success and failure is combined with knowledge about states of desire or avoidance to specify a unique conjunction of dimensions for each emotion. In this way, each emotion category is differentiated from all others.

Demonstrating that a particular emotion corresponds to a unique combination of appraisal components is not enough to consider a particular emotion basic. Additional conditions must be met. Basic emotion categories are easily instantiated in experience, emerge early in development, occur frequently, and subsume a class of related emotions that vary in intensity, certainty, and importance. In this sense, basic emotions resemble central prototypes of categories (Averill, 1982; Rosch, Mervis, Johnson, & Boyes-Braem, 1976; Shaver, Schwartz, O'Connor, & Kirson, 1987). Basic emotions are discriminable and are the most similar to or the least distant from other related members of their category. Instances of each basic emotion category share one or more features. In this regard, emotion category boundaries are defined by necessary and sufficient conditions. Thus, judgements about the cognitive dimensions underlying each basic emotion category should be discrete rather than continuous (see Ekman, this issue; Roseman, 1991).

In summary, then, the set of features used to discriminate between each basic emotion category is causally and temporarily linked to the status of goals and their outcomes. Goal states reflect either desired or undesired end-states, objects or activities. Activating internal goal states in conjunction with perceiving changes in the ability to attain/maintain these goal states provide some of the necessary antecedent conditions for the elicitation of an emotion. A consideration of goals and outcomes, however, must be augmented by additional meaning analyses in order to provoke a particular emotion. For example, wanting something and not attaining/ maintaining it or wanting to avoid something and not succeeding at it are necessary conditions for the elicitation of negative emotions. The presence of these conditions, in and of themselves, however, is not adequate to distinguish among the negative emotions. Further cognitive appraisals must be carried out to determine whether or not the change in goal status is certain. If the change is certain, then one class of emotions will be elicited. If the change is not certain, then a second class of emotions will be elicited.

Our contention that different appraisal patterns underlie the indentification of each of the basic emotion categories, however, does not rule out the existence of flexible correspondences between overt events and particular emotions. Because certain emotions are highly associated with goal success and maintenance (e.g. happiness and related positive emotions), and others are associated with goal failure and reinstatement (e.g. anger and sadness), each category of emotions normally takes certain types of initiating events. Stein and Jewett (1986), Stein and Levine (1989), Stein and Trabasso (1989), Stein, Trabasso, and Liwag (1991), and Trabasso et al. (1981) have found that children and adults react in predictable ways: happiness for goal attainment or maintenance, sadness for failure to attain or maintain goals, anger when agents cause these same losses, and fear when such failures have not as yet occurred but have a high probability of occurrence. Similarly, these several studies find that predictable goal plans of action occur for each basic emotion: maintenance when goals are attained, goal reinstatement when loss occurs, revenge on agents that cause goal loss or blockage, and avoidance of events or persons that threaten goal attainment or maintenance.

To the extent that a precipitating event is believed to aid or result in the *attainment-maintenance* of valued goal states, one set of positive emotions, of which happiness is prototypic, will be experienced. To the extent that the same precipitating event is believed to result in the *obstruction* of a valued set of goals, a second set of negative emotions, of which anger or sadness is prototypic, will be experienced. To the extent that *uncertainty* exists as to whether or not a goal will be attained-maintained, a third set of negative emotions, of which fear is prototypic, will be experienced. Once a person has determined whether failure, success, or uncertainty prevails with respect to a valued goal, then beliefs (expectations) about prior experience associated with attaining-maintaining the goal and beliefs about whether or not the goal can be reinstated will be accessed to further constrain the specific emotion experienced as well as the actions taken. Thus, in our system, the predominant foci are on goal success or failure, current expectations about *what* the status of a goal should be, and current expectations about the permanence or changeability of a goal state.

Our focus on succeeding or failing to attain goals necessarily entails a theory of social and personal understanding (F. Heider, 1958). Other theories as well have linked thinking and planning processes with the elicitation of different emotional states (Folkman & Lazarus, 1990; Lazarus, 1990; Mandler, 1990; Stein & Levine, 1987, 1990; Stein, Leventhal, & Trabasso, 1990). What we believe is different about our approach is that we focus on the content inferences made before and during the experience of emotion. We also specify the content of the antecedent conditions that leads to emotional reactions. Furthermore, we attempt to show how specific types of antecedent conditions affect the thinking, reasoning, and talking during an emotional episode.

As our procedures attempt to simulate the actual thinking processes that occur during emotional experience, they allow us to focus on both the temporal and causal constraints of the emotion episode. We call our procedures "on-line" assessments because subjects talk, plan, and explain their thinking during the reporting of an emotional experience. On-line assessments allow us to examine the immediate inferences made about changes in goal states during an episode (Stein & Trabasso, 1989), and we can determine whether or not subjects have changed or updated their beliefs about a particular event. We can also assess whether or not one or more emotions is experienced to a precipitating event, and we can control the presentation of appraisal dimensions such that single or multiple components of the appraisal process are presented (Stein & Trabasso, 1989). Furthermore, we are able to examine the active decision making and planning processes that occur before any action is undertaken.

Using these techniques, we have been able to assess how children and adults feel in response to both real life (Stein et al., 1991) and hypothetical events, their reasons for feeling a particular emotion, what they first thought when the precipitating event occurred, what they wished they could do, what they did, and how they expressed what they felt. Several examples of "on-line" interviews are found in our studies. For example, in order to determine the antecedent conditions that would evoke happiness, sadness, and anger, Stein and Levine (1989, 1990) systematically varied whether or not goals were attained or blocked, who or what caused the success or failure, and whether or not the outcome was intentional. Then, they asked children and adults to evaluate how they felt, why they felt this way, and what were their first thoughts, wishes, and plans.

Stein and Trabasso (1989) varied the frequency of success or failure over two successive episodes and asked children to evaluate intensity as well as other aspects of their feelings. Repeated success led to people feeling an emotion more intensely. Mixed success and failure increased the likelihood of these children reporting an experience of the co-occurrence of emotions. Trabasso et al. (1981) asked 3- and 4-year-old children to generate causes or consequences to 6 basic emotions. A cluster analysis of these free-generation responses indicated that the causal antecedents and consequences of positive and negative emotions were highly differentiated. Emotions having the same valence shared common antecedents and consequences. In particular, happiness overlapped but was discriminable from surprise and excitement; anger and sadness shared the most common antecedents and consequences but were differentiated from fear.

Understanding Emotions and Emotional Experience

Ortony and Turner (1990) have indicated that there are three views with respect to basic emotions: Those that treat them as basic-level concepts, those who view them as primitive and not decomposable, and those that look at them as biologically given. Our position is closest to the first view, namely that emotions are concepts used by human beings to interpret and organise experience, and has elements of the second, as we have sought to identify underlying conditions and features of emotions. The knowledge that is used to understand and classify emotional experiences is derived from and mirrors actual experience. This knowledge is conceptual in nature and leads to interpretations that are shared across persons. This knowledge is also used to interpret and evaluate situations and constrain which emotions are felt. Basic emotions are, as we have said above, those emotions which closely accompany appraisals of experiences of goal attainment and maintenance or failure and loss. Our analysis decomposes emotions into a sequence, beginning with the current goal states (desires to attain and maintain, and to avoid or escape an object, state or activity) and an appraisal of the environmental changes that may affect the status of these goals, including the probability of these changes. Together, these conditions specify a unique configuration of features (or components) that we regard as necessary for the occurrence of a particular emotion. In addition to the labelling of experience with an emotion, the appraisal process gives rise to goal plans of action and expression that deal with or express the emotional state. These thoughts, wishes, goals, plans, actions, and expressions are consequences of the antecedent change in goal status.

Because the change in a goal's status arises from a conjunction of conditions, the set of basic emotions come from mutually exclusive sets of conjunctions of necessary conditions (Mackie, 1980). As such, our analysis is componential. However, our causal theory allows for conditions and consequences to be "disassociated" from or to occur in the absence of an emotion. Ortony and Turner (1990) take such lack of correlation or dissociations to be evidence against basic emotion theories. That is, if a condition is a part of an experience other than the particular emotion, it is disassociated. This would be a problem for a basic emotion theory if it required each condition to be necessary and sufficient for an emotion; it is not a problem if it is a jointly necessary but not a sufficient condition. Ortony and Turner (1990), by their stance, seem to be adhering to a single cause model where a condition is necessary and sufficient. Disassociation, in our analysis, is allowable in that one can have either a particular goal or a particular environmental change without feeling an emotion. However, in order to feel a positive or negative emotion, one has to have a conjunction of a goal with the detection of a change in its status through environmental circumstances. The goal alone or the environmental change alone are neither necessary nor sufficient. Both are required for the emotion. On this matter, we seem to be in substantial disagreement with Ortony and Turner's (1990) criteria and basis for criticising theories of basic emotion.

We also show that basic emotions are related but they do not arise out of each other. We are, therefore, in some accord with Ortony and Turner's (1990) position that some emotions need not be building blocks for one another. In our view, basic emotions are related through conditions that give rise to common valences. Differences in emotions depend upon other conditions such as the goal's value or importance and which plans of action have been socialised by the culture to deal with the changes. Thus contentment, happiness, joy, and elation are related through goal success. They differ in terms of intensity and their focus of attention. Intensity of an emotion is related to the importance of the goal that was attained or maintained, and focus of attention is related to the unique conditions causing goal success.

Differences in some negative emotions can arise in the appraisal process. For example, it makes a difference as to whether one's thinking is directed towards the cause of goal failure or towards the consequences to one's goals. Anger arises out of focusing one's attention on the agent or on the external conditions responsible for the blockage or failure to attain or maintain a goal. Sadness is related to focusing on the consequences of goal failure—either to the lost goal or to further consequences to other goals. Variations can also be attributed to differences in goal plans and actions. Anger does not always result in revenge (fight or approach), and fear does not always result in flight (avoidance). These are not, we believe, invariant properties respectively associated with these two emotions. Fight or flight may also depend upon knowing or being able to infer the agent of the emotion and evaluating whether or not one can fight or take flight. For example, in Stein and Levine's (1989) study, children wished that they could be aggressive against an adult who caused a problem but offered plans of action that did not involve direct aggression against these powerful agents. On the other hand, if the agent was another child, fighting was one of the most frequent actions taken. Trabasso et al. (1981) replicated this finding on anger in 3-year-old children.

Similarly, variations in facial expressions that accompany particular emotional states do occur, but they can be caused by several factors and are not necessarily uniquely associated with a particular emotion. One source of variation is the intensity with which an emotion is experienced. A second source is a voluntary effort to inhibit a particular facial expression, and a third source is the rapid shifts in attention that occur during the experience of emotion so that a second emotion is experienced in rapid succession to the first.

Given a view of emotion as determined by mutually exclusive sets of conjunctions of conditions, the presence or absence of a particular expression or action is not evidence against a theory. Rather, what is required is to determine what configurations occur and why they occur. This does not abandon determinism but allows for the determinants of emotions to be disjunctive sets of multiple conditions. Variation in goal importance and conflicts or co-occurrences of goals also present problems for prediction as well as for study. However, they are not evidence against a theory unless the theory requires a particular expression or action to follow invariantly from an emotional state. The variation in means or plans pertaining to coping with emotions certainly argue against requiring a theory of emotion to be wed to one unique form of expression or action (see also Ellsworth, 1991; Folkman & Lazarus, 1990; Stein & Levine, 1990 for process-oriented approaches to studying the cognition-emotion relationship, and for descriptions of the dynamic nature of emotional experience).

Theories of goal-directed action have played a major role in the study of thinking processes, especially those that accompany problem solving (see Stein & Glenn, 1979; Stein & Trabasso, 1982; Trabasso, Secco, & van den Broek, 1984). In our approach, we have attempted to integrate the problem solving process with the experience of emotion. When the unfolding of emotional experience is documented in more detail over a temporal sequence, a goal-directed approach will help us explain the nature of the changes that occur in the values placed upon goals, the beliefs that are formed about goal maintenance and attainment, the decision making process that regulates the way in which two or more goals are co-ordinated, the plans and actions brought to bear in attaining a goal, and the accuracy of memory for the decision making and planning process (Stein & Levine, 1990). This focus differs from the components approach of critics of the "basic emotions" approach (e.g. Cacioppo, Petty, & Morris, 1985; Ortony, Clore, & Collins, 1987; Ortony & Turner, 1990; Smith, 1989). The difference is that we have attempted to characterise the organisation of emotional experience by analysis of the content that accompanies or determines the thinking, learning, and language associated with the experience over its time course. This analysis has forced us to give more consideration to what is a mental state, how these mental states operate, what types of knowledge are used during the experience of an emotional state, how this knowledge maps onto emotion categories, or how mental states are co-ordinated with other neurological processes. We hope that concordance between reports of basic emotional experience and patterns of facial expression associated with emotional experience can be discovered.

At least four different emotions taken to be "basic" by many investigators, can be shown to have a specific set of defining characteristics. Our descriptions of these features for each emotion, however, does not include specific plans of action like approach or avoidance because different emotions can lead to the same plan of action depending upon the context in which the emotion is experienced. What we have argued for (Stein & Jewett, 1986; Stein & Levine, 1987, 1990; Stein & Trabasso, 1989) and what we have demonstrated empirically (Stein & Levine, 1989; Stein & Trabasso, 1989; Stein et al., 1991) is that an emotion such as fear results from an appraisal that a valued goal is being threatened and the likelihood of maintaining the goal (or avoiding an aversive state) is minimal. In our conceptual analysis, when fear is elicited, a negative outcome has not yet occurred. Therefore, the higher-order goal that should co-occur with fear is the desire to *prevent* the onset of an aversive state or the desire to *prevent* the loss of a valuable goal. Sometimes prevention requires withdrawal, and sometimes it requires an approach. The sub-goals, plans, and overt actions accompanying fear are determined by those that result in prevention. We (Stein & Jewett, 1986; Stein & Levine, 1987, 1990) have proposed similar analyses for anger, sadness, and happiness. For example, the higher-order goal associated with anger is the reinstatement of a goal that has been blocked. In some situations, reinstatement will necessitate approach, and in others it will necessitate withdrawal. The main point, however, is that anger always carries some form of desire to reinstate the original goal and fear always carries a goal to prevent a negative (aversive or loss) state from occurring.

A small set of higher-order goals (e.g. maintenance, attainment, avoidance, prevention, abandonment, substitution of goals) may regulate those components that are appraised in situations, independent of the variation in contexts. Thus, the same sequence of thinking and decision making may be carried out within a given type of higher-order goal plan. What may vary, then, are those components of the sequence people choose to highlight, but the sequence and much of the experience may remain similar across people. This points to the necessity to consider the constraints on thinking and problem solving, decision making, and planning that occur during the emotional experience.

We have found that most investigators studying basic emotions postulate different numbers of basic emotion categories partly because they define emotion and cognition in different ways. Thus, variation in the number of emotion categories might have little to do with whether or not basic emotions exist. Rather than focus on the existence or non-existence of basic emotions, we have first focused on what we mean by cognition and emotion. The study of the vocabulary of emotion *per se* is a study of variation in labels attached to different experiences (e.g. Ortony, Clore, &

Foss, 1987). The emotion lexicon may help us to access knowledge and organisation of emotional experience. However, the structure of emotion concepts or the discriminations that are made amongst them in everyday emotion situations require considerably more than similarity analyses among emotion terms. To us, the question of what determines the semantic distinctions among emotion terms is of interest. That is, what features or components are there in the conditions that give rise to the emotion or in the consequences of the evaluation process that colour the differences in terms used to convey that experience? We have suggested that the value of goals and intensity are two aspects that contribute to differences in labels attached. People try to communicate the sense of the emotion through the selection of different labels. However, the core set of conditions that define the core emotions may still be present, giving rise to a family of emotional experiences and labels.

We have, in our approach, developed an analysis of emotional experience that goes well beyond simple expressions or actions. For us, the representation and meaning of emotions is referential and relational. We believe that people use emotional words to refer to knowledge about the environmental and motivational antecedents of emotions; thoughts, feelings, and wishes that occur during the emotion; plans and actions they took to deal with the emotion in addition to how they might express these thoughts, feelings, and beliefs. The meaning of emotion, then, depends upon the relationships between sets of environmental conditions and internal states as well as the appraisal of changes that affect goals and the formulation of goal plans of action to deal with these conditions and changes in state. Our studies have reflected attempts on our part to investigate and test how people access and use this knowledge to understand emotional experience as it unfolds over time. This approach makes emotional understanding, knowledge, and experience appear rich, and complicated. However, from our work thus far, we feel that this complexity is open to systematic analysis and understanding.

Similarities and Differences in Emotional Experience: Developmental and Cultural Variation

We believe that similarities as well as differences can be found in the organisation of emotional experience across cultures and over different developmental periods. The similarities would be directly related to the success-failure-uncertainty distinctions made in reference to valued goal states. Monitoring the environment with reference to the attainment of specific goal states should further constrain the organisation of emotion categories and provide common knowledge about emotional experience within and across cultures. The appraisals that people make about the status of their goals should directly influence expressive systems: the face, voice, hands, body, as well as language. Although variability exists in the correspondence between appraisal processes and different expressive systems, the number of variations may turn out to be quite small.

Because the emotional experience that occurs depends upon one's goal states as well as the environmental circumstances, cross-cultural variation as to what is believed to be important or valued become central to understanding the variation in how people appraise these circumstances. Our approach is sensitive to the content of these beliefs and to the contexts in which they occur. Goal content is crucial and very likely to be influenced culturally. However, similarities exist as to what is evaluated as well as to what thought processes occur. Similarities are also revealed when one moves up a level of generalisation above the particular context and contents. The generalisation, however, readily finds its instantiation in narrative categories, such as settings, initiating events, internal reactions and states, goals, goal plans, attempts, and outcomes, and in the causal and temporal relations that organise them (see, for example, Trabasso, van den Broek, & Suh, 1989). We have successfully used these categories and relations in the study of narrative understanding and production, and in how narrative content is structured and organised in memory. These analyses assume that people use naïve theories of intentionality to construct representations of goal plans of action and to understand and organise personal and interpersonal experience. The interested reader is referred to several of our studies for the details of this discourse analysis (Stein, Albro, & Rodkin, 1992; Stein & Glenn, 1979; Stein & Trabasso, 1982; Trabasso & van den Broek, 1985; Trabasso & Sperry, 1985; Trabasso & Nickels, in press; Trabasso et al., 1984, in press).

Differences in the content of what is important leads one to believe that there are differences in culture or development. However, contrasting age or cultural analyses highlight such differences, particularly at the level of the language of emotions. Our analysis suggests that there are important, general similarities of emotional experience. These similarities may occur because of common goals across age and culture. By reference to the values, goals, and mental representations, emotions can take on universal and common experiences to persons in all cultures. We assume that a small number of higher-order goals exist that are related to survival and self-regulation. These common goals guide behaviour and regulate the universal aspects of the appraisal and planning process. They may also guide and act as pointers in regulating the interleaving of expressive systems during emotional experience.

As an example, consider the knowledge and actions that might be used to monitor and attain physical and psychological survival. Despite differences in degree of the value placed on survival, people in all cultures can be assumed to at least place some value on it. We assume that all people have conceptions about positive states of well-being, about what these states should be and about how they should feel. We also assume that they develop strategies to maintain or attain these desired states. They also have definitions of harm and develop strategies for classifying events that are dangerous and ones that are safe. They learn how to avoid harm and develop strategies for coping with pain. They probably come into conflict with other people in their society, and they develop rules for avoiding and resolving conflicts. Moreover, they acquire beliefs about the substance and predictability (or lack of predictability) of other people's acts, and they also develop beliefs about their own skill and how other people view them. Thus, to the extent that people think about harms and benefits, they acquire knowledge and rules for carrying out valued personal and social actions. This kind of learning makes people quite similar both across and within cultures.

The sequence of mental processes carried out with respect to harms and benefits is also assumed to be similar across cultures. People in all societies are assumed to consider and think about the conditions under which they desire to attain, maintain, escape, or avoid particular states, activities or objects. Given failures in these, they should think about the conditions under which a particular goal could be reinstated, substituted or abandoned. Furthermore, they form specific expectations about how the world is organised and structured, and they carry out everyday action within the contexts of these beliefs.

Basic categories of human experience thus seem to exist and are shared. The processes of appraisal, planning, and acting are also shared across cultures. Positive or negative values are universally placed on any event affecting goal states, and a very small number of higher-order goals form the basis for commonalities or universals in emotional experience. These are attaining, maintaining, escaping, avoiding, as well as reinstating, abandoning or substituting goals. The variation in emotion categories, both across *and* within cultures, lies in the importance given to particular harms and benefits, the relative importance or value that is attached to the events, and the conditions under which the value of an event or goal will change. For example, many individuals in our culture attach a positive value to attaining or maintaining one's physical survival. However, one would attach positive value only under conditions where specified levels of mental and physical agility can be maintained. Even when physical survival is valued to a considerable degree, the presence of disease, impairment, or unremitting pain may be considered conditions for no longer maintaining but rather for ending life. The amount of suffering and pain that a person must undergo may decrease the value of life such that ending one's life assumes greater value than sustaining one's life. Other people in the culture, however, may value the maintenance of life at all costs, despite the suffering a person might endure. The presence of such limiting conditions or restrictions or constraints does not, in our view, deny the operation of the goals and processes detailed above. Rather, their presence is what one studies when one tries to understand how, why and under what conditions particular emotions are experienced. A single goal or value may not be sufficient in the understanding. Rather, conflicts in values or goals may occur and lead to different and unexpected actions. These conditions of goal conflict also contribute variability in what is taken to be of universal importance.

Within any culture, the value of a goal is relative to the ability to attain, maintain, or avoid other states, activities or objects. If the maintenance (or avoidance) of other goals is threatened or compromised, then the first goal may lose its value, even though it assumes great importance under some operating conditions. These relative values and qualifying conditions may form coherent sets of beliefs and expectations. Within any given culture, the value of a goal state is always conditional. Therefore, constructing value systems and updating beliefs about the conditions under which a goal remains valuable can be shown to be a fundamental part of everyday thinking in a culture. Everyone acquires expectations about psychological and physical survival. They also form beliefs about the ideal conditions under which they want to live, how they want to live, and under what conditions they do not want to live. They think about the conditions under which they want to interact with other people, they think about the value of objects and the meaning that different objects carry, they think about the development of their skills and abilities, the changes that occur in these abilities, and the changes that occur in the interpersonal relationships that they have formed.

The topics of survival, interpersonal interaction, and development provide a starting point for describing the common knowledge that is acquired about human social understanding. Lutz (1985), for example, has shown that talk about anger among the Ifaluk, a South Sea Island people, is heavily value- and goal-laden. One form refers to those instances where anger occurs without a justifiable cause. The second form refers to socially acceptable anger reactions that are preceded by the recognition that intentional harm to the self or others has been enacted. In empirical studies on how adults and children evaluate intentional or unintentional action leading to goal failure, Stein and Levine (1989, 1990) found similar distinctions made by their American sample. Furthermore, in studies of naturalistic occurrences of anger, American women, acting in the role of mothers, discriminate, categorise, and cope differently when either of these two forms of anger are displayed by their children (Radke-Yarrow & Kochanska, 1990). Unintentional harm or loss is occasioned by different forms of socialisation than is intentional harm.

Variation in the contents of events that are classified as harms and benefits does not imply that different types of structural representations and categories are constructed to remember and act upon these events.

The relative number and types of harms and benefits may vary within each category. The number of subordinate categories for each classification may also vary. Different means might be used to maintain or to attain a goal. But, the appraisal and planning processes may still be the same, despite all of these variations. In other words, variation in the relative value of a goal or in the particular means used to achieve a goal does not change the structural properties or its sequence (see also Folkman & Lazarus, 1990, for examples of such sequences). In any situation, where valence parameters have been set with respect to a goal, and the goal's value has been determined in relationship to other goals, the decision to move forward in the process of maintaining the most valued goal will be activated. If people in a given culture are successful at attaining valued goals, then a set of expectations regarding the value of these goals and the means by which to achieve the goals will be developed and learned. If failure ensues, then a set of expectations about overcoming failure will be developed.

Despite the variation in knowledge about ways of achieving important goals, circumstances are such that unexpected outcomes always accompany the success or failure of valued goals. The very nature of human interaction and the way in which the world is perceived guarantees that people will continually experience novelty (unexpected outcomes) regarding the conditions under which goals succeed and fail. The type of novelty or unexpectedness may vary across cultures, but the way in which novelty and unexpected outcomes are understood is extremely constrained, limited only to a few possibilities. We have found that children try to focus on coping with unexpected goal success and failure in free narrative generation (Stein et al., under review), in understanding sequences of events where goal success is followed by goal failure or vice versa (Stein & Trabasso, 1989) or in children's reports of real-life, autobiographical experiences involving basic emotions (Stein et al., 1991).

Unexpected outcomes are such an integral part of knowledge about goal-directed action. As a result, we have found that children as young as 3 years include unexpected outcomes in their talk about emotional episodes, be they positive or negative. The necessity of incorporating knowledge about unexpected, novel outcomes, in combination with other conditions, lead to the experience of emotions that we would call "basic" and universal. This knowledge and language of emotion encompass many of Wierzbica's (this issue) observations and ideas about the what is common across cultures.

The emphasis in cross-cultural studies has generally been on the unique aspects of a culture rather than on the similarities that might exist among cultures (e.g. Markus & Kitayama, in press; Lutz, 1988). These kinds of studies do not provide the kind of data that we would require to test claims about universality. We hope that systematic, verbal interviews that assess knowledge and understanding of the conditions that give rise to emotions such as we have employed on children of different ages as well as on adults would be carried out in cultures other than the one we have studied. In addition, we hope that observations of the circumstances under which emotions are experienced and reconstructed later in time could be carried out in studies on autobiographical memory, such as that done by Stein et al. (1991) on very young children. K. Heider (1988) provides a model of what we have in mind for combining of verbal reports with observations, interviews, or conversations in an effort to understand how people interpret their social and physical worlds. These convergent methodologies, if applied to the exploration of the ways in which emotion is experienced, understood, and displayed across cultures, would provide the kind of data necessary for comparisons of similarities as well as differences and would also test our claims.

In future cross-cultural or development studies, we would like to see the inclusion of more children younger than 3 or 4 years of age. We also make a plea for the documentation of the *changes* that occur in emotional experience as a function of development or learning across cultures. Although socialisation and the social construction of emotion are primary topics of concern in cultural and ethnic studies (e.g. Gumperz, 1982; Lutz, 1988; Rosaldo, 1980; Schieflin & Ochs, 1986; Shweder & LeVine, 1984), we feel that it is desirable to have investigations that describe the learning and conceptual changes that result from experiences in the socialisation of emotion. We would also like to see studies carried out that describe the way in which talking and thinking are interco-ordinated with different modalities of emotional expression, such as those conducted by Bloom (1990); Bloom and Beckwith (1989); Bloom and Capatides (1987); and Capatides (1989). Active appraisal and planning, in conjunction with the interco-ordination of thinking and different modes of expression, might account for the reliable differences in the experience and evocation of different emotional states, both within and across cultures. Emde (1980), Stein and Levine (1990), and Sroufe (1979) have each expressed similar sentiments.

It would be of interest to understand how expressive systems are interco-ordinated across cultures in infants before there is much socialisation of emotional behaviour. The socialisation of emotion is frequently co-ordinated with adult beliefs about the age at which children will best profit from training in culturally appropriate practices. The development of memory skill and the ability to learn the social consequences of action are probably considered to be essential before many children are subjected to systematic socialisation practices. In many cultures, adults believe that children do not develop these skills until a particular age. Thus, in the very early years of childhood, many cultures are more lenient about the variety of emotional behaviour they will tolerate from the young child (Lutz, 1985; Radke-Yarrow & Kochanska, 1990).

By the time socialisation practices begin, children may have already formed conceptions about their social and physical worlds, and they may act on these conceptions prior to and during the process of learning what practices are socially appropriate. Thus, the knowledge children bring to the situation, and their preferences and beliefs may dramatically influence what and how they learn. We need to consider the child's role in influencing the socialisation situation. Children may well contribute as much to the socialisation process as do their socialisers (see, for example, Davidson et al., 1990).

Our studies have been aimed at finding out children's perceptions or accounts of emotional experience. In this research, we hope to study the acquisition of an emotion vocabulary, or the voluntary control exerted over expressive behaviour in these experiences. Because parents are frequently involved as participants in these studies, they attempt to socialise the child's reactions. Hence, autobiographical studies allow us to study how the child and the parent interact in the emotional episode and during the parent's attempts at socialisation. Although cultures may differ in the way in which emotion is conceived and taught (Lutz, 1988; Markus & Kitayama, in press; Miller & Sperry, 1987), it would be useful to observe and analyse the *learning* and *socialisation* processes that co-occur with emotional experience. In this way, one could describe the changes that result from socialisation in the children's understanding before and after socialisation. To this end, we might benefit from the kind of work carried out on adults by Folkman and Lazarus (1990). Here, coping and the reconstruction of values systems with stressful emotional experiences received careful attention. These kinds of adult coping strategies may be the learned products of socialisation of emotion. One question for research, then, is to what extent do parents actually teach their children strategies for dealing with particular emotional or stressful contexts?

If enculturation is conceived of as the learning of knowledge systems that organise and classify emotions, thought, and behaviour, then a systematic account of what information is learned, how it is categorised, and how it is labelled are of value. The study of socialisation through analyses of multiple channels of communication would also be of interest as some information is more easily conveyed through one channel (e.g. the face), whereas other information is more easily conveyed through a second channel (e.g. prosody or language). For example, studies that explore the spontaneous way in which mothers and children use the emotion lexicon (Capatides, 1989; Dunn, Bretherton, & Munn, 1987; Huttenlocher & Smiley, 1990) have shown that words labelling the specific feeling state are used infrequently during interactive conversations. When discussing emotion interactions with their children, mothers focus primarily on the outcomes of success when positive emotions are experienced, and they focus on ways to reinstate goals when failure is experienced (Capatides, 1989). Moreover, studies on young preschool children's reconstruction of emotional episodes (Stein et al., 1991) also indicate a restricted use of the emotion lexicon.

However, when children are asked to label emotion faces, to talk about the causes and consequences of different emotion states in the presence of faces that express emotions, and to generate real-life experiences correspondent with particular emotion states after making a face, we have found that (Stein et al., 1991; Trabasso et al., 1981) children as young as 3 years of age are able to perform at a high level of proficiency. In the data collected by Stein et al. (1991), our current analyses of the taped interviews with the children suggest that different channels of expression are analysed (e.g. the face, hand gestures, and prosody) in conjunction with children's appraisal of an emotional experience. The appraisals are often accompanied by the facial expressions directly in accord with which emotion is expressed, based upon the circumstances of the episode. In our work, we hope to go beyond a focus on only the interactive discourse that occurs during spontaneous exchanges between mothers and children in order to access children's skill at understanding and reconstructing emotional experience.

If an interchange between a mother and child is considered in terms of the goals that the mothers and children want to achieve, then our approach would be to focus on the outcomes and strategies for goal reinstatement that the mother or the child might make. These interactive situations may reflect ongoing attempts by the mother and child to solve problems, and not be focused on the emotional aspects. Hence, one would not find much talk about emotions or the use of emotion words, a finding reported by Miller and Sperry (1987). Rather than focusing on emotion, the interchange may be aimed at bringing two people's goals into accord with one another, resolving conflicts or dealing with the problem that precipitated the emotion. Focusing on the outcomes of episodes and the ways of coping with failed or successful goals is a kind of problem solving. Focusing on an emotional reaction *per se* is not likely to result in a satisfactory problem solution. Rather, it can intensify or deepen the emotional interchange between the two parties. Focusing on feelings, *per se*, without specifying the causes or the consequences of those feelings does not lead to a problem solution. Telling someone about why one has angry feelings allows that person to understand which personal goals may not have been attained and can assist problem solution as strong beliefs exist that goals can and should be reinstated. However, merely labelling feelings as one of anger does not allow another person to understand exactly what event caused the anger and what expectations were violated. Moreover, labelling feelings as ones of anger does not allow a rapid assessment of whether or not the goal can be reinstated.

In sum, it may be useful to distinguish among the many ways in which people talk about emotional experience (e.g. labelling emotional feelings vs. talking about outcomes and strategies for reinstatement or maintenance), to characterise the functions of these types of talk, and to indicate how talk is interleaved with other expressive systems that carry information about emotion. This correspondence between emotional understanding and the emotion lexicon could possibly then be more clearly specified. Talk about preferences, values, goals, and outcomes, in combination with the nonverbal expression of emotion, may be an indicator of how the lexicon of emotion words is represented along with other emotional knowledge conceptually.

Manuscript received 30 March 1991
Revised manuscript received 27 November 1991

REFERENCES

Averill, J.R. (1982). *Anger and aggression: An essay on emotion.* New York: Springer.

Bloom, L. (1990). Developments in expression: affect and speech. In N.L. Stein, B. Leventhal, & T. Trabasso (Eds), *Psychological and biological approaches to emotion.* Hillsdale, NJ: Lawrence Erlbaum Associates Inc.

Bloom, L. & Beckwith, R. (1989). Talking with feeling: integrating affective and linguistic expression in early language development. *Cognition and emotion, 3,* 313–342.

Bloom, L. & Capatides, J. (1987). Sources of meaning in the question of complex syntax: The sample case of causality. *Journal of Experimental Child Psychology, 43,* 112–128.

Cacioppo, J.T., Petty, R.E., & Morris, K.J. (1985). Semantic, evaluative, and self referent processing: Memory, cognitive effect, and somatovisceral activity. *Psychophysiology, 22,* 371–384.

Capatides, J. (1989). *Mothers' socialization of children's affect expression.* Unpublished doctoral dissertation. Teachers College, Columbia University.

Davidson, R.J., Ekman, P., Saron, C.D., Senulis, J.A., & Friesen, W.V. (1990). Approach/ withdrawal and cerebral asymmetry: Emotional expression and brain physiology, I. *Journal of Personality and Social Psychology, 58,* 330–341.

Dunn, J., Bretherton, I., & Munn, N. (1987). Conversations about feeling states between mothers and their young children. *Developmental Psychology, 23*(1), 132–139.

Ellsworth, P.C. (1991). Some implications of cognitive appraisal theories of emotion. In K.T. Stongman (Ed.), *International review of studies on emotion,* Vol. 1. New York: Wiley.

Emde, R. (1980). Levels of meaning in infant development. In W.A. Collins (Ed.), *Minnesota symposium on child psychology,* Vol. 13. Hillsdale, NJ: Lawrence Erlbaum Associates Inc.

Folkman, S. & Lazarus, R.S. (1990). Coping and Emotion. In N.L. Stein, B. Leventhal, & T. Trabasso (Eds), *Psychological and biological approaches to emotion.* Hillsdale, NJ: Lawrence Erlbaum Associates Inc.

Gumperz, J. (1982). *Language and social identity.* Cambridge University Press.

Heider, F. (1958). *The psychology of interpersonal relations.* New York: Wiley.

Heider, K. (1988). Paper presented at the NICHHD meeting on the *Socialization of emotion*. May. Bethesda, Md.

Huttenlocher, J. & Smiley, P. (1990). The developmental of the concept of person. In N.L. Stein, B. Leventhal, & T. Trabasso (Eds), *Psychological and biological approaches to emotion*. Hillsdale, NJ: Lawrence Erlbaum Association Inc.

Lazarus, R.S. (1990). What is a cognitive relational theory of emotion? In N.L. Stein, B. Leventhal, & T. Trabasso (Eds), *Psychological and biological approaches to emotion*. Hillsdale, NJ: Lawrence Erlbaum Associates Inc.

Levine, L.J. (1991). *Cognitive processes associated with anger and sadness: Evidence from kindergarten children*. Unpublished doctoral dissertation, University of Chicago, U.S.A.

Lutz, C. (1985). Cultural patterns and individual differences in the child's emotion meaning system. In M. Lewis & C. Saarni (Eds), *The socialization of affect*. New York: Plenum, pp. 161–186.

Lutz, C. (1988). *Unnatural emotions*. University of Chicago Press.

Mackie, J.L. (1980). *The cement of the universe*. Oxford: Clarendon Press.

Mandler, G. (1990). A constructivist theory of emotion. In N.L. Stein, B. Leventhal, & T. Trabasso (Eds), *Psychological and biological approaches to emotion*. Hillsdale, NJ: Lawrence Erlbaum Associates Inc.

Markus, H.R. & Kitayama, S. (In press). Culture and the self: Implications for cognition, emotion, and motivation. *Psychological Review*.

Miller, P. & Sperry, L. (1987). The socialization of anger and aggression. *Merrill Palmer Quarterly*, *33*, 1–31.

Ortony, A. & Turner, T.J. (1990). What's basic about basic emotion? *Psychological Review*, *97*, 315–331.

Ortony, A., Clore, G.L., & Foss, M.A. (1987). The referential structure of the affective lexicon. *Cognitive Science*, *11*, 341–364.

Ortony, A., Clore, G., & Collins, A. (1988). *The cognitive structure of emotion*. Cambridge University Press.

Radke-Yarrow, M. & Kochanska, G. (1990). Anger in young children. In N.L. Stein, B. Leventhal, & T. Trabasso (Eds), *Psychological and biological approaches to emotion*. Hillsdale, NJ: Lawrence Erlbaum Associates Inc.

Rosaldo, M.Z. (1980). *Knowledge and passion: Ilongot notions of self and social life*. Cambridge University Press.

Rosch, E., Mervis, C.B., Gray, W., Johnson, D., & Boyes-Braem, P. (1976). Basic objects in natural categories. *Cognitive Psychology*, *8*, 382–439.

Roseman, I.J. (1991). Appraisal determinants of discrete emotions. *Cognition and Emotion*, *5*, 161–200.

Schiefflen, B.B. & Ochs, E. (1986). *Language socialization across cultures*. Cambridge University Press.

Shaver, P., Schwartz, J., O'Connor, C., & Kirson, D. (1987). Emotion knowledge: Further explanations of a prototype approach. *Journal of Personality and Social Psychology*, *52*, 1016–1086.

Shweder, R.A. & LeVine, R.A. (1984). *Culture theory: Essays on mind, self, and emotion*. Cambridge University Press.

Smith, C.A. (1989). Dimensions of appraisal and physiological response in emotion. *Journal of Personality and Social Psychology*, *56*, 339–353.

Sroufe, A. (1979). Socioemotional development. In J. Osofsky (Ed.), *Handbook of infant development*. New York: Wiley.

Stein, N.L. & Glenn, C.G. (1979). An analysis of story comprehension in elementary school children. In R.O. Freedle (Ed.), *New directions in discourse processing*, Vol. 2. (In the series *Advances in discourse processes*.) Norwood, NJ: Ablex.

Stein, N.L. & Jewett, J. (1986). A conceptual analysis of the meaning of negative emotions: Implications for a theory of development. In C.E. Izard and P. Read (Eds), *Measurement of emotion in infants and children*, Vol. 2. Cambridge University Press, pp. 238–267.

Stein, N.L. & Levine, L.J. (1987). Thinking about feelings: The development and organization of emotional knowledge. In R.E. Snow & M. Farr (Eds), *Aptitude, learning, and instruction: Cognition, conation and affect*, Vol. 3. Hillsdale, NJ: Lawrence Erlbaum Associates Inc, pp. 165–198.

Stein, N.L. & Levine, L. (1989). The causal organisation of emotional knowledge: A developmental study. *Cognition and Emotion*, 3(4), 343–378.

Stein, N.L. & Levine, L.J. (1990). Making sense of emotion: The representation and use of goal-structured knowledge. In N.L. Stein, B. Leventhal, & T. Trabasso (Eds), *Psychological and biological approaches to emotion*. Hillsdale, NJ: Lawrence Erlbaum Associates Inc.

Stein, N.L. & Trabasso, T. (1982). What's in a story: An approach to comprehension and instruction. In R. Glaser (Ed.), *Advances in instructional psychology*, Vol. 2. Hillsdale, NJ: Lawrence Erlbaum Associates Inc.

Stein, N.L. & Trabasso, T. (1989). Children's understanding of changing emotion states. In C. Saarni & P.L. Harris (Eds), *Children's understanding of emotion*. Cambridge University Press.

Stein, N.L. & Trabasso, T. (1991). *A theoretical framework for understanding the co-ordination of expressive systems*. Working paper, University of Chicago, June.

Stein, N.L., Leventhal, B., & Trabasso, T. (1990). *Psychological and biological approaches to emotion*. Hillsdale, NJ: Lawrence Erlbaum Associates Inc.

Stein, N.L., Trabasso, T., & Liwag, M. (1991). *Children's and parents' memory for real life emotional events: Conditions for convergence or polarization*. Paper presented at Society for Research in Child Development, Seattle, Washington, April.

Stein, N.L., Albro, E., & Rodkin, P. (1992). *Building complexity and coherence: Children's use of goal-structured knowledge during storytelling*. Unpublished manuscript. University of Chicago.

Trabasso, T. & van den Broek, P. (1985). Causal thinking and the representation of narrative events. *Journal of Memory and Language*, 24, 612–630.

Trabasso, T. & Nickels, M. (In press). The development of goal plans of action in the narration of picture stories. *Discourse Processes*.

Trabasso, T. & Sperry, L.L. (1985). Causal relatedness and importance of story events. *Journal of Memory and Language*, 24, 595–611.

Trabasso, T., Stein, N.L., & Johnson, L.R. (1981). Children's knowledge of events: A causal analysis of story structure. In G. Bower (Ed.), *Learning and motivation*. Vol. 15. New York: Academic Press, pp. 237–282.

Trabasso, T., Secco, T., & van den Broek, P. (1984). Causal cohesion and story coherence. In H. Mandl, N.L. Stein, & T. Trabasso (Eds), *Learning and comprehension of text*. Hillsdale, NJ: Lawrence Erlbaum Associates Inc.

Trabasso, T., Stein, N.L., Rodkin, P.C., Munger, G.P., & Baughn, C. (In press). Achieving coherence in narration: Children's use of goal plans of action to encode pictorial events. *Cognitive Development*.

COGNITION AND EMOTION, 1992, 6 (3/4), 245–268

Prolegomenon to the Structure of Emotion: Gleanings from Neuropsychology

Richard J. Davidson

Department of Psychology, University of Wisconsin-Madison, U.S.A.

This article presents a model of the structure of emotion developed primarily from a consideration of neuropsychological evidence and behavioural data which have bearing on neuropsychological theories. Valence is first considered and highlighted as a defining characteristic of emotion. Next, the use of facial behaviour and autonomic nervous system patterns as defining characteristics of discrete emotions is questioned on empirical and conceptual grounds. The regulation of emotion is considered and proposed to affect the very structure of emotion itself. If there is an invariant pattern of biological activity across different instantiations of the same emotion, it is likely to be found in higher-order associative networks of central nervous system activity, the very same networks that subserve goal-directed behaviour and other cognitive functions. Drawing upon evolutionary considerations, it is argued that what is basic about emotion are the dimensions of approach and withdrawal. The nature of the linkage between such action tendencies and emotion is discussed.

INTRODUCTION

The purpose of this article is to begin to sketch a model of what we know about the structure of emotion. A sizeable portion of the evidence from which I draw is neuropsychological or psychophysiological. The analysis I present also makes liberal use of non-biological evidence, but considers the relevance and import of this corpus of data for biological theories of

Correspondence concerning this article should be addressed to Richard J. Davidson, Department of Psychology, University of Wisconsin-Madison, 1202 West Johnson Street, Madison, WI 53706, U.S.A.

The research described in this article was supported in part by an NIMH Research Scientist Development Award MH00875, NIMH grants MH40747 and MH43454, and by a grant from the John D. and Catherine T. MacArthur Foundation. I wish to thank Paul Ekman, Leonard Berkowitz, Yoshi Nakamura, and the members of my lab group for helpful comments on earlier drafts of this paper.

emotion. I first consider the role of valence in emotion and highlight this as a defining characteristic of emotion. I then consider the ways in which emotions differ from one another. Specific questions are raised about the utility of using facial behaviour and autonomic nervous system activity as defining characteristics of specific emotions. The issue of emotion regulation and its relevance for understanding the structure of emotion is considered next. Here, I ask the question of *whether* and *what* invariance is preserved across different instantiations of the same emotion when different regulatory processes are invoked. In other words, is there a basic emotion structure that is preserved irrespective of the nature of the regulatory manœuvres called into play to cope with the emotion? Although we clearly do not have the requisite evidence at this time to firmly answer this question, I introduce a variety of data which suggest that at least for expressive behaviour and autonomic physiology the answer is likely to be no. The possibility that certain components of central nervous system functioning are invariant across different instantiations of the same basic emotion is considered and the level at which such invariance might occur is described. Finally, drawing upon evolutionary considerations, I argue that what is basic about emotion are the dimensions of approach and withdrawal. The role of these action tendencies in different emotions is considered and the nature of the linkage between the action tendency and the emotion is described.

I wish to note at the outset that I am focusing upon data and theory which bear upon the actual production of emotion. Evidence relating to the perception of emotional information, although interesting and important in its own right, is in most cases irrelevant to a consideration of emotion production. Moreover, we know from an extensive literature that the neural circuits implicated in the perception of emotional information are different from those required for the production of emotion (see Davidson, 1984, for a review).

The Role of Valence in Emotion

Many theorists have suggested that emotion must be valenced, that a given emotion must either be positive or negative in hedonic tone (e.g. Ortony & Turner, 1990; Woodworth & Schlosberg, 1954). It is instructive to consider the emotion surprise because it raises critical problems for the valence criterion and suggests a related, but alternative view. As Ortony and Turner (1990) have noted, surprise appears to be an emotion that is positively valenced in certain situations (e.g. "John was surprised to learn that he won the award") and negatively valenced in others (e.g. "John was surprised to learn that his tumour was malignant"). As a consequence of this, Ortony and Turner (1990) question whether surprise should be considered an emotion.

In general, I agree with those theorists who suggest that affective valence is a characteristic of emotion. However, I prefer to describe this dimension as an approach/withdrawal one rather than as positive/negative. The reasons for this will be elaborated in a later section. For the present purposes, let me underscore that the fact that approach and withdrawal are, in an important sense, the fundamental psychological decision an organism will make in relation to its environment. Approach and withdrawal behaviour are seen at every level of phylogeny where behaviour itself is present. The over-arching importance of approach and withdrawal was clearly underscored by the pioneering syntheses of the great comparative psychologist, Schneirla (1959), who illustrated its fundamental importance for promoting adaptive responses in situations of survival relevance.

In this context, and in general agreement with Ekman's (this issue) intuition, I regard the emotion of surprise as an approach emotion. Surprise is often associated with an orienting response (Donchin, 1981) and many theorists have suggested that an orienting response reflects a "call for further processing" (e.g. Ohman, 1979). In this sense, then, surprise would arise in contexts where the organism requires additional information prior to a final decision about appropriate action. Because of this, surprise is probably an emotion which is more likely than most to be followed by another emotion, as soon as the organism processes the additional information required to resolve a discrepancy. According to this analysis, at the *moment* of its occurrence, surprise is an approach emotion. It is associated with an accentuation of information processing to resolve a discrepancy. However, it is likely that in certain contexts, it is quickly replaced by a negative emotion if the additional information warrants such a response.

This analysis highlights the dynamic temporal unfolding of emotions. It also implies that retrospective self-report, the primary source of evidence for many emotion researchers (e.g. Ortony & Turner, 1990), is simply incapable of resolving the rapidly shifting, often preconscious changes in emotion that occur in response to real world challenges. Just as new methods were developed in cognitive psychology to address processes that are automatic and inaccessible to conscious awareness, so must new methods be utilised in the emotion domain for the very same reason.

In What Ways do Emotions Differ?

Like any other natural phenomenon, the topic of emotion has attracted a variety of taxonomic schemes designed to parse the terrain into meaningful units. A major impetus for this Special Issue is the continuing controversy over so-called "basic emotions". A number of theorists have proposed that complex emotions are comprised of different combinations of elemental or basic emotions. This colour palette scheme has been a dominant one in the theoretical writings of a number of discrete emotion theorists, most notably Izard (1972). Ekman (this issue), in his most recent statement on the topic, suggests that basic emotions share nine distinguishing characteristics. The first four, which Ekman regards as the most robust, include: (1) distinctive universal signals; (2) distinctive physiology; (3) presence in other primates; and (4) universal, distinctive antecedent events. Different instantiations of the same basic emotion are said to preserve the invariant characteristics of distinctive signals, distinctive physiology, and distinctive antecedent events.

Although aesthetically appealing, I wish to raise several questions about this general approach and suggest that nature does not conform to this idealised scheme. I will argue that there is considerable within-family variability in the response systems which specify emotion. Furthermore, I will suggest that different emotions may have differential access to certain response systems. If this is so, it further complicates the notion that each discrete emotion is associated with a relatively invariant pattern of expressive behaviour and physiological activity.

It is instructive at the outset to consider the sources of evidence that have most often been used to argue for the presence of discrete emotions. The most convincing and substantial evidence is from studies on facial expression where Ekman (e.g. Ekman & Friesen, 1971; Ekman, Sorenson, & Friesen, 1969) and others (Izard, 1971) have demonstrated that observers clearly choose the "appropriate" facial expression when asked to pick the one that displays a particular emotion. Moreover, if told a story with a universal theme (e.g. loss) and asked to choose an emotional face that depicts the most likely emotion experienced by the story's protagonist, subjects throughout the world choose the correctly matching facial expression (e.g. sadness). Finally, if subjects are asked to show how their face would appear if they were the protagonist in an emotion episode, New Guineans pose expressions which are judged moderately accurately by US college students. Ekman (1972) reported that the percentage of correct judgements ranged from a high of 73% for happiness to a low of 18% for fear. The mean level of accuracy across six emotion situations was 47.2%. This corpus of evidence establishes that certain facial expressions are associated with particular emotions and that this association is indeed universal. What such studies do not address, however, is whether such prototypical expressions invariably mark the occurrence of the emotions they denote when such emotions occur spontaneously. Even though Ekman (1972) has studied the spontaneous display of happiness and disgust expressions in the United States and Japan, virtually nothing is

known about the differential incidence of displaying other facial expressions in contexts where those emotions are reported. For example, when
subjects report experiencing fear, what is the likelihood of them expressing
a fear face compared with the expression of a disgust face when reporting
disgust?

A recent study performed in my laboratory addresses this issue and
raises a fundamental question about whether emotions may differ in their
likelihood of being expressed on the face. In this study, we (Tomarken &
Davidson, in prep.) unobtrusively videotaped subjects' facial
behaviour while they viewed short emotional film clips designed to elict
happiness, disgust, and fear. The film clips were carefully selected based
upon extensive prior ratings from several hundred subjects. I will focus
here on the responses to the fear and disgust clips. These clips (two per
emotion) were chosen to be matched on self-reported intensity of the
target emotions ($M = 6.30$ and 5.39 on disgust for the two disgust clips; $M
= 6.44$ and 5.40 for the two fear clips, on 9-point scales). The intensities of
the non-target emotions in response to these clips was also matched. For
the disgust clips, the emotion reported more intensely after disgust was
fear; similarly, for the fear clips, disgust was the second most intense
emotion reported. The mean fear rating for the disgust clips was 3.31, and
the mean disgust rating for the fear films was 3.10. In addition, the variance
of the ratings in response to the disgust and fear film clips was matched. A
total of 86 subjects were exposed to these clips in counterbalanced order.
Subjects viewed the clips alone in a darkened room, while physiology was
recorded. The facial behaviour was scored from the videotapes with
Ekman and Friesen's (1984) EM-FACS system. This system is designed to
code the facial actions which comprise emotional expressions and allows
for the derivation of the frequency and duration of specific discrete
expressions. We simply tabulated the percentage of subjects showing facial
signs of disgust in response to the disgust clips and facial signs of fear in
response to the fear clips. We found that 62% of the subjects showed at
least one disgust expression in response to either of the two disgust film
clips. The mean number of disgust expressions displayed by subjects (who
had at least one expression) to the disgust clips was 2.58, with a range from
1 to 8 expressions. In response to the fear clips, *not a single subject showed a
facial expression of fear or questionable fear* according to the EM-FACS
criteria. If we just use the most common element of the facial prototype of
fear, eye widening, 8.5% of subjects show this action unit [either alone or
in combination with any other action unit(s)] in response to the fear clips.
If we adopt the most inclusive possible facial criteria and determine the
percentage of subjects who show any action unit (either alone or in
combination with any others) that is part of the fear prototype (i.e. eye
widening, lips pulled back, eyebrows raised), a total of 18% display such

behaviour. It is important to underscore the fact that subjects' reported experiencing fear as intensely in response to the fear clips as they reported experiencing disgust in response to the disgust clips. Thus, using self-report criteria, they were experiencing the relevant target emotion in each case. However, the facial responses to these stimuli differed dramatically.

One objection that might be raised about this evidence is that film clips may simply be incapable of eliciting "genuine" fear. The film clips we selected to elicit fear did contain vivid depictions of threats of bodily harm, an antecedent event proposed by a number of theorists to be universally associated with fear (e.g. Lazarus, 1991). However, the subjects viewing the videoclips clearly were not threatened in this way.

To address this issue, we performed another study with small animal phobics (Tomarken & Davidson, in prep.). Such subjects report intense fear to their phobic object. In the context of an exposure treatment protocol, we exposed phobics (who met DSM-III-R criteria for simple phobia) to their phobic object *live* (either a boa constrictor or a tarantula) while their facial behaviour was again videotaped unobtrusively. All of our phobic subjects in this context reported being threatened with imminent physical harm. Here again, despite their self-reports indicative of intense fear, we rarely observed facial signs of fear. However, we did see a large percentage of subjects displaying facial signs of disgust to the phobic stimuli. Thus, in both a normal and a clinical sample, we found that when subjects are exposed to stimuli which they rate as eliciting moderately to extremely intense fear, little evidence of facial signs of fear are observed. Disgust, however, is much more likely to be displayed on the face.

Another objection that might be raised about this body of evidence is that it has been obtained from adults who have been socialised to mask their expressions, even in situations where they believe they are not being observed. What about fear expressions in infants? The literature on this point is again consistent with that obtained in adults. When young infants are exposed to classes of stimuli that are expected to elicit fear (e.g. placement over the deep side of visual cliff), they show behavioural signs of wariness (e.g. lack of approach) and autonomic signs generally believed to be consistent with fear (e.g. high heart rate), but they show little evidence of facial signs of fear (see reviews by Camras, this issue; Campos et al., 1983; Camras, Malatesta, & Izard, 1991).

These findings in diverse populations suggest that certain forms of fear exist that are not associated with the prototypical facial expression of fear. Although not readily testable, one obvious hypothesis which presents itself is that there may be adaptive advantages to not displaying fear on the face because its expression may signal vulnerability to a predator. It must also be noted that full, protypic facial expressions of fear probably do occur, but rarely in the laboratory. When the intensity of the frightening stimulus reaches a certain level, all available response systems may be recruited. The notion that different response systems may become engaged at different levels of affect intensity is consistent with recent findings of Cacioppo (see Tassinary & Cacioppo, 1992). At low levels of stimulus intensity, he observed differentiation between positively and negatively valenced stimuli in recordings of the electrical activity of muscles (but a relative lack of differentiation for discrete expressions). These findings suggest that facial differentiation of emotion varies directly with the intensity of the elicited emotion. Interestingly, the differentiation between positively and negatively valenced stimuli at low levels of stimulus intensity was not observable in recordings of autonomic activity.

In future research, it will be important to ascertain whether the lack of recruitment of particular response systems at low levels of affect intensity is a function of different gain thresholds present in the different response systems, or rather different patterns of efferent signals to the various effector systems at different stimulus intensities. This question is very important theoretically because if it is found that the pattern of efferent commands to the various effector systems maintain their differentiated activity and specify different discrete emotions, the relative lack of emotion-specific patterning in particular instances would be attributed to effector-specific (i.e. local) threshold and sensitivity factors. According to this view, different effector systems have different gain requirements and only become recruited when the input gain reaches a certain level. Lack of consistency across response systems may arise as a function of variability among effector systems in the gain requirement parameter.

An alternative view holds that the very pattern of efferent outflow to the effectors varies with intensity. Such a view implies that as the "same" emotion at different intensity levels is associated with a different pattern of efferent responses, the central physiology is not invariant across different intensities within an emotion. In fact, for certain components of physiology, the variability within a family may be as large as the variability between emotion families. The empirical question must be to specify precisely what is invariant across the many different instantiations of an emotion within a family. Of the first four characteristics which Ekman (this issue) has proposed are shared by each of the basic emotion families, only the first two, expressive signals and physiology, have been extensively evaluated. Certainly, the question of distinctive appraisals has received a considerable amount of research attention, but as Ekman (this issue) has noted, this research is mostly based upon the retrospective recollections of subjects about processes that occurred during prior emotional states, or that might occur during hypothetical emotional episodes. In the light of the automatic and often unconscious nature of appraisal, it is highly unlikely that retrospective self-report methodology is capable of addressing this question.[1]

For the first characteristic expression, I have tried to raise questions earlier about the degree of isomorphism between expression and emotion and to suggest that the package is indeed not a tidy one. There are many other questions of a similar nature that might be raised about expression, but an exhaustive cataloguing would go beyond the purpose of this paper. I wish to note only one other complication in the view that different discrete emotions have distinctive facial expressions. The complication has to do with the question of whether there are different types of positive emotion which may be as different from one another as negative emotions are among themselves. It seems that there is only one basic form of positive facial expression. Thus, if there are different types of positive emotion and if each is marked by the same expression, then the first characteristic shared by emotion families is violated. Ekman (this issue) clearly acknowledges this point and asks how crucial it is that each basic emotion share every one of the characteristics predicted to define such emotions. However, more important than the taxonomic question is the issue of meaningful differentiation within the positive emotions. We have suggested that one important distinction within the category happiness may be the degree to which it is associated with an approach action tendency. We have therefore distinguished between approach and non-approach happiness and have proposed that each is associated with distinctive central nervous activity (Davidson et al., 1990). Contentment and amusement may represent positive affective states that contain no approach component. Unambiguous "approach-happiness" is observed when 10-month-old infants observe their mothers walking toward them and smiling. Such infants show frank signs of approach action (e.g. reaching toward mother) and dramatic changes from baseline in brain activity (e.g. Fox & Davidson, 1988). The wrinkle is that each of these different forms of positive affect appears not to have a distinctive universal facial expression.

Consideration of the question of whether different emotion families are associated with distinctive patterns of physiology underscores the complexity of this problem and further highlights the substantial variability we can

---

[1]In a landmark paper on the nature of verbal reports as data, Ericcson and Simon (1980) specifically delineate the conditions in which verbal reports might provide veridical information about ongoing mental activity. They clearly note that automatic processes are relatively unavailable to verbal report. If such processes are rendered conscious, it is likely that significant transformations of the "heeded" information take place. In most contexts where subjects are asked to introspect about automatic processes, the verbalisations they produce reflect their a priori theories or knowledge about the information requested (Nisbett & Wilson, 1977).

expect to find *within* emotion families. I will address several issues as examples, but do not intend for this to be an exhaustive review of the problem.

In considering the physiology associated with emotion, it is essential to distinguish between peripheral and central physiology, as well as among different components of the latter. The autonomic responses associated with emotion presumably occur to facilitate the action associated with the emotion. Thus, Levenson, Ekman, and Friesen (1990, p. 379) suggest that autonomic changes associated with different discrete emotions "produce patterns of activity that will support the behavioral adaptations and associated motor programs that are most likely for that emotion". Levenson et al. (1990) ask but do not answer the question of whether the same emotion accompanied by different action tendencies is likely to be associated with an invariant or differing pattern of autonomic activity. Fortunately, other relevant data may be brought to bear on this problem.

Kalin and Shelton (1989) studied different behavioural manifestations of fear in infant rhesus monkeys and found that certain fear-related behaviours (e.g. freezing) are selectively reduced by administration of a benzodiazepine, whereas other fear-related behaviours are selectively reduced by administration of morphine (e.g. vocalisation). These findings underscore the differentiated nature of the various subcomponents of fear and suggest that different patterns of central neurochemistry underlie distinct behavioural components of fear.

Unfortunately, there is a paucity of literature reporting on research with humans that has direct bearing on this important question. However, there are other animal studies which are relevant, although they certainly were not originally designed to address this question. Almost 20 years ago, Goesling and Brener (1972) reported on a study that was designed to address a critical problem in the literature at that time on operant conditioning of heart rate. The problem was whether heart rate control was "somatically mediated". Goesling and Brener (1972) trained one group of rats to run (in a running wheel) in response to a particular discriminative visual stimulus and to remain still in response to a second visual cue. In another phase of the experiment, the animals were administered curare, a peripheral neuromuscular blocking agent. Thus, while under the influence of curare, the animals were paralysed: They received one of the two discriminative stimuli that had been previously paired with either running or remaining still. Then, the animals received training to either increase or decrease their heart rate using standard operant techniques. They found that when the rats were exposed to the stimulus previously paired with running, they showed large magnitude increases in heart rate compared with exposure to the stimulus previously paired with remaining still, even though the animals were unable to move at all under the influence of curare. This suggests that the cardiac-somatic linkage was central and did not depend upon the overt expression of the action. Interestingly, the operant training failed to override the massive effects of the discriminative stimulus on heart rate.

Although this study did not involve emotion in any way, it does underscore the potency of autonomic changes which are action-specific. From this study, one would certainly expect that a fear state accompanied by freezing would differ from a fear state associated with fleeing; just as the rats exposed to a stimulus previously paired with running showed much higher heart rates than animals exposed to a stimulus previously paired with freezing. Of course, this is only a prediction and the requisite empirical studies have not been performed. However, if the predicted finding did emerge, it would seriously call into question the idea that a *single* pattern of autonomic activity remains invariant across different manifestations of the same emotion.

In this discussion, I have addressed the first two characteristics that Ekman has suggested are shared by basic emotions—distinctive universal signals and distinctive physiology. Of course, it should be apparent that signals other than the face are likely to be important and that failure to differentiate among emotional states on the basis of facial expression does not imply that such states do not have distinctive, universal signals of another type (e.g. vocalic expression). Also, the fact that different forms of the same emotion are likely to differ on certain parameters of physiology does not indicate that other aspects of physiology will not be found which are invariant across different types or expressions of the same underlying emotional state (e.g. fear associated with fleeing vs. freezing; anger associated with striking out vs. withdrawing; happiness associated with approach vs. non-approach, etc.). My comments are meant more to raise questions than to provide answers, to underscore where future research must be directed and not to draw firm conclusions on the basis of extant data. I have not considered the third and fourth characteristics that have been proposed to be shared among the basic emotions because of the paucity of available data in the case of primate emotion and the methodological limitations of the evidence that is available on the issue of appraisal.

The empirical challenge that confronts us is the specification of reliable patterns of coherence across multiple response systems. If a 10-month-old infant exposed to the deep side of the visual cliff reliably displays a cardiac acceleration and behavioural signs of withdrawal in the absence of a protypical fear facial expression, it would seem that such a state would have a status equal to that of any other emotion. The name we assign to that state is not the issue. In fact, it is likely that the very act of assigning a name to the state obfuscates rather than clarifies, as we tend to unwittingly assume that states given the same name are indeed the same state (see

Kagan, 1988). What is important is the establishment of repeatable patterns of multi-systemic coherence in response to well-defined incentive conditions. Only through such efforts will it be possible to identify which, if any, components of the emotional response remain invariant across different instantiations within an emotion family.

It is instructive in this regard to consider other characteristics which some theorists propose as the basis of the invariant features for different emotions. Stein and Trabasso (this issue) underscore the importance of higher-order goals associated with different emotions and propose that such goals remain invariant across different instantiations of basic emotions. If they are correct, then it is likely that the patterns of central physiology which might retain their invariance within an emotion family reflect activity in brain circuits associated with the formulation of goals and plans. Such a possibility is consistent with our emphasis on the importance of frontal cortical function in emotion (e.g. Davidson, in press), as the dorsolateral frontal cortex has been directly implicated as the critical structure in the mediation of such behaviour (Fuster, 1989; Nauta, 1971). This issue will be considered in more detail in a subsequent section.

Emotion Regulation: Can it be Disentangled from Emotion Structure?

Regulatory influences on the various components of emotion begin early in development and continue throughout the life-span. Some theorists (e.g. Izard, 1990) have postulated a core emotion process that remains relatively invariant under the pressure of these influences. Contextual factors are held to influence display rules and coping, but the core emotion remains unchanged, a Platonic essence which exhibits deep universality. Although aesthetically elegant, I wish to take issue with this position and to suggest instead the inevitability of the core changing as much as the shell. The evidence that I will bring to bear in support of this position is derived from studies on emotion, as well as studies on neighbouring phenomena, such as cultural variations in pain sensitivity, as many of the most important questions on the psychobiological consequences of emotion regulation have not been asked, let alone answered.

I will consider two forms of emotion regulation, borrowed from the cross-cultural work of Shweder (1985). The first he termed the *communication question*. This refers to cultural differences in emotional expressivity. Some cultures reinforce the overt, full-blown expression of certain emotions whereas others place constraints on the expression of some emotions. The relevant question in the context of this article is the impact of such regulation on the structure of emotion. Where do such cultural influences exert their effect? Do they simply amplify or attenuate the motor expressive component? Are they associated with differences in the subjective intensity of the experienced emotion? Are they associated with different magnitudes of physiological response?

There have been a number of studies of ethnic differences in pain responsivity. Although some of the differences observed are undoubtedly in part genetic, it is also likely that experiential effects play some role. In a classic experiment, Sternbach and Tursky (1965) demonstrated ethnic differences in pain tolerance levels, which were paralleled by differences in autonomic responsivity. Women of Italian descent tolerated less shock and showed heightened electrodermal responses compared with women of Old American origin.

The data on ethnic differences in pain responsivity are relevant to the emotion domain for they suggest that cultural differences in the reinforcement of expressivity[2] will likely have both behavioural *and* physiological consequences, particularly if such influences are long-standing. If cross-cultural differences in the physiology of emotion are found, it would again pose challenges for the proposition that there are unique, invariant, and universal patterns of physiology which specify each discrete emotion. If certain action tendencies varied in their association with particular emotions across cultures, it would unquestionably be associated with different patterns of physiology.

The claim that culture can importantly modify the physiology of emotion is simply an extension of the more basic proposition that experience influences the brain. Since the experiments of Rosenzweig and his colleagues nearly 30 years ago (e.g. Rosenzweig, Krech, Bennett, & Diamond, 1962; see Diamond, 1988, for a review) on the effects of environmental enrichment on basic brain organisation, anatomy, and neurochemistry, we know that even at the level of gene expression, experiential determinants abound (see e.g. Kandel, 1983 for a more modern statement on this issue). On this view, biological processes are no closer to the genotype than are behavioural processes. And, therefore, it should come as no surprise that considerable variability may exist in the

---

[2]It is also conceivable that such cultural differences in physiological reactivity to pain are, at least in part, a product of cognitive differences in reaction to the pain challenge between the ethnic groups. The Italian women might ruminate more in response to such stimuli compared with women of Old American origin. Such differences in rumination might amplify or attenuate both expressive and physiological responses to the painful stimuli. In the depression literature, individual differences in ruminative tendencies have been proposed to account for differences in the duration of depressive symptoms (Nolen-Hoeksema, 1991). Individuals who engage in ruminative responses and focus attention on their symptoms are likely to have longer depressive episodes than people who distract themselves from their symptoms. Similar regulatory influences are likely to occur in both the pain and emotion domains.

biological concomitants of emotion and be determined, in part, by the differing action tendencies with which the emotion is associated. Having said this, I must hasten to add that I view it as likely that certain emotions have hard-wired action tendencies that emerge early in ontogeny, but may be modifiable with experience. Also, the possible pairings of action tendencies with emotion is not random, but is likely to be biologically constrained in much the same way as has been demonstrated for preparedness in classical conditioning (e.g. Seligman & Hager, 1972). Thus, it is very unlikely that a strong approach action can be coupled with the emotional state of fear. Attempts at such pairing would likely change either the emotion itself, or the nature of the action tendency.

Another form of emotion regulation considered by Shweder (1985) is what he termed the *management question*. This refers to techniques and/or strategies utilised to deal with emotions that cannot be directly expressed. The issue most directly relevant to the theme of this article is the level at which such management occurs and the question of whether long-term habitual use of certain management strategies changes the very core of the emotional response. More specifically, do prohibitions on emotional expression change the physiological concomitants of emotion? As will be described below, the answer to this question depends upon the level at which the management occurs. The level, in turn, reflects the duration of time the management strategy has been practised.

I will again borrow here from the literature on pain, as the requisite studies in the emotion domain have not yet been performed. Several studies have been conducted to evaluate the claim that the adoption of certain meditative states can dramatically attenuate pain responsivity (e.g. Anand, Chinna, & Singh, 1961). Another, related literature (e.g. Hilgard, 1973, 1977) concerns the effects of hypnotic analgesia on behavioural and physiological responses to pain. Both meditation and hypnotic analgesia have been proposed as effective strategies for managing pain. However, it appears as if the level at which such management effects are exerted differs substantially between these two forms of self-regulation. Meditation has been found to significantly attenuate certain physiological responses to pain (e.g. Anand et al., 1961). Although hypnotic analgesia results in profound decreases in reported pain and objective increases in pain tolerance (i.e. subjects can withstand a painful stimulus for a longer duration of time), it has not been found to reduce the autonomic concomitants of pain (Hilgard, 1973, 1977). Thus, it appears that hypnotic analgesia in contrast to other forms of self-regulation, such as long-term meditation, change those components of pain responsivity over which we have the most direct voluntary control. Other, more automatic response components, such as physiological changes, remain unaltered. This is consistent with the findings on signal detection and pain responsivity under hypnotic analgesia where it has been found that alterations are produced in measures of response bias (β), but not in measures of sensitivity (d') (Clark, 1974). One important question raised by these data for the emotion domain concerns the differences between phasic and long-term regulation strategies.

Pennebaker and his colleagues (Pennebaker & Chew, 1985) have examined the effects of a short-term management strategy on one component of autonomic physiology—skin conductance. They tested subjects in a standard guilty knowledge paradigm (Lykken, 1959) where they had to deceive an experimenter. One group of subjects was instructed to specifically inhibit all overt expressive signs, and another group was not given specific instructions about the inhibition of expressive behaviour. Pennebaker and Chew (1985) found that the inhibit group displayed significantly higher skin conductance activity compared with the control group. The very act of inhibition exacted a biological cost reflected in increased skin conductance activity. An identical pattern of results was obtained in a recent study by Gross and Levenson (1991), where they found that when subjects were asked to suppress expressive signs of affect in response to a disgust-producing film clip, greater sympathetic activity was observed compared with a non-suppression control group.

These findings suggest that a short-term management strategy may actually accentuate certain physiological manifestations of emotion. What we do not know from such experiments is whether the long-term deployment of such strategies results in changes in physiology over time. Based upon the very limited corpus of available evidence, I offer two related hypotheses concerning the effects of expression management on the underlying psychobiology of emotion. The first hypothesis states that short-term (i.e. those which are only occasionally deployed for short periods of time) prohibitions on expression may not attenuate physiological changes that normally accompany emotion. In fact, for certain emotions, they may accentuate such changes (Pennebaker & Chew, 1985; Gross & Levenson, 1991). Such short-term changes are also likely not to have much effect on the neural activity which normally accompanies the emotion. The efferent patterning to various effector systems is likely to be intact in such cases. Inhibitory strategies are overlaid on and may potentially mask such effector changes, but the input to the effector systems is thought to be largely unchanged. In contrast to this is the second hypothesis which holds that prohibitions occurring early in life and persisting for a long period of time are likely to modify the very pattern of efferent commands normally associated with that emotion. In other words, long-term exposure to a cultural context requiring certain forms of management and inhibition of emotional expression will modify the underlying structure of the emotion (see also Shweder, 1985).[3] To evaluate these hypotheses, longitudinal research in different cultures which differ in prohibitions on expressivity is needed. Early in life, substantial universality in expression and physiology is expected. However, with development, significant departures from universality are predicted. On this view, the structure of emotion reflects an irrevocable mix of innate and experiential influences.

Carving Nature at its Joints: Approach/Withdrawal as the Basic Emotion-relevant Dimension

The analysis just presented questions the special status of emotions that putatively possess distinguishing characteristics proposed to denote basic emotions. Both expression and physiology were shown to be quite variable within an emotion family. Rather than characterise any particular emotion or set of emotions as basic, I wish to argue that approach and withdrawal are two dimensions along which emotions differ and these dimensions should properly be regarded as basic. They are basic principally because of their phylogenetic primacy. Organisms approach and withdraw at every level of phylogeny where behaviour itself is present. To approach or to withdraw is the fundamental adaptive decision in situations or conditions that have recurred during our evolutionary past (Tooby & Cosmides, 1990). In very primitive organisms with simple nervous systems, rudimentary forms of approach and withdrawal behaviour occur in the absence of any emotion. The very structure of the nervous system in such species precludes any reasonable ascription of emotion in the presence of approach and withdrawal behavioural states (see Schnierla, 1959, for examples) as they contain none of the circuitry found to be essential for the generation of emotional responses in vertebrates. Thus, it is important to distinguish between approach and withdrawal action *per se*, and approach and withdrawal behaviours that occur in the context of emotion. Over the course of evolution, approach and withdrawal action emerged prior to the appearance of emotions to solve adaptive problems in simple species.

As the nature of adaptive problems became more complex (for examples, see Tooby & Cosmides, 1990) and co-ordination among perceptual, cognitive, and action systems was required, emotions evolved and became associated with already established approach and withdrawal action sys-

---

[3]It may be that long-term exposure to particular cultural constraints on emotional expression exert their effects indirectly through modification of certain cognitive processes such as appraisal and coping mechanisms, rather than by (or in addition to) direct effects via the inhibition of emotional expression. Indeed, certain technologies for emotion regulation, such as cognitive therapy for depression, are predicated on this view.

tems. The co-ordination and integration among these various systems required a convergence zone (Damasio, 1989) in the brain. According to current accounts of convergence zones, these brain regions contain codes to "bind" together information from widely distributed neural networks. In the case of an emotion arising in response to an external stimulus, perceptual information about the stimulus must be combined with the output of various specialised processing regions in the brain, including those that code valence, formulate action plans, and generate the requisite autonomic supports. This integration of multiple components of emotion depends upon "phase-locked coactivation of geographically separate sites of neural activity" (Damasio, 1989, p. 127). As Damasio (1989) notes, more complex combinatorial codes are inscribed in more anterior cortical zones. In the light of the extensive multi-system coherence apparent in emotion, the frontal lobes are likely the major site of the emotion convergence zone (for supporting evidence, see Davidson, in press, Fuster, 1989; Nauta, 1971).

Elsewhere (e.g. Davidson & Tomarken, 1989; Davidson, in press), I have dealt with the evolutionary significance of separating approach and withdrawal systems in each hemisphere. I have suggested that one effective way in which competitive interactions between response systems could be minimised is to separate them geographically in the brain. Hemispheric specialisation is perhaps the most effective geographical separation which has been achieved in vertebrate nervous system evolution. And, recent evidence of hemispheric specialisation in a number of different species consistently confirms the direction of the effects found in humans and indicates that lateralisation for approach- and withdrawal-related emotion is considerably more robust across phylogeny than is cognitive lateralisation (e.g. Denenberg, 1984). In fact, some investigators have implied that cognitive lateralisation in certain primate species, including humans, has emerged from the more basic lateralisation for emotion (e.g. Kinsbourne, 1978).

We (Sobotka, Davidson, & Senulis, in press) have recently completed an experiment in which we attempted to disentangle approach/withdrawal action components from the positive and negative emotional states with which they are usually associated. According to the model of the emotion convergence zone I just sketched, only during the actual production of emotion should distinct activation patterns in the frontal region be present. We had subjects play a video-type game in which they could win and lose money as a function of their performance. At the start of the experiment, they were given $5 and told that they could add to this amount or decrease the amount, depending on their performance. On certain trials they received a cue (an arrow in the up position) that denoted a potential reward trial. Four seconds following the cue, they received an imperative stimulus to which they were to respond as quickly as possible. If they responded sufficiently quickly, they received a monetary reward. If their response was slow, there was no change in their cumulative earnings. On other trials, the initial arrow was in the down position. On such trials, if they responded too slowly money would actually be taken away from them. If they responded quickly, there was no change in their earnings. We confirmed that such reward and punishment contingencies indeed produced marked changes in their emotional state during the playing of the game.

In addition to manipulating reward and punishment contingencies, we also manipulated the nature of the motor response subjects were asked to make in response to the imperative stimulus. On half the trials, subjects were instructed to make approach responses—their index finger was held above a button and they were instructed to make a button press when they saw the imperative stimulus. On the remaining trials, subjects were instructed to make withdrawal responses—their index finger depressed the button prior to trial onset and they were instructed to lift their finger off the button when they detected the imperative stimulus. The reward and punishment contingencies were fully crossed and counterbalanced with the movement instructions. Brain activity was examined in the four second period just prior to making the motor response.

The results indicated that approach and withdrawal responses (averaged across reward and punishment conditions) did differ in the lateralised pattern of brain activation that preceded the response, but only in the temporoparietal region and not in more anterior regions. Approach responses were associated with more relative left-sided activation in this region compared with withdrawal responses. When the reward and punishment conditions were compared, we confirmed what we had found on many previous occasions—reward trials were associated with more left-sided frontal activation compared with punishment trials, and the latter were associated with more right-sided activation than the former. We expected that the movement condition might interact with the reward and punishment contingencies. We did not find this to occur, largely because the effects of the reward and punishment contingencies were so large that they swamped any additional variance contributed by the rather subtle manipulation of movement.

The results of this experiment suggest that as simple a manipulation of approach and withdrawal responding as a finger press vs. a finger lift is enough to produce differential lateralised effects in posterior processing regions. This finding suggests that approach and withdrawal action plans themselves, stripped of their usual pattern of associated emotion, are segregated into different hemispheres. However, recruitment of the frontal convergence zone occurs only in response to the incentives that produce emotion.

Although within an experimental context we can dissociate rudimentary action plans from the emotions with which they might normally be associated, naturally occurring emotion is likely to be more tightly coupled to specific action tendencies. And conversely, when approach and withdrawal action occur, they usually are associated with an emotional state. As I noted earlier, the nature of this coupling is not rigidly fixed,[4] but rather probably biologically constrained in a fashion similar to that observed in the literature on biological preparedness and learning (Seligman & Hager, 1972).

What is the utility of highlighting approach and withdrawal as the fundamental basic dimensions relevant to emotion? Below I will briefly summarise the powerful analytical advantages afforded by this conceptual approach. Following this summary, I will then consider where discrete emotions fit within this model and how research on their neural substrates should proceed.

We have proposed that those negative emotions, affective traits, and psychopathology that include a strong withdrawal component—distancing the organism from the source of stimulation—will be associated with right-sided anterior cortical activation. Both fear and disgust protypically involve withdrawal. Certain anxiety disorders, such as phobias, also include a strong withdrawal component. In our research, we have consistently found that the experimental arousal of these negative emotions is associated with an accentuation of right-sided frontal activation compared with either a non-emotional baseline or a positive emotional state (e.g. Davidson et al., 1990). Moreover, in three separate studies we found that those individuals with tonically elevated right-sided frontal activation report more intense levels of fear and disgust in response to short film clips designed to elicit these emotions compared with subjects who show left-sided activation (Tomarken, Davidson, & Henriques, 1990; Wheeler, Davidson, & Tomarken, in press). Among social phobics, the anticipation of making a public speech is associated with pronounced right anterior activation (Davidson et al., in prep.). In contrast to these withdrawal-related negative emotions and psychopathology is depression, a negative

---

[4]Although some theorists argue for a more isomorphic relation between action tendencies and emotions (e.g. Frijda, 1986), their own data do not support such a strong linkage (cf. Frijda, Kuipers, & ter Schure, 1989). Using self-report measures of action tendencies, these investigators found that an average of only 40% of the emotion names used across two studies were correctly predicted from descriptions of action tendencies.

affect state or trait that we have proposed is predominantly associated with deficits in the activation of an approach system. This suggestion is based upon numerous and diverse sources. The phenomenology and symptomatology of depression specifically includes references to approach-related deficits (see Depue & Iacona, 1989, for a review). For example, psychomotor retardation and loss of interest and pleasure are all symptoms we would logically expect to follow from deficits in the activation of an approach system. Moreover, factor analytical studies of mood in depressed and normal subjects indicates that the most pronounced difference between these groups is not an increase in negative affect among depressives, but rather a decrease in positive affect in this group compared with normals (Watson, Clark, & Carey, 1988). In comparisons of baseline levels of frontal activation in depressives and controls, we have consistently found that depressives show decreased activation in the left frontal region (Henriques & Davidson, 1990, 1991; Schaffer, Davidson, & Saron, 1983). We have also found that toddlers who have a temperamental style characterised by reticence to approach novel and unfamiliar people and objects show decreased left frontal activation compared with their uninhibited counterparts (Davidson, Finman, Straus, & Kagan, submitted). Most recently, we have found that the administration of diazepam, a benzodiazepine that increases approach-related behaviour in novel and unfamiliar situations, also increased left-sided frontal activation in rhesus monkeys (Davidson, Kalin, & Shelton, submitted).

Within the positive affect category, we have distinguished between approach and non-approach forms of happiness. In response to short film clips which depict amusing positive events, subjects report increases in the intensity of happiness and amusement and also show facial signs of felt happiness (Duchenne smiles). However, these positive affect states rarely include an approach component. Contrast this with a situation where a 10-month-old infant is exposed to an episode of its mother approaching and smiling. In addition to showing a Duchenne smile, the vast majority of infants of this age show unambiguous and frank signs of approach behaviour, e.g. reaching out toward the mother. We have observed different patterns of brain activity in these situations. During approach positive affect, we find increases in left frontal activation above baseline (Fox & Davidson, 1987, 1988), whereas in the film clip example, anterior asymmetry does not differ significantly from that found at baseline (Davidson et al., 1990). Thus, we have two positive affect states, both of which are associated with the same pattern of facial expressive behaviour and of self-reported emotion. However, behaviourally these states differ and they also differ in patterns of frontal brain activity.

We believe, although we do not yet have the requisite data, that a similar distinction between approach and non-approach forms of the emotion can be made for anger. When anger is elicited within the first year of life it is typically associated with a strong approach component. For example, one of the most reliable procedures for the experimental elicitation of anger in the first year is the moderate restraint procedure (Stenberg, Campos, & Emde, 1983). In this procedure, the infant is placed on its back while the wrists of the infant are held to the ground. Infants will typically struggle against this restraint (presumably to overcome a goal blockage) and will show facial signs of anger. During this procedure, when facial signs of anger are present in the absence of crying, infants show left frontal activation (Fox & Davidson, 1988).

We have not yet directly compared the experimental arousal of approach and non-approach forms of anger in the laboratory. We are currently performing such a study by comparing brain activity during the experimental arousal of anger in subjects who habitually express their anger and in those who habitually withdraw from anger-producing situations. Only through such a comparison, or by experimentally manipulating these different forms of anger will a more definitive answer emerge.

It is my hope that this discussion underscores the salience of the approach and withdrawal dimensions for understanding the structure of different emotions. As I tried to illustrate, for at least some emotions (e.g. anger, happiness) the magnitude of engagement of the approach and withdrawal systems is not fixed but rather varies with the context and across different individuals. Certain emotions may have a high probability of being associated with either approach or withdrawal (e.g. disgust), although one may imagine scenarios in which the opposite action tendencies may be associated with even these emotions. It is clear that approach and withdrawal are dimensions which are basic to emotion, appear throughout many levels of phylogeny, emerge early in ontogeny, and are mediated by separate brain systems found in all vertebrate species.

This analysis should not be taken as inconsistent with a focus on discrete emotions. The fact that certain forms of anger and happiness both include an approach component does not imply that they are the same emotion. They may share certain important neural substrates in common, but it seems clear that they also must differ in important respects too. The dimensional perspective articulated above should be regarded as complementary to the discrete emotions perspective. They are simply addressing different levels of a complex process.

If physiology and expressive behaviour vary within emotion families, then what remains invariant across different instantiations of the same discrete emotion? In agreement with the theoretical position articulated by Stein and Trabasso (this issue), the invariance is carried in the higher-order goal with which the emotion is associated. Thus, for example, Stein and Trabasso argue that fear *always* is associated with "the desire to prevent the onset of an aversive state or the desire to prevent the loss of a valuable goal". According to their analysis, each emotion has its own unique higher-order goal which is *necessary* for the experience of that emotion. A similar emphasis on higher-order goals is implicit in the analysis of basic emotions proposed by Johnson-Laird and Oatley (this issue). Given that different discrete emotions are associated with different higher-order goals and these goals represent the invariant core of the emotion, I would expect there to be central states which subserve these mental events. However, it is likely that the neural networks which subserve these core goals will be constituted in cortical sites that participate in the generation of other, non-emotional beliefs and desires. Thus, the patterns of neural activity that might reflect the core invariance within emotion families and differentiate among different emotion families will likely be found to occur in those brain regions—such as the dorsolateral frontal cortex—that are not specifically implicated in the emotion generation process, but rather participate in the integration of basic cognitive and emotional operations associated with belief and desire states.

SUMMARY AND CONCLUSION

In this article, I have attempted to raise questions about some of the characteristics of emotions given special status as basic. I have focused here on expression and physiology. The strength and isomorphism of the linkage between expression and emotion was considered and several examples were brought to bear to support the conclusion that the expression-emotion package is neither simple nor tidy. Similarly, considerable variability within an emotion family in physiology was suggested. Most physiological patterning was claimed to be more action-specific than emotion specific, although it is clear that the requisite studies to fully address this question have not been performed. Invariance across the many different instantiations of an emotion within a family may be found centrally, but are likely to be found in neural circuits that subserve the basic cognitive processes associated with beliefs and desires because it is at this higher-order level that the best case for invariance within emotion families can be made. Finally, the dimensions of approach and withdrawal were proposed as basic, fundamental building blocks of emotion. The application of these dimensions to a number of different emotions and to individual differences in affective style was illustrated.

Manuscript received 15 March 1991
Revised manuscript received 25 November 1991

REFERENCES

Anand, B.K., Chinna, G.S., & Singh, B. (1961). Some aspects of electroencephalographic studies in yogis. *Electroencephalography and Clinical Neurophysiology, 13*, 452–456.

Campos, J.J., Barrett, K.C., Lamb, M.E., Goldsmith, H.H., & Stenberg, C. (1983). Socioemotional development. In P.H. Mussen (Ed.), *Handbook of child psychology*, Vol. II. New York: Wiley, pp. 783–915.

Camras, L.A., Malatesta, C., & Izard, C. (1991). The development of facial expressions in infancy. In R. Feldman & B. Rime (Eds), *Fundamentals of nonverbal behavior.* Cambridge University Press.

Clark, W.C. (1974). Pain sensitivity and the report of pain: An introduction to sensory decision theory. *Anesthesiology, 40*, 272–287.

Damasio, A.R. (1989). The brain binds entities and events by multiregional activation from convergence zones. *Neural Computation, 1*, 123–132.

Davidson, R.J. (1984). Affect, cognition and hemispheric specialization. In C.E. Izard, J. Kagan, & R. Zajonc (Eds), *Emotion, cognition and behavior.* Cambridge University Press.

Davidson, R.J. (In press). Anterior cerebral asymmetry and the nature of emotion. *Brain and Cognition.*

Davidson, R.J. & Tomarken, A.J. (1989). Laterality and emotion: An electrophysiological approach. In F. Boller & J. Grafman (Eds), *Handbook of neuropsychology.* Amsterdam: Elsevier.

Davidson, R.J., Ekman, P., Saron, C., Senulis, J., & Friesen, W.V. (1990). Approach/ withdrawal and cerebral asymmetry: Emotional expression and brain physiology. I. *Journal of Personality and Social Psychology, 58*, 330–341.

Davidson, R.J., Finman, R., Straus, A., & Kagan, J. (Submitted). Patterns of frontal asymmetry differentiate between wary and outgoing children: A neurobiological substrate of childhood temperament.

Davidson, R.J., Kalin, N.H., & Shelton, S.E. (Submitted). Lateralized effects of diazepam on frontal brain electrical asymmetries in rhesus monkeys.

Davidson, R.J., Marshall, J., Tomarken, A.J., Straus, A., & Henriques, J.B. (In prep.). While a phobic waits: Brain electrical patterning in social phobics during anticipation of making a public speech.

Denenberg, V.H. (1984). Behavioral asymmetry. In N. Geschwind & A.M. Galaburda (Eds), *Cerebral dominance: The biological foundations.* Cambridge, MA: Harvard University Press, pp. 114–133.

Depue, R.A. & Iacona, W.G. (1989). Neurobehavioral aspects of affective disorders. *Annual Review of Psychology, 40*, 457–492.

Diamond, M.C. (1988). *Enriching heredity: The impact of the environment on the anatomy of the brain.* New York: The Free Press.

Donchin, E. (1981). Surprise! . . . Surprise? *Psychophysiology, 18*, 493–513.

Ekman, P. (1972). Universals and cultural differences in facial expressions of emotion. In J. Cole (Ed.), *Nebraska symposium on motivation, 1971*, Vol. 19. Lincoln, NE: University of Nebraska Press.

Ekman, P. & Friesen, W.V. (1971). Constants across cultures in the face and emotion. *Journal of Personality and Social Psychology, 17*, 124–129.

Ekman, P. & Friesen, W.V. (1984). *Emotion Facial Action Coding System (EM-FACS).* San Francisco: University of California.

Ekman, P., Sorenson, E.R., & Friesen, W.V. (1969). Pan-cultural elements in facial displays of emotions. *Science, 164*, 86–88.

Ericcson, K.A. & Simon, H.A. (1980). Verbal reports as data. *Psychological Review*, 87, 215–251.

Fox, N.A. & Davidson, R.J. (1987). Electroencephalogram asymmetry in response to the approach of a stranger and maternal separation in 10 month old infants. *Developmental Psychology*, 23, 233–240.

Fox, N.A. & Davidson, R.J. (1988). Patterns of brain electrical activity during facial signs of emotion in ten month old infants. *Developmental Psychology*, 24, 230–236.

Frijda, N.H. (1986). *The emotions*. Cambridge University Press.

Frijda, N.H., Kuipers, P., & ter Schure, E. (1989). Relations among emotion, appraisal and emotional action readiness. *Journal of Personality and Social Psychology*, 57, 212–228.

Fuster, J.M. (1989). *The prefrontal cortex* (2nd edn). New York: Raven.

Goesling, W.J. & Brener, J. (1972). Effects of activity and immobility conditioning upon subsequent heart-rate conditioning in curarized rats. *Journal of Comparative and Physiological Psychology*, 81, 311–317.

Gross, J.J. & Levenson, R.W. (1991). *Emotional suppression in males and females*. Paper presented at the Annual Meeting of the Society for Psychophysiological Research, Chicago.

Henriques, J.B. & Davidson, R.J. (1990). Regional brain electrical asymmetries discriminate between previously depressed subjects and healthy controls. *Journal of Abnormal Psychology*, 99, 22–31.

Henriques, J.B. & Davidson, R.J. (1991). Left frontal hypoactivation in depression. *Journal of Abnormal Psychology*, 100, 535–545.

Hilgard, E.R. (1973). A neodissociation interpretation of pain reduction in hypnosis. *Psychological Review*, 80, 396–411.

Hilgard, E.R. (1977). *Divided consciousness: Multiple controls in human thought and action*. New York: Wiley.

Izard, C.E. (1971). *The face of emotion*. New York: Appleton-Century-Crofts.

Izard, C.E. (1972). *Patterns of emotions: A new analysis of anxiety and depression*. New York: Academic Press.

Izard, C.E. (1977). *Human emotions*. New York: Plenum.

Izard, C.E. (1990). Facial expressions and the regulation of emotions. *Journal of Personality and Social Psychology*, 58, 487–498.

Kagan, J. (1988). The meaning of personality predicates. *American Psychologist*, 43, 614–620.

Kalin, N.H. & Shelton, S.E. (1989). Defensive behaviors in infant rhesus monkeys: Environmental cues and neurochemical regulation. *Science*, 243, 1718–1721.

Kandel, E.R. (1983). From metapsychology to molecular biology: Explorations into the nature of anxiety. *American Journal of Psychiatry*, 140, 1277–1293.

Kinsbourne, M. (1978). The biological determinants of functional bisymmetry and asymmetry. In M. Kinsbourne (Ed.), *Asymmetrical functions of the brain*. Cambridge University Press.

Lazarus, R.S. (1991). *Emotion and adaptation*. Oxford University Press.

Levenson, R.W., Ekman, P., & Friesen, W.V. (1990). Voluntary facial action generates emotion-specific autonomic nervous system activity. *Psychophysiology*, 27, 363–384.

Lykken, D.T. (1959). The validity of the guilty knowledge technique: The effects of faking. *Journal of Applied Psychology*, 44, 258–262.

Nauta, W.J.H. (1971). The problem of the frontal lobe—A reinterpretation. *Journal of Psychiatric Research*, 8, 167–187.

Nisbett, R.E. & Wilson, T.D. (1977). Telling more than we can know: Verbal reports on mental processes. *Psychological Review*, 84, 231–259.

Nolen-Hoeksema, S. (1991). Responses to depression and their effects on the duration of depressive episodes. *Journal of Abnormal Psychology*, *100*, 569–582.

Ohman, A. (1979). The orienting response, attention and learning: An information processing perspective. In H.D. Kimmel, E.H. Van Olst, & J.F. Orlebeke (Eds), *The orienting reflex in humans*. Hillsdale, NJ: Lawrence Erlbaum Associates Inc, pp. 443–471.

Ortony, A. & Turner, T.J. (1990). What's basic about basic emotions? *Psychological Review*, *97*, 315–331.

Pennebaker, J.W. & Chew, C.H. (1985). Behavioral inhibition and electrodermal activity during deception. *Journal of Personality and Social Psychology*, *49*, 1427–1433.

Rosenzweig, M.R., Krech, D., Bennett, E.L., & Diamond, M.C. (1962). Effects of environmental complexity and training on brain chemistry. *Journal of Comparative and Physiological Psychology*, *55*, 429–437.

Schaffer, C.E., Davidson, R.J., & Saron, C. (1983). Frontal and parietal electroencephalogram asymmetry in depressed and nondepressed subjects. *Biological Psychiatry*, *18*, 753–762.

Schneirla, T.C. (1959). An evolutionary and developmental theory of biphasic processes underlying approach and withdrawal. In M.R. Jones (Ed.), *Nebraska symposium on motivation*. Lincoln: University of Nebraska Press.

Seligman, M.E.P. & Hager, J.E. (Eds) (1972). *Biological boundaries of learning*. New York: Appleton-Century-Crofts.

Shweder, R.A. (1985). Menstrual pollution, soul loss and the comparative study of emotions. In A. Kleinman & B. Good (Eds), *Culture and depression*. Berkeley: University of California Press, pp. 182–215.

Sobotka, S.S., Davidson, R.J., & Senulis, J.A. (In press). Anterior brain electrical asymmetries in response to reward and punishment. *Electroencephalography and Clinical Neurophysiology*.

Stenberg, C., Campos, J., & Emde, R. (1983). The facial expression of anger in seven month old infants. *Child Development*, *54*, 178–184.

Sternbach, R.A. & Tursky, B. (1965). Ethnic differences among housewifes in psychophysical and skin potential responses to electric shock. *Psychophysiology*, *1*, 241–246.

Tassinary, L.G. & Cacioppo, J.T. (1992). Unobservable facial actions and emotion. *Psychological Science*, *3*, 28–33.

Tomarken, A.J. & Davidson, R.J. (In prep.). Fear and the face: Differential accessibility of fear and disgust to the face.

Tomarken, A.J., Davidson, R.J., & Henriques, J.B. (1990). Resting frontal brain asymmetry predicts affective responses to films. *Journal of Personality and Social Psychology*, *59*, 791–801.

Tooby, J. & Cosmides, L. (1990). The past explains the present: Emotional adaptations and the structure of ancestral environments. *Ethology and Sociobiology*, *11*, 375–424.

Watson, D., Clark, L.A., & Carey, G. (1988). Positive and negative affectivity and their relation to anxiety and depressive disorders. *Journal of Abnormal Psychology*, *97*, 346–353.

Wheeler, R.E., Davidson, R.J., & Tomarken, A.J. (In press). Frontal brain asymmetry and emotional reactivity: A biological substrate of affective style. *Psychophysiology*.

Woodworth, R.S. & Schlosberg, H. (1954). *Experimental psychology*. New York: Holt.

COGNITION AND EMOTION, 1992, 6 (3/4), 269–283

Expressive Development and Basic Emotions

Linda A. Camras

Department of Psychology, DePaul University, Chicago, U.S.A.

One important emotion theory currently postulates an innate tie between specific infant facial expressions and a set of discrete basic emotions. The arguments and evidence relevant to this assertion are reviewed. New data are presented from a naturalistic study of one infant's early expressive development and a judgement study of infant facial, vocal, and body activity. These data challenge the innate tie hypothesis. Based on dynamical systems systems theory, an alternate conceptual framework is presented that may allow us to usefully retain the concept of basic emotions while accommodating the data on infant expressive development.

INTRODUCTION

Although basic emotions may be viewed as either psychological entities (in the mind of the beholder) or real world entities (in the mind/body of the emoter) (Ortony & Turner, 1990), current developmental theories generally adopt the latter perspective. Extended into the domain of development, the strongest form of the basic emotions hypothesis is embodied in Izard's differential emotions theory (Izard, 1977), which argues that discrete emotions are present in infancy corresponding to a set of biologically basic emotions proposed for adults. Infant emotions are indexed by a set of distinct facial expressions resembling configurations universally identified as adult expressions of emotion. In this article, I will argue that a considerable body of data on infant facial expressions challenges this theory's current description of infant emotional and expressive development. Alternative hypotheses regarding the affective underpinnings of some particular expressions will be proposed. Beyond this, however, I will also present an alternative conceptual framework incorporating elements of dynamic sys-

Requests for reprints should be sent to Linda Camras, Department of Psychology, DePaul University, 2323 N. Seminary, Chicago, IL 60614, U.S.A.

I would like to thank Sol Rappaport and Richard Lawton for their devoted coding of the videotapes of my daughter, Justine, as described in this article.

tems theory that, I contend, may allow us to usefully retain the concept of basic emotions while also accommodating data that can not be easily accounted for by the current formulation of differential emotions theory.

Basic Emotions in Adulthood

Like several other basic emotions theories (e.g. Ekman, 1972, 1984; Frijda, 1986; Plutchik, 1980; Tomkins, 1962, 1963, 1984), Izard's differential emotions theory (DET) stems from Darwin's (1872/1965) early research on emotional expression and rests importantly on recent evidence for universality in the identification of a number of emotional facial expressions (Ekman, Friesen, & Ellsworth, 1982). Basic emotion theorists have argued that universal recognition of facial expression could only be explained by assuming an underlying innate emotion "programme" or "discrete set of neural processes" (Izard & Malatesta, 1987) for each basic or "primary" emotion. Reflecting state-of-the-art thinking in neurobiology during the time these theories were initially established (i.e. the 1960s), affect programmes were assumed to control various aspects of emotion output. For DET, these include expressive responses (e.g. facial and vocal behaviour) and phenomenological experience.

Although emotions were also considered to include an important motivational component, specific instrumental behaviours were not dictated by the emotion programme. The assumption implicit in these theories was that instrumental behaviours, or coping responses, were determined through a hierarchical system in which decisions regarding alternatives were influenced by both emotion and also extra-emotion influences. Thus, with regard to instrumental behaviours, emotions were viewed as flexible systems rather than hard-wired instincts. Regarding expressive responses, a degree of flexibility was also admitted to accommodate anthropological reports of cross-cultural variability in emotional displays and to acknowledge our ability to voluntarily produce or inhibit facial expressions in accord with social and personal display rules (Ekman, 1972; Ekman & Friesen, 1969). Nonetheless, underlying this variability in facial behaviour was assumed to be an affect programme which automatically sent neural messages dictating an emotion-specific facial expression although these messages might be subject to interference before they ultimately reached the output system. In summary, basic emotions theories initially established during the late 1960s adopted explanatory principles similar to those characterising molecular biology and neurobiology at the time (Oyama, 1989), i.e. control was assumed to flow from the centre to the periphery with a set of core emotion responses being automatically prescribed by the central affect programme.

Basic Emotions in Development

Although the study of ontogeny would seem critical to informing theories of adult basic emotions, only differential emotions theory (DET) contains an explicitly articulated developmental component.[1] According to DET (Izard & Malatesta, 1987), basic emotions emerge according to a maturational timetable. After their emergence, emotions may be elaborated in a variety of ways including their association with new eliciting situations and cognitive appraisal processes. In addition, individuals may learn to inhibit the expressive component of emotions in accordance with cultural and personal display rules. More sophisticated instrumental or coping behaviours may be developed. Lastly, basic emotions may become components of "affect-cognitive" structures representing non-basic, often culturally specific emotions. However, regarding the issue of basic emotions in infancy, DET's most important hypotheses are that: (1) basic emotions emerge as structured wholes rather than being created through developmental processes; (2) there exists an innate tie among the three components of emotion, with an emotion-specific neurophysiological programme presumably orchestrating emotion-specific expressive, physiological, and phenomenological responses; and (3) infant facial expressions are direct "automatic read-outs" of infant emotions, at least until the age at which voluntary control over them begins to be exerted. One important implication of these assertions is that researchers may use facial expressions as both necessary and sufficient indices of infant emotions.

Infant Facial Expression and Emotion

Both a critical re-evaluation of the previous literature and several recent studies to be described below suggest that DET's view of emotional and expression development in infancy requires modification. Herein, I will briefly review this material as it relates to both the innate tie and automatic read-out hypotheses (see Camras, Malatesta, & Izard, 1991, for further detail).

Differential emotions theorists have generally provided two types of arguments as evidence for the innate concordance of expression and feeling. First, they have reported that adults judge infant facial expressions (as described in Izard's Max and Affex coding systems, Izard, 1979; Izard, Dougherty, & Hembree, 1983) to be expressions of discrete emotions. This is presumed to reflect their adaptional value as evolved signals

---

[1]For example, Ekman (personal communication 1991) takes no position on development.

eliciting appropriate responding in adults (Izard et al., 1980). Secondly, theorists have argued that the Affex-specified expressions occur in situations in which the hypothesised emotion would be an appropriate or at least plausible response (Malatesta-Magai & Izard, 1991).

Each of these assertions, however, has been questioned. Regarding adult judgements of emotion, Oster, Hegley, and Nagel (in press) recently found that—when given the opportunity—adults judge most Affex-specified expressions of discrete negative affects as reflecting either blends of several negative emotions or distress (which is not itself a discrete affect according to DET). Oster points out that the Affex-specified negative expressions for infants differ morphologically to some extent from the expression prototypes described for adults. In addition, negative expressions described for infants share features that are not shared by prototype adult expressions, for example, contraction of orbicularis oculi (the muscle encircling the eye). Furthermore, two infant expressions (the "anger" and "distress-pain" configurations) are morphologically indistinguishable save that the eyes are open for anger and closed for distress-pain. The morphological differences between adult and infant expressions as well as the morphological commonalities among the Affex-specified infant negative affect expressions might be interpreted as evidence for less differentiated negative emotion experiences in infants. Furthermore, these morphological features may be responsible for adults' failure to differentiate as clearly among the expressions in their judgements as would be predicted by DET.

With regard to situational occurrence of the Affex-specified emotional expressions, over a decade ago, Hiatt, Campos, and Emde (1979) argued that to demonstrate the discrete emotion status of a facial configuration, one must demonstrate discrimination in its occurrence across situations producing the target emotion vs. other emotions from which it is to be discriminated. However, thus far there has been no demonstration that several negative affect expressions (i.e. distress-pain, anger, and sadness) are differentially produced in response to appropriate pain, anger, and sadness elicitors. Instead, laboratory studies (reviewed in detail in Camras et al., 1991) have shown that the Affex-specified anger configuration is the most common discrete negative facial expression in all studies presenting any form of negative elicitor to infants over 2 months of age: e.g. DPT inoculation, arm restraint, cookie removal, separation from mother, contingency interruption, and mothers' facial and vocal expressions of sadness. The Affex-specified sadness expression is also produced with lesser frequency in all these circumstances but has not been found to be the most frequent facial response to any eliciting situation. Although distress-pain expressions are the predominant response shown by 2-month-olds to clearly painful DPT inoculations, these expressions have also been observed in circumstances where physical discomfort would seem unlikely, such as face-to-face interactions between mothers and 4-month-old infants. These laboratory studies thus suggest that, at least in young infants, the Affex-specified expressions of distress-pain, anger, and sadness do not reflect the discrete emotions with which they are associated according to differential emotions theory.

Based on this review of the literature in conjunction with a recent naturalistic investigation of my daughter Justine's expressive development I have proposed a more distress-oriented interpretation for the Affex-specified expressions of distress-pain, anger, and sadness. To briefly describe the latter study (see also Camras, 1988, 1991; Camras et al., 1991) during the first several weeks of Justine's life, I kept diary records in which I described the circumstances under which I observed the Affex-specified facial expressions. Furthermore, after the third week, I videorecorded examples of a number of situations that I had previously observed to elicit these expressions. Thus far, coding has been completed for 167 minutes of videotape taken during the fourth through ninth weeks. Tapes were coded by research assistants who identified all instances of Affex-codeable facial configurations ($n = 401$, reliability = 0.90). Coders then made judgements regarding the elicitors for these expressions using a provisional list of elicitors that I extracted from the diary records and expanded to include additional elicitors observed on the videotapes (reliability = 0.82). Using a very conservative confidence criterion, elicitors were identified for 135 Affex-specified expressions.

Given the informal recording procedure, these data were considered more appropriate for qualitative rather than quantitative analysis. Inspection of the elicitors identified for each facial configuration (see Table 1) revealed a number of observations inconsistent with the differential emotions theory interpretation of several expressions. Of particular note, considerable overlap was observed among elicitors for the Affex-defined expressions of distress-pain, anger, sadness, and to some extent, disgust. Furthermore, some of these expressions were observed in situations in which one would not expect the corresponding emotion to be produced. For example, the distress-pain pattern was seen in response to elicitors that were not likely to be causing physical pain or discomfort (e.g. termination of physical contact with mother; bathing; being moved, lifted or leaned; pacifier removal). Lastly, the distress-pain, anger, and sadness patterns were frequently seen together in a single episode of crying. During these episodes, the three facial configurations appeared to be differentially associated with opening vs. closing the mouth and thus the waxing and waning of the crying response. Together, these observations suggest that the anger and distress-pain patterns are distress responses of increasing intensity while the sadness pattern may reflect a waning or relatively low level of distress. Similar proposals regarding limited differentiation of

TABLE 1
Affex-specified Facial Configurations Observed for Each Eliciting Circumstance

Elicitor	Affex-specified Configuration					
	DP^a	AN	SD	DR	SU	EJ
Pacifier removed	+^{b}	x	x			
Physical contact terminated	x^b	x	+			
Inoculation	+	+	+			
Hunger	x	x	+			
Swing/Motion stops	+	+	+			
Head/Limb restraint	x	x	+	+		
Aspirate nostrils	x	x	x	+		
Vitamin (sour)	+	+	x	x		
Bath	x	x	x	x		
Reject/Eject pacifier	+					
Waking up	+	x	x			
Move/Lift/Lean	x	+	x			
Light in eyes	x				+	
Gentle bouncing	+					x
Takes nipple					x	
Sleep	+		+			x
Stretch						+
After yawn, sneeze, feeding						x
Visual attention to object/Env					x	x
Stroke cheek, body						+
Mild auditory stimulations (Voice, Rattle)						+

^{a}DP, distress-pain; AN, anger; SD, sad; DR, disgust; SU, surprise; EJ, happy.
^{b}+, 1–2 data records; x, 3 or more data records.
Note: Both diary and videotaped observations are included.

negative affect expressions in early infancy have been made by Matias and Cohn (1991) and Oster, Hegley, and Nagel (in press).

It is interesting to note that all of the observations regarding this situational occurrence of the Affex-specified expressions can be regarded as consistent with differential emotions theory if one assumes its major premise to begin with. That is, as has been argued by differential emotions theorists, these data would merely indicate that infants experience non-predicted emotions in some situations and also (like adults) can experience multiple affects in response to the same situation (Malatesta-Magai & Izard, 1991). To support this argument, however, sources of evidence other than elicitor-specificity must be sought. One potential source of such evidence would be specificity and appropriateness in the nonfacial actions accompanying infant facial expressions.

In an attempt to examine this issue, Sullivan, Camras, and Michel (in prep.) conducted a study in which nonfacial behaviours accompanying the

Affex-specified expressions of distress-pain, anger, and sadness were both objectively coded and judged by naïve undergraduate raters. As part of this study, raters were shown brief segments of videotape extracted from Camras' tapes of her daughter at 4 to 9 weeks in which both the facial expression and whole body of the infant were seen. Judges were told to focus on the infant's nonfacial body behaviours and rate each segment on a set of unipolar 7-point scales.

Similar to findings reported by Oster, Hegley, and Nagel (in press) for judgements of infant facial expressions alone, distress ratings were the highest negative emotion rating for all three types of segments and ratings of pain, anger, and sadness did not significantly differ for any of the expression types. In contrast to the differential emotions theory interpretation, the Affex-specified distress-pain segments were rated as significantly more angry than the Affex-specified anger and sadness segments. Both the Affex-defined pain and anger segments were rated as reflecting significantly more pain, disgust, sadness, distress, and fear than the Affex-defined sadness segments. This pattern of results suggests that raters judged the "pain" and "anger" segments as involving more negative affect of all types than the "sadness" segments. Objective coding of the infant's body movements similarly revealed few significant differences among the segments. During the "pain" and "anger" segments, the infant held her arms more flexed and closer to her side than during the "sadness" segments. In addition, there was a nonsignificant tendency for the infant to kick more during the "pain" and "anger" segments than during the "sadness" segments.

In conjunction with the morphology and elicitor studies described earlier, these data suggest that Affex-specified expressions of distress-pain, anger, and sadness reflect differences in intensity of negative affect rather than discretely different emotions in early infancy. Based on similar analyses, elsewhere I have suggested (Camras et al., 1991) that surprise expressions reflect excited attention and disgust expressions are responses to physical intrusiveness. In a separate study (Michel, Camras, & Sullivan, in press), evidence was obtained suggesting that the raised brow form of interest expression is part of a co-ordinative motor structure involved in raising the eyes and head. Several other investigators (e.g. Emde & Harmon, 1972; Wolff, 1987) have argued that neonatal smiles are tied to REM state rather than the emotion of enjoyment. Thus, the Affex-specified infant facial expressions are not initially random but neither are they innately tied to discrete emotions as described for adults.

With regard to the automatic read-out hypothesis, differential emotions theory asserts that facial expressions should inevitably accompany emotion responding at least during the infant's first year. Yet it is particularly striking that two of the emotional expressions described for infants, surprise and fear, have only rarely been observed in situations that commonly are believed to elicit the corresponding emotion. For example, Hiatt et al. (1979) found 10-month-old infants to seldom display components of the surprise and fear expression patterns although these same infants produced nonfacial responses indicating that they were indeed surprised and frightened by the experimental manipulations. Even in adults, facial behaviour has been observed that may not be completely consistent with an automatic read-out hypothesis even in conjunction with the notion of display rules. For example, Davidson (this issue) found that phobics exposed to their phobic stimuli showed disgust expressions (rather than fear or fear-disgust blends), although experiences of both emotions were reported. Several studies of both adults and young infants have found that smiles are more often shown in social as opposed to nonsocial pleasurable situations (Fridlund, 1991; Jones, Collins, & Hong, 1991; Kraut & Johnson, 1979). In their coding system for adult emotional expression, Friesen and Ekman (1984) list a number of variant configurations hypothesised to be spontaneous expressions for each emotion. If such variability in both form and production of spontaneous expressive behaviour indeed exists, one might well argue that a theory of emotional expression must account for it. Current theories have not yet attempted to do so. In the next section, I will argue that dynamical systems theory provides an alternative approach to conceptualising basic emotions that potentially could account for such variability as well as accommodate those data challenging the innate tie hypothesis.

Dynamical Systems Theory

Dynamical systems theory is a general model that can be used to account for the organised co-ordination of complex systems of various sorts (Fogel & Thelen, 1987; Prigogine & Stengers, 1984; Schoner & Kelso, 1988; Thelen & Ulrich, 1991). Within the domain of behaviour and development, dynamical systems theory was primarily developed to overcome certain problems with traditional accounts of motor control and development (Bernstein, 1967). Like emotion, motoric action involves the organised co-ordination of a large set of components (muscles) that in theory can be combined in a virtually limitless number of ways. Yet body movement appears to be organised into a restricted finite number of co-ordinated patterns. At the same time, these co-ordinated patterns are enacted with an almost infinite number of minor variations. For example, no two acts of reaching are precisely alike even when one is reaching twice for the same object. Many small-scale features of a co-ordinated act involve compensation or accommodations to features of the action context (e.g. position of the body when reaching is initiated).

What type of theory can best describe the control of such a system? Traditional accounts reflecting the "central dogma" have proposed a command programme for each basic pattern that (through a hierarchical control system) selects and sequences the constituent components of each instantiation of an organised action. More recently, however, movement scientists have rejected such a model as a complete solution in part because it requires the command system to perform a monumental number of computations to adjust for variability in task demand and action context, and thus produce the myriad variants of organised action.

Instead, motor action has been modelled as a dynamical system in which a significant degree of control comes from contextual and other "bottom-up" influences as well as more central "top-down" forces (Kelso & Scholz, 1986; Kugler, Kelso, & Turvey, 1980). One important mechanism through which co-ordination is maintained is a set of synergistic relationships among lower-order (muscular) components termed co-ordinated motor structures. For example, when an individual traverses slightly uneven ground, this surface directly impacts his muscular actions. In response to this, co-ordination and balance are maintained through synergistic compensations among lower-order muscle groups rather than continuous monitoring and adjustment by a higher-level motor programme.

Dynamical systems theorists have envisioned the distribution of "top-down" vs. "bottom-up" system control in a variety of ways (Kelso, 1989; Thelen, 1989a). In the most radical versions of dynamic systems theory, the central executive agent may be completely eliminated. Organisation of control is viewed as emanating solely from the interaction between contextual variables (i.e. task demands) and component synergies. These synergistic relationships create a set of "preferred states" or organisational patterns. Enactment of one or another pattern may be produced "from the bottom" if some feature of the action context directly affects an element of the system which then recruits the system's other components, thus producing the particular organisational state. In most versions of dynamical systems theory, enactment of one or another pattern is produced by a more complex interaction of higher and lower influences. In all versions of dynamical systems theory, contextual factors are considered to critically determine behavioural output. Thus, to use a favourite dynamical systems dictum: The task assembles the behaviour.

Dynamical systems theory may be literally applicable to the domain of emotion or may provide us with a heuristic impetus toward appropriate but more limited modifications of current emotion theories. According to dynamical systems theory, basic emotions might be conceived of as "preferred states", i.e. universally observed organisations of emotion components. However, these preferred states might in theory result from either top-down (central) influences, bottom-up (contextual) influences or some interaction of the two. With particular regard to facial expression, this view might accommodate the possibility that emotional facial expressions are not automatic read-outs of emotion and thus may not be produced even under some circumstances allowable by display rules. Instead, facial expressions, like other components of emotion, might be recruited for an emotion episode when they are specifically appropriate (i.e. adaptive) to the action context. In addition, consistent with the recent work of Levenson, Ekman, and Friesen (1990) on ANS correlates of voluntarily produced facial expressions, facial expressions might themselves recruit other components of the emotion system through a set of synergistic relationships.

With regard to development, dynamical systems theorists propose that the emergence of new developmental structures (e.g. motor abilities, cognitive abilities) need not imply the emergence of new executive control systems (Fogel, 1987; Thelen, 1989b; Fogel & Thelen, 1987). Instead, co-ordination patterns may develop when a constituent non-central variable reaches a critical value and catalyses a reorganisation of a system. Thelen's recent analysis of the development of walking, persuasively illustrates the potential value of the dynamical systems perspective. Thelen (1989b; Fogel & Thelen, 1987) has argued that a critical co-ordinative motor structure underlying walking can be seen early in development and produces the rhythmic leg cycling seen in both early infant kicking and in later walking. Walking does not begin when a new central programme matures but rather when the fat : muscle ratio in the leg changes such that the infant can lift its legs against gravity while in an upright position. In dynamical systems terms, the fat : muscle ratio functions as a "control" variable; when it reaches its critical threshold, previously present components can be reorganised and a new developmental structure (i.e. "walking") emerges.

As seen in the system described by Thelen, elements of an organised co-ordination pattern can develop heterochronically, i.e. independently and at different rates. Thus some components (e.g. leg cycling) may be present before they function as part of the larger system (e.g. walking). Furthermore, such heterochronic development can result in periodic reorganisations (e.g. creeping, crawling, walking) by changes in different variables. That is, the control variables underlying system change may be different at different points in development. For example, fat : muscle ratio in the leg may serve as a control parameter for walking but not for running.

With respect to emotional development, the dynamical systems perspective would suggest that basic emotions need not emerge as structured wholes according to a maturational timetable. Components of emotions may develop heterochronically and at some point in time be organised into emotion systems. Furthermore, emotional development may involve periodic reorganisations as different parameters (e.g. motor abilities, cognitive appraisal capacities) reach critical values. Such periodic reorganisations are in fact acknowledged by differential emotions theory. However, they are viewed as elaborations superimposed upon an inherently unified neurophysiological, expressive, and phenomenological core. In contrast, the dynamical systems perspective can accommodate the possibility that relationships among these components are established in the course of development.

Beyond this, the dynamical systems perspective with its emphasis on heterochronicity and varying control parameters suggests that emotional or expressive development itself may not be best conceptualised as a unified whole involving synchronous changes across all emotions. Instead, the developmental story may differ for different emotions depending upon their particular expressive, cognitive, and instrumental constituents. For example, data reviewed above suggests that anger-related facial configurations are seen earlier than anger-related actions, whereas fear-related actions (e.g. withdrawal from strangers) may occur at a younger age than the "fear" facial expression.

Although it would be premature to propose a fully articulated developmental theory at the present time, it may be useful to present a hypothetical example to illustrate how a dynamical systems account of emotional development might differ from current views. Accordingly, I offer the following highly speculative proposal regarding the development of anger and sadness. As indicated above, I have previously suggested that the Affex-specified anger configuration initially reflects a high intensity of distress, whereas the sadness configuration reflects a lower intensity or waning of distress. Furthermore, based on informal observations of my daughter at older ages (see Camras, 1991), I have also suggested that by 1–2 years of age these configurations to some extent become more differentially associated with situational appraisals and action responses consistent with adult distinctions between anger and sadness. Nevertheless, even at older ages, the anger configuration is sometimes seen in conjunction with circumstances and behavioural responses appropriate to distress rather than anger.

How might a dynamical systems perspective attempt to account for such a developmental picture? One possibility involves an analogy to Thelen's description of the development of walking. Such an analogy might suggest that a common core of negative hedonic experience (tentatively referred to as "distress") may underly the anger and sadness expressions both at younger and older ages. During the course of development, other components of fully developed emotion systems (e.g. action capabilities, appraisal capabilities, self-regulation capacities) may develop heterochronically. As these emerge, the child may go through a series of sub-stages (analogous to creeping and crawling) as components of the systems achieve their critical values and catalyse successive reorganisations of the system. Thus, the basic emotions of anger and sadness might be viewed as end-points of a developmental process rather than entities that emerge at a particular point in development. This view is not incompatible with previously offered differentiation views (e.g. Sroufe, 1979) save that such accounts have implicitly assumed the differentiation process to result in a set of distinct central affect programmes. According to this radical dynamical systems account, the ultimate discreteness of anger vs. sadness may instead be in the contextually determined organisational patterning of their non-central constituents.

For the less radically inclined, versions of dynamic systems theory might also be proposed in which discrete central affect programmes are retained. During the course of development, facial expressions as well as other forms of response would become available for recruitment by such emotion programmes during the course of their heterochronic development. However, in each emotion "episode", the selection of particular responses would depend on the action context. This view differs from the current formulation of differential emotions theory in that facial expressions would not be considered automatic read-outs of emotion. Instead, facial expressions—like other responses—would be recruited in a task-specific manner, i.e. the emotion task would assemble the emotion behaviour. Such a model might be deemed desirable if future research produces further examples of situations in which we believe emotions to be present yet facial expressions do not occur despite the absence of inhibitory display rules. In contrast to other alternative theories which retain a central dogma orientation (e.g. Fridlund, 1991) this dynamical systems model would suggest that we relinquish the automatic read-out hypothesis while retaining the notion of facial expression as emotion signal.

CONCLUDING REMARKS

As noted at several points, the dynamical systems perspective outlined earlier shares some characteristics with previous proposed alternatives to differential emotions theory (e.g. differentiation theories: Bridges, 1932; Sroufe, 1979; and Barrett & Campos', 1987, functionalist view). Why then consider this new alternative? I believe that several strong arguments can be made. First, adopting a dynamical systems perspective will encourage us to conceptualise emotion and emotional development with minimal recourse to homunculus-like entities that monitor and dictate emotion responding from above (i.e. the "ghost in the machine"). This would be consistent with current efforts by molecular and developmental neuro-biologists to replace analogous preformist assumptions embodied in the "central dogma" with principles of self-organisation (e.g. Purvis, 1988). Secondly, dynamical systems theory offers an alternative conceptualisation of emotion that will allow us to usefully preserve the concept of "basicness" from a biological point of view rather than dictate a retreat to earlier notions of undifferentiated arousal. Thirdly, adopting a dynamical systems perspective will encourage us to address those "orphan phenomena" of facial expression highlighted earlier as well as explore possible linkages among and contextual determinants of the constituent components of emotion episodes. As such, dynamical systems theory can—at minimum—serve as a valuable heuristic, stimulating new and productive avenues of research on expression, emotion, and development.

Manuscript received 1 March 1991
Revised manuscript received 29 October 1991

REFERENCES

Barrett, K. & Campos, J. (1987). Perspectives on emotional development. II: A functionalist approach to emotions. In J. Osofsky (Ed.), *Handbook of infant development* (2nd edn). New York: Wiley, pp. 555–578.

Berstein, N. (1967). *Coordination and regulation of movements*. New York: Pergamon.

Bridges, K.M.B. (1932). Emotional development in early infancy. *Child Development, 3,* 324–341.

Camras, L.A. (1988). *Darwin revisited: An infants first emotional facial expressions*. Paper presented at the International Conference on Infant Studies. Washington, DC.

Camras, L.A. (1991). Conceptualizing early infant affect: View II and reply. In K. Strongman (Ed.), *International review of studies on emotion*. New York: Wiley, pp. 16–28, 33–36.

Camras, L.A., Malatesta, C., & Izard, C. (1991). The development of facial expressions in infancy. In R. Feldman & B. Rime (Eds), *Fundamentals of nonverbal behavior*. Cambridge: Cambridge University Press.

Darwin, C. (1872). *The expression of the emotions in man and animals*. [Reprinted, 1965.] University of Chicago Press.

Ekman, P. (1972). Universals and cultural differences in facial expressions of emotion. In J. Cole (Ed.), *Nebraska symposium on motivation, 1971*. Lincoln, NE: University of Nebraska Press, pp. 207–283.

Ekman, P. (1984). Expression and the nature of emotion. In K. Scherer & P. Ekman (Eds), *Approaches to emotion*. Hillsdale, NJ: Lawrence Erlbaum Associates Inc, pp. 319–344.

Ekman, P. & Friesen, W.V. (1969). The repertoire of nonverbal behavior: origins, usage, and coding. *Semiotica, 1*(1), 49–98.

Ekman, P., Friesen, W., & Ellsworth, P. (1982). What are the similarities and differences in facial behavior across cultures? In P. Ekman (Ed.), *Emotion in the human face* (2nd edn). Cambridge University Press, pp. 128–144.

Emde, R. & Harmon, R. (1972). Endogenous and exogenous smiling systems in early infancy. *Journal of Child Psychiatry, 11*(2), 177–200.

Fogel, A. (1987, October). *Dynamic systems in human development: The inhibition of attention to mother in early infancy*. Paper presented at the Dynamic Patterns in Complex Systems Conference, Fort Lauderdale, FL.

Fogel, A. & Thelen, E. (1987). The development of early expressive and communicative action. *Developmental Psychology*, 23, 747–761.

Fridlund, A. (1991). Evolution and facial action in reflex, social motive and paralanguage *Biological Psychology*, 32, 1–96.

Friesen, W. & Ekman, P. (1984). *EMFACS: Emotion Facial Action Coding System* (Available from W. Friesen, Department of Psychiatry, University of California, San Francisco).

Frijda, N. (1986). *The emotions*. Cambridge University Press.

Hiatt, S., Campos, J., & Emde, R. (1979). Facial patterning and infant emotional expression: Happiness, surprise and fear. *Child Development*, 50, 1020–1035.

Izard, C. (1977). *Human emotions*. New York: Plenum.

Izard, C. (1979). *The maximally discriminative facial movement coding system (MAX)*. Newark, DE: University of Delaware, Instructional Resources Center.

Izard, C., Dougherty, L., & Hembree, E. (1983). *A system for identifying affect expressions by holistic judgments (AFFEX)*. Newark, DE: Instructional Resources Center, University of Delaware, Newark, Delaware.

Izard, C., Huebner, R., Risser, D., McGinnes, G., & Dougherty, L. (1980). The young infant's ability to produce discrete emotion expressions. *Developmental Psychology*, 16, 132–140.

Izard, C. & Malatesta, C. (1987). Perspectives on emotional development. I: Differential emotions theory of early emotional development. In J.D. Osofsky (Ed.), *Handbook of infant development*. New York: Wiley, pp. 494–554.

Jones, S., Collins, K., & Hong, H. (1991). An audience effect on smile productions in 10 month old infants. *Psychological Science*, 2(1), 45–49.

Kelso, J.A.S. (1989). A tutorial on dynamical systems and application to behavioral studies. In B. Bertenthal, A. Fogel, L. Smith, & E. Thelen (Chairpersons), *Dynamical systems in development*. Society for Research in Child Development. Pre-conference Workshop, Kansas City.

Kelso, J. & Scholz, J. (1986). Cooperative phenomenon in biological motion. In H. Haken (Ed.), *Synergetics of complex systems in physics, chemistry, and biology*. New York: Springer-Verlag.

Kraut, R. & Johnson, R. (1979). Social and emotional messages of smiling: An ethological approach. *Journal of Personality and Social Psychology*, 37(9), 1539–1553.

Kugler, P., Kelso, J., & Turvey, M. (1980). On the concept of coordinative structures as dissipative structures: I. Theoretical line. In G. Stelmack & J. Requin (Eds), *Tutorials in motor behavior*. Amsterdam: North-Holland, pp. 3–48.

Levenson, R., Ekman, P., & Friesen, W. (1990). Voluntary facial action generates emotion-specific autonomic nervous system activity. *Psychophysiology*, 27, 363–384.

Malatesta-Magai, C. & Izard, C. (1991). Conceptualizing early infant affect: View I & Reply. In K. Strongman (Ed.), *International review of studies on emotion*. New York: Wiley, pp. 1–15, 29–32.

Matias, R. & Cohn, J. (1991). *Evidence for the differentiation of positive but not negative affect during the first half year*. Unpublished manuscript.

Michel, G., Camras, L., & Sullivan, J. (In press). Infant interest expressions as coordinative motor structures. *Infant Behavior and Development*.

Ortony, A. & Turner, T. (1990). What's basic about basic emotions? *Psychological Review*, 97, 315–331.

Oster, H., Hegley, D., & Nagel, L. (In press). Adult judgments and fine-grained analysis of infant facial expressions: Testing the validity of a priori coding formulas. *Developmental Psychology*.

Oyama, S. (1989). Ontogeny and the central dogma: Do we need the concept of genetic programming in order to have an evolutionary perspective? In M. Gunnar & E. Thelen

(Eds), *Systems and development: The Minnesota symposium on child psychology*, Vol. 22. Hillsdale, NJ: Lawrence Erlbaum Associates Inc, pp. 1–34.

Plutchik, R. (1980). *Emotion: A psychoevolutionary synthesis*. New York: Harper & Row.

Prigogine, I. & Stengers, I. (1984). *Order out of chaos: Man's new dialogue with nature*. New York: Bantam.

Purvis, D. (1988). *Body and brain: A trophic theory of neural connections*. Cambridge, MA: Harvard University Press.

Schoner, G. & Kelso, J. (1988). Dynamic pattern generation in behavioral and neural systems. *Science, 239*, 1513–1520.

Sroufe, L.A. (1979). Socioemotional development. In J. Osofsky (Ed.), *Handbook of infant development*. New York: Wiley, pp. 462–516.

Sullivan, J., Camras, L., & Michel, G. (In prep.). *Nonfacial body movements accompanying Affex-specified expressions of distress-pain, anger, and sadness*.

Thelen, E. (1989a). Conceptualizing development from a dynamical systems perspective. In B. Bertenthal, A. Fogel, L. Smith, & E. Thelen (Chairpersons), *Dynamical systems in development*. Society for Research in Child Development. Pre-conference Workshop, Kansas City.

Thelen, E. (1989b). Self-organization in developmental processes: Can systems approaches work? In M. Gunnar & E. Thelen (Eds), *Systems and development: The Minnesota symposia on child psychology*, Vol. 22. Hillsdale, NJ: Lawrence Erlbaum Associates Inc, pp. 77–118.

Thelen, E. & Ulrich, B. (1991). Hidden skills. *Monographs of the Society for Research in Child Development, 56*(1), whole issue.

Tomkins, S.S. (1962). *Affect, imagery, and consciousness*, Vol. 1. *The positive affects*. New York: Springer.

Tomkins, S.S. (1963). *Affect, imagery and consciousness*, Vol. 2. *The negative affects*. New York: Springer.

Tomkins, S.S. (1984). Affect theory. In K. Scherer & P. Ekman (Eds), *Approaches to emotion*. Hillsdale, NJ: Lawrence Erlbaum Associates Inc, pp. 163–196.

Wolff, P. (1987). *The development of behavioral states and the expression of emotions in early infancy*. University of Chicago Press.

COGNITION AND EMOTION, 1992, 6 (3/4), 285-319

Talking about Emotions: Semantics, Culture, and Cognition

Anna Wierzbicka

Australian National University

The author argues that the so-called "basic emotions", such as *happiness*, *fear* or *anger*, are in fact cultural artifacts of the English language, just as the Ilongot concept of *liget*, or the Ifaluk concept of *song*, are the cultural artifacts of Ilongot and Ifaluk. It is therefore as inappropriate to talk about human emotions in general in terms of *happiness*, *fear*, or *anger* as it would be to talk about them in terms of *liget* or *song*. However, this does not mean that we cannot penetrate into the emotional world of speakers of languages other than our own. Nor does it mean that there cannot be any universal human emotions. Universality of emotions is an open issue which requires further investigation. For this further investigation to be fully productive, it has to be undertaken from a universal, language and culture-independent perspective; and it has to be carried out in a universalist framework that is language and culture-independent. The author proposes for this purpose the "natural semantic metalanguage" based on universal (or near-universal) semantic primitives (or near-primitives), developed over two decades by herself and colleagues, and she argues that the use of this metalanguage facilitates such a perspective and offers such a framework.

INTRODUCTION

Ortony, Clore, & Collins (1988, p. ix) open their book *The cognitive structure of emotions* with the remark that "As cognitive psychology established itself in the 1970s, it became increasingly apparent that it was a 'cold' approach to cognition, and doubts began to arise as to whether or not it could provide the machinery necessary to account for affect and emotion", and describe their own volume as "an attempt to explore the extent to which cognitive psychology could provide a viable foundation for the analysis of emotions".

Requests for reprints should be sent to Professor Anna Wierzbicka, Department of Linguistics, The Australian National University, GPO Box 4, Canberra ACT 2601, Australia.

I would like to express my gratitude to Cliff Goddard and to Lisette Frigo, who have discussed with me an earlier version of this paper and made a number of very valuable criticisms and suggestions.

Despite my profound respect for much recent work that has been done by psychologists investigating emotions I believe that cognitive psychology will never be able to provide a viable foundation for the analysis of emotions until it faces squarely the fundamental question of the role of language in the conceptualisation of emotions, and tries to overcome the obstacles which language erects between the investigator of emotions and the emotions themselves.

In the last decade, there has been an explosion of psychological literature on emotions, and a number of different schools of thought have emerged. However, despite their merits, most of them suffer from one important flaw: They seem oblivious to the problem of language. In particular, most of them take English emotion terms for granted and use English words such as *anger, happiness, fear* or *disgust* as if they stood for universal concepts and were reliable tools in the investigation of emotions.

For example, Johnson-Laird and Oatley (1989, p. 90) write: "According to our theory, there is a set of basic emotion modes that correspond to internal signals that can impinge on consciousness. These modes— happiness, sadness, anger, fear, disgust—should be universally accepted as discriminable categories of direct experience." The authors overlook the fact that words such as *happiness, sadness, anger, fear,* and *disgust* encode concepts which are specific to English, and different from those encoded in the emotion terms of other languages (cf. Wierzbicka, 1986, 1988a,c).

For example, it has been established that the Ilongot language of the Philippines, or the Ifaluk language of Micronesia, do not have words corresponding in meaning to the English word *anger*, just as English does not have words corresponding in meaning to the core Ilongot emotion concept of *liget* (cf. Rosaldo, 1980, 1984; Wierzbicka, 1988c, and in press c), or to the core Ifaluk emotion concept *song* (cf. Lutz 1982, 1983, 1987; Wierzbicka, 1988a and 1992; see also discussion below on pp. 303–307).

By using English emotion words as their basic analytical tools scholars are imposing on their subject matter an ethnocentric, Anglocentric perspective. Why should *anger* be any better placed as a tool for identifying "basic human experiences" than either *liget* or *song* (which are different in meaning from both *anger* and from each other)? Had Johnson-Laird and Oatley been born Ilongots, or Ifaluks, rather than Englishmen, *liget* and *song* would have seemed as natural candidates for "basic human emotions" as *anger* seems to them now.

Similar criticisms can be made of the work of most other psychologists investigating emotion. For example, Ekman (1973, pp. 219–220) writes:

The evidence now proves the existence of universal facial expressions. These findings require the postulation of some mechanism to explain why the same facial behavior is associated with the same emotion for all peoples. Why are observers in all these cultures familiar with a particular set of facial expressions (a set which is only a fraction of the anatomically possible facial muscular configurations)? But they are not merely familiar with these facial expressions. Regardless of the language, of whether the culture is Western or Eastern, industrialized or preliterate, these facial expressions are labelled with the same emotion terms: happiness, sadness, anger, fear, disgust, and surprise.

Ekman's reasoning seems almost to imply that the whole world speaks English: In the East as well as in the West, in preliterate as well as in industrialised socities, photographs of facial expressions bring to mind "the same emotion terms: happiness, sadness, anger, fear, disgust, and surprise", *regardless of language*. This can only mean that although the actual words used by different observers are different (belonging to different languages), these words can be matched neatly across language and culture boundaries with the English words *happiness*, *sadness*, and so on.

However, in fact, there are *no* emotion terms which can be matched neatly across language and culture boundaries; there are *no* universal emotion concepts, lexicalised in all the languages of the world. In particular, it is certainly not the case that all the languages of the world have words corresponding to the so-called basic emotion concepts: happiness, sadness, anger, fear, surprise, and disgust. This point will be illustrated and further documented below, although in essence it has already been documented in the literature. (In fact, Ekman, 1975 p. 39, himself notes that, for example, the Dani people of the New Guinea Highlands "don't even have words for the six emotions".)

The absence of universal emotion terms does not mean that there cannot be any universal emotions, or that certain emotions cannot be matched, all over the world, with certain identifiable facial expressions. It only means that *if* there are certain emotions which can be matched, universally, with the same (identifiable) facial expressions, these emotions cannot necessarily be identified by means of English emotion terms, such as *sadness* or *anger*, because these terms embody concepts which are language- and culture-specific.

Because of the dominant position of English in international science, most psychologists, including those investigating emotion concepts, write in English and conduct their research via English. There is, of course, nothing inappropriate about this. However, to reach language-independent and culture-independent psychological realities it must first be recognised that the medium that they are using (a particular ethnic language) has certain limitations.

SEMANTIC PRIMITIVES AND LEXICAL UNIVERSALS

Fortunately, not all English words are equally language-specific and culture-specific. Generally speaking, the more simple a concept is, the less culture-dependent it is going to be, and the wider the language range is going to be in which it has been lexicalised. For example, complex concepts, such as "baptise", "excommunicate", or "vote" are highly culture-dependent, and the range of languages in which they have been lexicalised is relatively narrow. However, simple concepts, such as "say", "want", "good", and "bad" are relatively, if not absolutely, culture-free (of course, not in the sense that, for example, the standards of what is good and what is bad are the same in all cultures, but in the sense that all cultures seem to rely on the concepts "good" and "bad").

If we could assume that concepts such as these have been lexicalised in all natural languages, that is, if the English lexicon included a subset that has isomorphic subsets in the lexicons of all other human languages, then we could use this subset as a language-independent semantic metalanguage, suitable for a psychological and philosophical study of human emotions, as well as for cross-cultural comparisons of emotions (and indeed of any other semantic domain). However, even remaining sceptical or agnostic as to which words are universal or whether universals even exist, one should at least seek out near-universals. It is much safer to rely in our descriptions on concepts such as "want" and "say", which find lexical expression in an enormous range of unrelated languages, than on concepts such as "disgust", "fear", and "shame", which are highly language- and culture-specific.

Ortony et al. (1988, p. 173) have claimed similarly that their focus "has been on trying to characterize emotion types in as language-neutral a fashion as possible":

> Thus, instead of selecting as its theoretical terms particular English emotion words (e.g. 'fear'), the theory purports to be a theory about emotions themselves—what we have called 'emotion types'—characterized in terms of their cognitive eliciting conditions.

However, the terms that the authors have actually chosen for talking about "emotion types" are not as "language-neutral" as they might be. For example, "anger" is characterised in terms of the following two "eliciting conditions", as they call them: "disapproving of someone else's blameworthy action (reproach)" and "(being) displeased about an undesirable event (distress)"; "gratitude" is characterised in terms of "approving of someone else's praiseworthy action (admiration)" and being "pleased about a desirable event (joy)"; and "remorse" is characterised in terms of "disapproving of one's own blameworthy action (shame)" and being "displeased about an undesirable event (distress)" (Ortony et al., 1988, p. 147).

But the words *approve* and *disapprove*, *praise* and *praiseworthy*, *blame* and *blameworthy*, or *desirable* and *undesirable*, are also culture-specific English words, which encapsulate very complex language-specific concepts (for a detailed analysis of *praise*, *blame*, *approve*, and *disapprove*, see Wierzbicka, 1987); and they cannot, therefore, be regarded as "language-neutral" analytical tools.

What applies to *blame*, *praise*, or *approve*, applies even more to *pleased* and *displeased*, which are English emotion terms, specific to English, and without precise semantic equivalents in most other languages of the world. Using the "natural semantic metalanguage", based on universal semantic primitives or near-primitives,[1] we would sketch something like this:

X is grateful to Y
when X thinks of Y, X thinks something like this:
    this person did something good for me
because of this X feels something good (when X thinks of Y)

X feels remorse
X thinks something like this:
    I did something bad
    because of this, I can't not think: I am bad
    I would want: I didn't do it
    (idiomatically: I wish I hadn't done it)[2]
because of this, X feels something bad

("Anger" will be explicated later, as will be the twin concepts "pleased" and "displeased".)

However, an analysis based entirely on the "cognitive eliciting conditions" is not sufficient because it does not tell us what exactly the experiencer felt: One could, after all, think: "this person did something good for me" and feel something other than gratitude. The concept of gratitude does imply the thought "this person did something good for me", and it does imply a feeling (a "good" feeling), but it also implies a feeling

---

[1]For a further discussion concerning this metalanguage see, e.g. Wierzbicka, 1987, 1988b, 1989a,b, 1990b, 1991b, 1992; Goddard, 1989a,b.

[2]The metalanguage of universal semantic primitives is a semi-artificial language: It is based on natural language (any natural language) and its formulae should be understandable via a natural language, but they are not meant to be idiomatic or elegant. In this particular case, idiomatic English would require the use of *wish*, not *want*. But *wish* is not a lexical universal (that is, many languages do not have a word corresponding to it in meaning), whereas *want* is a universal or a near-universal.

of a particular kind. To capture this special quality of the feeling of gratitude we have to refer not simply to the actual "cognitive eliciting conditions" but to certain *prototypical* eliciting conditions; it is a feeling similar to that which is usually (typically, prototypically, etc.) caused by the thought "this person did something good for me". This leads us to the following, expanded explication:

> *X is grateful to Y*
> when X thinks of Y, X feels something
> sometimes people think something like this of someone:
>   this person did something good for me
> because of this, they feel something good
> (when they think of this person)
> X thinks something like this
> because of this, X feels something like this

DO ALL EMOTION CONCEPTS INVOLVE THOUGHTS?

Emotional experience can be conceptualised in many different ways, and the languages of the world encode—in their lexicon and in their grammar—different types of conceptualisation. Some words, and some grammatical constructions, present the experiencer's emotion as caused by a particular thought, or chain of thoughts; others, however, do not imply any particular thoughts. This is shown, for example, by the following contrast:

> A. For some reason, I feel happy/sad today—I don't know why.
> B. ?For some reason, I feel grateful/disappointed today—
>   I don't know why.

Johnson-Laird and Oatley (1989) have suggested that sentences of type A are possible only in the case of their five basic emotions, and that the contrast between A and B helps to establish these five emotions as basic. But this is not the case. One can also say, for example:

> For some reason, I feel anxious/depressed/excited today—
>   I don't know why.

On the other hand, as Ortony and Clore (1989) point out, one can hardly say:

> ?For some reason I feel disgusted today—I don't know why.

To account for this contrast, we can postulate for some emotion concepts (e.g. for *grateful*, *disappointed*, or *disgusted*) the component "X thought something like this", and to refrain from postulating this component for other emotion concepts (e.g. for *sad* or *happy*).

Ortony and Clore (1989) have also pointed out that it is usually easier to say "I feel X (sad, etc.)—I don't know why" than "I am X (sad etc.)—I don't know why". I think this is correct; but I cannot agree with the further claim that only the frame "I feel X" is compatible with the comment "I don't know why". Ortony and Clore argue (1989, p. 127) that "to be an emotion, the feelings must signify the results of an appraisal of some kind. Thus, sadness is not simply a particular kind of feeling, but a particular kind of feeling for a particular kind of reason". But this claim seems incompatible with the fact that one *can* say:

A'.   I am sad/happy today—I don't know why.

although certainly not:

B'.   *I am disappointed/disgusted today—I don't know why.

It appears, therefore, that for some emotion concepts (e.g. for *disappointed, grateful,* or *disgusted*) we do need a reference to a particular thought ("X thought something like this"), whereas for others (e.g. for *sad, happy,* or *anxious*) we do not—although for the latter, too, we need a reference to a prototypical thought ("sometimes people think something like this"). In both cases, however, there has to be a reference to a prototypical scenario, which identifies, indirectly, the emotion in question. For example, for *sad* and *happy* the following formulae can be proposed:

X is sad
X feels something
sometimes people think something like this:
    something bad happened
    I would want: it didn't happen
    because of this, if I could, I would want to do something
    I can't do anything
because of this, they feel something bad
X feels like this

X is happy
X feels something
sometimes people think something like this:
    something good happened to me
    I wanted this
    I don't want other things
because of this, they feel something good
X feels like this

This format seeks to reconcile a number of apparently contradictory positions in the analysis of emotions, in particular, the controversy relating to the question of whether feelings are precognitive (cf. Zajonc, 1980) or postcognitive (cf., for example, Ortony et al., 1988). It also removes the apparent conflict between definitions on the one hand and prototypes and scenarios on the other (cf., for example, Fehr & Russell, 1984; Russell & Bullock, 1986; Conway & Bekerian, 1987; Fehr, 1988; Medin, 1989). To compare concepts with any degree of precision we need to have definitions, which, if they are to have any explanatory power, cannot be, directly or indirectly, circular. This in turn requires that they are based on a set of listed indefinables or primitives. On the other hand, most emotion terms are referentially indeterminate or "fuzzy", which means that they cannot be defined simply by listing necessary and sufficient conditions. If one cannot envisage a different form of definition than such a listing of conditions, then one is tempted to conclude that no definitions of emotion terms are possible.

But the conclusion does not follow from the premise. As I have tried to demonstrate elsewhere (cf. Wierzbicka, 1985), a prototype can be built into the structure of the definition itself. For example, a reference to flying can be built into a definition of *bird* in such a way as not to exclude ostriches and emus.

In the case of words referring to actions, events, and states, the prototype will often take the form of a script or scenario, such as those sketched above (sometimes very complex ones; cf. Wierzbicka 1988a,c).

Johnson-Laird and Oatley (1989, p. 91) have recently objected to this mode of analysis, arguing as follows:

> Where we disagree is over the status of words that denote basic emotion modes, such as sadness. Wierzbicka's strategy is reminiscent of the account of emotion in Frijda (1986): she defines an emotion by recounting a brief scenario of a possible cause of the feeling. But this analysis conveys only the conditions in which someone is likely to feel sad; it does not convey anything about what it feels like to be sad.

This is undeniably true: An analysis of the concept "sad" in terms of a prototypical script or scenario does not convey anything about what it feels like to be sad.[3]

---

[3]I argued this point two decades ago, in Wierzbicka (1972, pp. 59–60): "Thoughts have a structure which can be rendered in words, but feelings, like sensations, do not. All we can do, therefore, is to describe in words the external situations or thoughts which are associated in our memory or in our imagination with the feeling in question and to trust that our reader or listener will grasp what particular feelings are meant . . .

It may be objected that definitions based on this scheme are not really definitions, that they evade the question of the quality of different emotions. But this is precisely the point: the semantic structure of names of emotions is a comparative one; emotions can be identified only by a reference to a standard situation: X feels Z = X feels as one does when . . ." (see also Wierzbicka 1973, 1990b; Iordanskaja, 1974).

Johnson-Laird and Oatley ask: "Why, then, not accept that the meaning of 'sad' is given by a universal semantic primitive corresponding to one of the five basic emotion modes?" And they conclude that "sad" is indeed a universal semantic primitive.

However, first, "sad" is a complex concept, related to other complex concepts (such as *disappointed*, *upset*, *worried*, etc.) and sharing with them certain components; it cannot, therefore, be a semantic primitive. Secondly, it is certainly not a universal concept: There are languages (e.g. Tahitian) which have no word corresponding to anything like it (cf. Levy, 1973, p. 305), and other languages which have various words roughly comparable but none corresponding to it exactly. The following section will provide an illustration of this point. First, however, one further comment on the format of explications is in order.

If emotion concepts such as *sad* or *happy* are explicated here in terms of their "cognitive eliciting conditions" this is not because I have arbitrarily chosen this mode of analysis. The purpose of an explication is to *reveal* a semantic structure, not to *invent* one. There are some emotion concepts encoded in English, and in other languages, which involve the experiencer's will, or a volitional impulse (e.g. *anger*) and there are others which do not (e.g. *disappointment*). There are emotion concepts which refer to the experiencer's expressive behaviour and there are others which do not (e.g. *cheerful* differs in this respect from *happy*; one can be *happy*, but not *cheerful*, without showing it in some way). Semantic analysis reveals the conceptualisation of emotions encoded in language. If "cognitive eliciting conditions" play a particularly important role in the explication of emotion concepts this is not because of the analyst's fiat but because careful, methodical comparison of many emotion concepts encoded in language shows that they can be effectively and rigorously identified and compared in these terms. If these explications were not correct, they would not "work" (i.e. they would not be able to capture the similarities and the differences between different emotion concepts).

WHY SAD CANNOT BE A UNIVERSAL SEMANTIC PRIMITIVE

The Australian Aboriginal language Pintupi has the following words which have been compared to the English word *sad* (Morice, 1977, p. 105): *watjilpa, wurrkulinu, yiluruyiluru, yirraru, yulatjarra*. Morice describes the meaning of these words as follows:

> *watjilpa*: preoccupation with thoughts of country and relatives. To become sick through worrying about them. Other people may try to assuage worry, or traditional doctor may treat.

wurrkulinu: excessive concern for, and worry about, land or relatives, as for *watjilpa*.

yiluruyiluru: dejection caused by worrying too much for absent relatives, for example, if they are in hospital.

yirraru: as for *watjilpa*.

yulatjarra: sympathy or sorrow for sick or deceased relatives. If a death has occurred this state is accompanied by self-inflicted wounds—"sorry cuts". Not treated by traditional doctor.

However, glosses of this kind, useful as they are, cannot be taken as adequate definitions. To begin with, *yirraru* has not been defined at all, except for the unconvincing comment that it is like *watjilpa*, and *yiluruyiluru* has not really been differentiated from *watjilpa*. The other glosses are clearly not intended to be taken literally either. For example, *yulatjarra* can hardly mean "sympathy for deceased relatives" (if they are dead they are no longer a suitable target for *sympathy*). In the other glosses, too, words such as *preoccupation*, *worry*, *concern*, *sympathy*, *sorrow* or *dejection*, appear to be used almost indiscriminately.

All this half-hearted matching achieves is an ethnocentric look at Pintupi emotion concepts through the prism of English emotion concepts, not an understanding of Pintupi conceptualisation in its own right. As a result, the relations between the different Pintupi emotion words discussed remain obscure, and so do the relations between the Pintupi and the English emotion terms.

The data provided by Morice are not sufficient for well-justified explications of the relevant Pintupi concepts to be confidently posited (and there appear to be some inconsistencies between Morice's data and Myers' 1976 and 1979 data). As a first approximation, however, I will propose a tentative explication of the key concept of *watjilpa*, which Myers (1979, p. 361) describes as follows:

> The core of the concept refers to *separation* [Myers' emphasis] from objects or persons of security and familiarity—family and home—places and people among which and with whom one grew up and where one feels safe and comfortable . . . Time and again in the life histories collected, Pintupi talked of their travels and the 'homesickness' (*watjilpa*) that made them come back to their home country. One friend (who had not seen his country for a long time), explained to me, 'I close my eyes and I can see that place. It's very green. There's a rockhole and a hill where I used to play. My brother pushed me down—it makes me "homesick".'

watjilpa
X feels something
sometimes people think something like this of a place:

I am like a part of this place
I am not in this place now
I want to be in this place
I can't be in this place now
because of this, something bad can happen to me
because of this, they feel something bad
X thinks something like this
because of this, X feels something like this

It is easy to se that the closest English equivalent of *watjilpa* is in fact not *sad* but *homesick*, although the cultural salience of *watjilpa* in Pintupi may well bring it to mind as the principal Pintupi counterpart of the English *sad*.

The fact that the Pintupi language has "many words for sadness and depression" (Myers 1979, p. 350) which imply "that the sufferer is 'worrying' for his land or his relatives", does indeed support the general conviction of all observers that the Pintupi are strongly attached to their country and to their kin, and that they somehow identify with them; and that this attachment constitutes an important part of their culture. But this fact also suggests that the words in question are not really words "for sadness, depression or worry". They are really words for something else— each of them being somehow different in meaning from each other, as well as from the English words *sadness*, *depression*, and *worry*.

It is true that *watjilpa*—although a culturally key concept—is not the closest Pintupi counterpart of the English *sad*. As pointed out to me by Cliff Goddard (personal communication), a closer counterpart of the English *sad* is *tjituru-tjituru*. In his dictionary of the closely related language Pitjantjatjara, Goddard (1987) glosses this word as follows: (1) unhappy, dissatisfied, discontent; (2) sorrowful, sad. On the basis of a lengthy discussion with Goddard, I would explicate this concept as follows:

tjituru-tjituru
X feels something
sometimes people think something like this:
    something bad happened
    I wanted this not to happen
because of this, they feel something bad
X thinks something like this
because of this, X feels something like this

The main differences between *tjituru-tjituru* and *sad* are these: first, one can be *sad* without knowing why one is sad, but *tjituru-tjituru*, like *disappointed*, appears to imply a known cause (Goddard, personal communication); secondly, *sad* implies a kind of quiet resignation ("I can't do anything"), whereas *tjituru-tjituru* (often translated as *dissatisfied*, *discontent*) does not; and thirdly, *sadness* can be caused by events which do not affect the speaker personally and it does not imply unfulfilled wishes, whereas *tjituru-tjituru* does ("I wanted this not to happen"). One might say that *tjituru-tjituru* is a much more concrete concept referring to specific wishes; for example, I wanted someone not to die, but they died; I wanted my caravan to arrive but it didn't, whereas *sadness* is compatible with fully hypothetical wishes, e.g. someone else's dog died; I would want: it didn't happen (although I never thought of this before the event); and, as pointed out earlier, it does not imply that the experiencer thought anything at all.

Thus, although close, the concepts "sad" and "tjituru-tjituru" are undoubtedly different. So, if there is some universal human emotion associated with losses, tears, inability to laugh, and so on, why should it be identifiable via the English word *sad* rather than via the Pintupi/ Pitjantjatjara word *tjituru-tjituru*?

The concept of "sadness" is a European cultural construct, and for that reason alone, even if there were no others, it cannot be regarded as a "universal semantic primitive". The same argument holds, incidentally, for colour concepts, such as "blue" or "green", which Johnson-Laird and Oatley (1989) invoke as a parallel for "basic emotions". The English words *blue* or *green* cannot identify universal semantic primitives. Because the Russian words *sinij* and *goluboj* (both, roughly, "blue") or the Japanese word *aoi* (again, roughly "blue") do not correspond in meaning (or range of use) to the English word *blue*, there is no reason to think that *blue* has a privileged status and expresses some universal semantic primitive (cf. Wierzbicka, 1990a).

If we are to avoid ethnocentric illusions we have to give up the conviction that either *sad* or *blue* identify some universal semantic primitives. Hence the need for further decomposition of both *sad* and *blue*, of both colour concepts and emotion concepts.

Even within English, the choice of "sad" rather than "unhappy", "happiness" rather than "joy", or "fear" rather than "fright" or "afraid" seems arbitrary; from a universal perspective, the choice of *sad* over *watjilpa* or *tjituru-tjituru* or of *anger* over *liget* or *song* is of course all the more arbitrary.

The advocates of "basic emotions" will no doubt reply at this point that when they identify their "basic emotions" by means of English words such as *sad*, *happy*, *fear*, *anger*, or *disgust*, they do not take these words seriously: They really mean something else, something for which English has no words (cf. Johnson-Laird & Oatley, 1989, p. 85).

However, this raises a major problem: If the English labels chosen by the authors are offered only as an approximation, and if there are several thousand languages in the world, whose emotion lexicons differ enormously in scope and in meaning, then what exactly is being proposed as the

set of universal basic emotions? Without some universal points of reference the claim that there are five, or six, "basic human emotions" seems to
be void.

We could, of course, try to identify the hypothetical "basic emotions" in
terms of bodily behaviour. Thus, we could say that there is one basic
emotion associated with tears, another associated with smiling, another
one associated with fighting, another associated with running away, and yet
another associated with vomiting. But this would make nonsense of
theories that maintain that there are some universals in facial expression of
emotions: These theories would now mean that tears signal the kind of
emotion which is associated with tears, that smiling expresses the kind of
emotion which is associated with smiling, and so on.

The advocates of "basic emotions" and of "universals of facial expression of emotions" should be particularly interested in finding some universal
points of reference in terms of which their hypothetical basic emotions
could be identified; for without such points of reference their claims can be
seen as either ethnocentric or less than truly meaningful.

My point is that universal points of reference *can* be found: Not in
culture-specific English words such as *happiness* or *sadness*, but in lexical
universals such as "want", "think", "know", "say", "good", "bad", and
so on.

Psychologists writing about emotions usually feel free to disregard
differences between words which appear to be close in meaning, such as,
for example, *unhappy* and *sad*, *happy* and *joy*, *fear*, *fright*, and *afraid*, and
so on. But if we want to look for universals, we have to know what exactly
we are looking for. The use of universal semantic primitives allows us,
indeed forces us, to be precise in our statements and hypotheses.

WHAT DOES "SOMETHING LIKE **HAPPY**" MEAN?

Consider, for example, what appears to be the least controversial and the
"most easily recognisable" basic emotion, namely the one associated with
a ("genuine") smile. The English language writings on "basic emotions"
usually seek to identify this emotion by means of the word *happy*, or
happiness. Sometimes, however, the same writers use the word *joy* (or its
derivatives) as if there was no difference between *happiness* and *joy*, or
between *happy* and *joyful*.

In fact, however, there are two important differences here. One has to
do with the personal character of *happiness* (highlighted by expressions
such as *pursuit of happiness* or *personal happiness*), and the non-personal,
"selfless", character of *joy* ("something good happened to me" vs. "something good happened"). *Happy* is analogous in this respect to *unhappy*
("something bad happened to me"), and *joy* to *sad* ("something bad

happened"). The other difference is manifested in the following contrast in acceptability:

– Are you thinking of applying for a transfer?
– No, I am quite happy (*joyful, *joyous) where I am.

Sentences such as "I am quite happy where I am", suggest that *happy*—unlike *joy* and its derivates—contain the component "I don't want anything else". This conjecture is further supported by sentences such as:

The children were playing happily.

which imply not only something like "enjoyment" but also something like "contentedness". We can account for both the similarities and the differences between the two concepts by means of the following two formulae:

joy (e.g. X feels joy)
X feels something
sometimes people think something like this:
    something very good is happening
    I want this
because of this, they feel something good
X feels like this

X is happy
X feels something
sometimes people think something like this:
    something good happened to me
    I wanted this
    I don't want anything else
because of this, they feel something good
X feels like this

The advocates of "basic emotions" usually choose *happiness* rather than *joy* as the "nearest English word" for the emotion associated with smiling. The reason seems to be that in modern English, *happy* is an everyday word whereas *joy* and its derivates are more literary and stylistically marked. *Happy* is also much more frequent than *joy* (cf. *The American Heritage word frequency book*, 1971 and Kučera & Francis, 1967).

However, in many other European languages, the closest semantic equivalents of *joy* are much more common in everyday language than the closest semantic equivalents of *happy*. For example, in German the verb *sich freuen* and the noun *Freude* (roughly, "joy") are everyday words, unlike the adjective *glücklich* (roughly, "happy") or the noun *Glück* (roughly, "happiness"); and if some German psychologists were to draw a list of "basic emotions" they would probably choose *Freude* rather than *Glück*.

Similarly, French psychologists would no doubt choose *joie* rather than *bonheur* (roughly, "happiness") as the label for a basic emotion. Part of the problem is that both *Glück* and *bonheur* imply, primarily, permanent states rather than transient emotions, although they can also be used with reference to more fleeting experiences. So, looking for names of quintessential emotions one would no doubt think of *joie* and *Freude* rather than of *bonheur* and *Glück*.

But even leaving aside the question of permanence, *happy* does not mean exactly the same as *glücklich* or *heureux* (the adjective corresponding to *bonheur*).

I am happy. ≠
Je suis ("I am") heureux. ≠
Ich bin ("I am") glücklich.

If *glücklich* or *heureux* express a common European concept (realised also as *felice* in Italian, *sčastliv* in Russian, *szczęśliwy* in Polish, and so on), the modern English word *happy* expresses a "weaker", less intense, devalued version of this concept. Speaking metaphorically, emotions such as *bonheur*, *Glück*, *felicità*, or *sčast'e* fill a human being to overflowing, leaving no room for any further desires or wishes. The English noun *happiness* can still be used in this sense, but the adjective *happy* no longer implies this totality of emotion, this absolute "bliss".

This more limited, more "pragmatic" character of the English concept of "happy" manifests itself in its syntax. For example, one can say:

I am happy with the present arrangements.
I am happy with his answer. (An examiner speaking)

But in French, German, or Russian one could not use the words *heureux, glücklich*, or *sčastliv* in sentences of this kind. Instead, one would have to use semantically "weaker", less intense words such as *satisfait* (or *content*), *zufrieden*, or *dovolen* (roughly, "pleased"):

Je suis satisfait (*heureux) de sa réponse.
Ich bin zufrieden (*glücklich) mit seiner Antwort.
Ja dovolen (*sčastliv) ego otvetom.

Normally, words such as *heureux* or *glücklich* are used in an absolute way, that is, without complements specifying in what respect one is "heureux" or "glücklich". If one is *heureux*, one is *heureux*, not *heureux* "with something".

To account for the "absolute", "total" character of the concept encapsulated in words such as *heureux* or *glücklich*, I propose for them the following semantic formula:

X is heureux (glücklich, etc.).
X feels something
sometimes people think something like this:
    something very good happened to me
    I wanted this
    everything is good
    I can't want anything else
because of this, they feel something good
X feels like this

This explanation differs from that assigned to *happy* in three respects: first, it has one additional component: "everything is good" (by implication, "everything that is happening to me"); secondly, it includes the adverb *very* ("very good"); and thirdly, its last "thinking" component is phrased as "I can't want anything else" rather than as "I don't want anything else", as in the case of *happy*. The person who says: "I am quite happy where I am" implies something similar to contentedness ('I don't want anything else"). But in French or in German one could only use "weaker" adjectives in this kind of context, such as *content* "content/ pleased", *zufrieden* or *dovolen* "pleased/content", not *heureux*, *glücklich*, or *sčastliv*, which are at odds with the implication that someone could become "heureux" or "glücklich" or "sčastliv" if some particular need of theirs was satisfied.

1.   – Vous voulez demander une mutation?
     "Do you want to ask for a transfer?"
     ?Non, je suis complètement heureuse où je suis.
     "No, I'm quite happy where I am."
2.   – Sie wollen eine Versetzung?
     ?Nein, ich bin hier ganz glücklich.
3.   – Vy xotite perenestis' v drugoe mesto?
     ?Net, ja vpolne sčastliv zdes'.

Similarly, one would not use the words *heureux*, *glücklich*, or *sčastliv* in French, German, or Russian equivalents of the sentence "The children were playing happily".

?Les enfants jouaient heureusement.
*Die Kinder spielten glücklich miteinander.
*Deti sčastlivo igrali.

By comparison with *happily*, the words *heureusement*, *glücklich*, or *sčast-livo* sound almost euphoric, inappropriately so in sentences describing ordinary everyday behaviour.

Thus, the English word *happy* is not the same as *heureux* or *glücklich*, just as it is not the same as *joy* (or its French, German, and Russian counterparts: *joie, Freude*, and *radost'*).[4]

One might argue that the differences between *happy* and *heureux*, or between *happiness, joy*, and *joie*, are relatively minor, and that what is meant by the "basic emotion of happiness" is what corresponds to what they all have in common. The problem is that as one moves further afield from European languages, the closest counterparts of *happiness* and *joy* differ from them more sharply than does *bonheur* or *joie*. For example, the closest Ifaluk counterpart of *joy* and *happiness*, namely *ker*, glossed by Lutz (1987) as "happiness/excitement", also implies something like excitement, lack of self-control, a touch of euphoria, a touch of irresponsibility, and so on. (For a more precise analysis of this concept, see Wierzbicka, 1988a and 1992.) Thus identifying some "universal human emotion" by referring to words "such as *happy*" becomes more and more unrealistic the more languages one takes into account. Conversely, the fewer languages one takes into account the greater the danger of ethnocentrism.

This does not mean that there cannot be an identifiable universal emotion related to what is usually called "happiness". As one looks at the smiling faces in Ekman's photographs one is inclined to think that some conceptual structure associated with these expressions can perhaps be identified. As a first approximation, and a starting point for discussion, I would propose the following:

X feels something
sometimes people think something like this:
    something good is happening
because of this, they feel something good
X feels like this

This is less than what has been included in the explications of *happy*, *heureux*, or *joy* (or the Ifaluk *ker*), but is compatible with all of them.

But even here, for the phrase "something like happy" to be truly meaningful its intended meaning has to be specified in an explicit formula.

It is interesting to note that for the apparent opposite of the emotion under discussion, the English word *sad* rather than *unhappy* is usually used. We have seen that the core cognitive component of *sad* is "something bad happened". If *unhappy* is—as it appears to be—a semantic opposite of *happy*, its core cognitive component would be "something bad happened to me". Do people who postulate universal "basic emotions" have in mind

---

[4]It is possible that in the course of centuries, *happy* has undergone a devaluation, and that this is linked with the general "greying of the emotions" in the English-speaking world (cf. Wierzbicka, 1989c; Vértes, 1989).

emotions based on the thought "something bad happened" (like "sadness"), or emotions based on the thought "something bad happened to me" (like "unhappiness")? Or both? Or both these and some others as well? Without an answer to these questions the claim that "something like sadness" is a universal human emotion (recognisable through a universal range of facial expressions) is lacking in clear content.

CAN "PLEASED" AND "DISPLEASED" BE USED AS PRIMITIVES IN SEMANTIC ANALYSIS?

Let us now consider briefly the two English concepts chosen by Ortony et al. (1988) as their basic analytical tools: "pleased" and "displeased", which in fact are no less complex than "sad", "happy", or most other emotion concepts lexicalised in English. I would propose the following analysis for these concepts:

> pleased (≠pleasure)
> X feels something
> sometimes people think something like this:
>   something good happened
>   I wanted something like this
> because of this, they feel something good
> X thinks something like this
> because of this, X feels something like this

> displeased, displeasure
> X feels something
> sometimes people think something like this (of someone):
>   this person did something
>   it was not good
>   I wanted something not like this
>   because of this I did something
> because of this, they feel something bad
> X feels like this

It is interesting to note that although *pleased* and *displeased* may seem to be completely symmetrical in meaning, in fact *displeased* includes one additional constraint: it implies something like "misbehaviour", and so it appears to be restricted to human causes:

> She was pleased/displeased with her son.
> She was pleased/?displeased with the colour of her hair
>   (after it had been dyed).

This is why I have posited one additional component for *displeased*: "this person did something". I will note in passing that the closest Polish counterparts of *pleased* and *displeased*, namely, *zadowolony* and *niezado-wolony*, appear to be fully symmetrical, and, that, consequently, if *zadowolony* can be equated with *pleased*, *niezadowolony* cannot be equated with *displeased*.

This brief discussion of the concepts "pleased" and "displeased" should suffice to show that these concepts, too, are complex and language-specific—not less so than "happiness" or "sadness"—or than "anger", to which we will turn next.

"ANGER" AND "SOMETHING LIKE ANGER"

My explication of the English concept of *anger* is as follows (cf. Wierzbicka 1972, p. 62 and 1988c):

> *angry*
> X feels something
> sometimes people think something like this (of someone):
>   this person did something bad
>   I don't want this
>   because of this, I want to do something
>   I would want to do something bad to this person
> because of this, they feel something bad
> X thinks something like this
> because of this, X feels something like this

The English concept is not universal. As noted earlier, Ilongot, for example, does not have a word corresponding to *anger*. The Ilongot concept closest to anger—that is, *liget* (glossed by Rosaldo, 1980 as anger/energy/passion)—involves something like competition and a desire to prove oneself (in head-hunting, but also in "fierce" gardening), to show that one is not inferior to other people. These elements are totally absent from the concept of "anger".

Using the "prototypical" framework employed here for *anger* we can, tentatively, explicate *liget* as follows:

> *liget*
> X feels something
> sometimes people think something like this:
>   other people can do something
>   they could think that I can't do it
>   I don't want this
>   because of this, I want to do something
>   I can do it
> because of this, they feel something
> X feels like this

As this explication shows, *liget* has a competitive character and is related to envy and ambition; but there is nothing like that in the concept of *anger*. *Anger* has its basis in the thought that "someone did something bad"; but there is nothing like that in the concept of *liget*.

Consequently, *anger* implies a negative impulse directed at the target person ("I would want to do something bad to this person"), but *liget* does not. In fact, *liget* does not imply that there is any specific target person at all. Moreover, the feeling associated with *liget* does not have to be a "bad feeling". It *can* be a "bad feeling", but it can also be an intoxicatingly "good feeling" (depending on one's perception of one's chances of success).

It is true that both *anger* and *liget* are likely to hurt somebody, that is, to cause someone to "feel something bad". But in the case of *liget*, one does not necessarily have an urge to hurt somebody, as one does in the case of *anger* (regardless of whether or not one acts upon that urge). The fierce head-hunter kills not because he wants to hurt, to punish, to inflict pain, but because he wants to prove to himself and to others that he is as good as anybody else or better. There is nothing like that in the concept of *anger*.

Furthermore, the person who is likely to get hurt through *liget* may well be the experiencer of *liget* himself. When one is sweating and panting in "fierce" work, one is disregarding one's own "bad feelings" (tiredness, aches, pain, and so on). One is determined not to let such "bad feelings" (whether in oneself or in another person) interfere with one's action. This is a ruthless determination which "narrows vision on a task", not an urge to hurt.

Finally, *liget* spurs people to action, gives them strength and courage, enables them to go beyond their limits, and leads them to achievements and to triumphs. Because, however, *liget* can also lead to destructive and unplanned actions, for example, "basket-slashing, knife-waving violence", the things that one can do because of *liget* are not described in the explication as "good things", or as "things that one wants to do".

The explication of *liget* sketched here attempts to account for the entire range of this concept's use, as reported by Rosaldo, and, in particular, to explain "the ambivalence surrounding *liget*" deriving "from the fact that it can lead in a variety of directions" (Rosaldo, 1980, p. 47). Anger is not similarly ambivalent, and if it is not repressed or sublimated, it can lead only in one direction, that of intentionally "doing something bad to someone".

I conclude that the Ilongot concept of *liget* is indeed unique, and cannot be identified with the English concept of *anger*. If there are any "transcultural characteristics of a generic human mind" (Spiro, 1984, p. 334), conceptualisation of emotions in terms of either *anger* or *liget* is certainly not among their number. It is an illusion to think that "in the human being the expression of anger and the experiential phenomenon of *anger* are innate, pan-cultural, universal phenomena" (Izard, 1977, p. 64). There is no reason to think that *anger* is any more "innate", "pan-cultural", or "universal" than *liget*.

The Ifaluk language of Micronesia, described in a number of studies by Lutz (cf. for example, 1982, 1987) has neither a concept like *anger* nor *liget*, but instead has the concept of *song*, described by Lutz as something like "justified anger".

Lutz's discussion shows clearly, however, that this word does not mean the same as the English word *anger*, and not only because *song* is supposed to be "justified". *Song* is a less aggressive feeling than *anger*, a feeling which is less likely to lead to physical violence. Typically, *song* manifests itself in reprimands, refusal to eat, or in a pout. What is more, in some cases *song* can lead to suicide, or in any case to an attempted suicide. The hidden "goal" of *song* is, according to Lutz (1987, p. 301), "to change the situation by altering the behavior of the offending person", but the actions caused by *song* are often directed towards oneself rather than towards the guilty person (for example, an attempted suicide rather than an attempted murder). From an earlier article on the same subject (Lutz, 1982, p. 121) we learn that *song* is regarded as "good for people (and especially parents) to feel and express when a wrongdoing has occurred. It is only through the observation of their parents' *song* in particular situations that children are said to learn the difference between right and wrong". Accordingly, people in a higher position, who are responsible for other people's behaviour, can be expected to feel and to show *song* particularly frequently. "An elder is more often *song* (justifiably angry) at a younger person than at a peer or at a higher-ranked individual. The chiefs are often said to be *song* at those who have broken rules or taboos" (Lutz, 1982, p. 122).

All these observations indicate that the concept of "song" differs from the concept of "anger", and suggest the following conceptual structure:

song
X feels something
sometimes people think something like this of someone:
    this person did something bad
    this person should know this
    because of this, I should do something
    because of this, I want to do something
because of this, they feel something bad
X thinks something like this
because of this, X feels something bad

Both the concept of "song" and that of "anger" involve the thought "this person did something bad". But in the case of *anger*, the negative judgement leads to an urge to do something bad to that person ("because of this I would want to do something bad to this person"); in the case of *song*, the urge to do something is not oriented towards anyone, and it can express itself in a refusal to eat as much as in a reprimand ("because of this, I want to do something"). This does not mean, of course, that *song* can express itself in any action whatsoever. All the actions mentioned by Lutz (a reprimand, a refusal to eat, a pout, an attempted suicide) have a common denominator: X wants Y to know that Y has done something bad, and to draw consequences from this. Hence the need for the components "this person should know this" and "I should do something".

Lutz (1987, p. 300) observes that the Ifaluk culture enjoins people to avoid aggression, and that in its hierarchy of values it puts this injunction much higher than Western culture, and in particular, than American culture.

> . . . although both the Ifaluk and Americans may have the goal of avoiding violence, roles of physical aggression in the two societies and beliefs about those roles are in dramatic contrast, in part due to cultural differences in the importance attached to that goal.

The fact that the Ifaluk language has no word corresponding to the English word *anger* and that the closest Ifaluk counterpart of this concept is much "softer" and closer to *admonition*, seems to constitute a lexical confirmation of this difference between the two cultures. In the explications proposed above the conceptual relations in question are explicitly addressed.

Finally, let me mention the Polish concept of "złość"—a much more basic word in Polish than *gniew* (roughly, "anger", but a somewhat dignified kind of "anger"). For example, Ekman's photograph of a woman viciously baring her teeth as if she wanted to bite someone would bring to mind in Polish *złość* rather than *gniew*. Similarly, a child's tantrum would be linked with the word *złość*, not with the word *gniew*. *Gniew* (like *anger*) implies a judgement: "this person did something bad", and so it easily acquires somewhat intellectual and moral connotations; but *złość* is compatible with an almost animal aggression or with a childish rage. *Gniew* can be dignified and impressive, but *złość*—like *tantrum, temper,* or *"aggro"*— cannot. I would propose for the Polish *złość* the following explication:

złość
X feels something
sometimes people think something like this:
    something happened
    I don't want this
    because of this, I want to do something bad

because of this, they feel something bad
X feels like this

This differs from *anger*, and from *gniew*, in two respects: first, the experiencer doesn't make the judgement "this person did something bad" but simply is frustrated in his will ("something happened—I don't want this"); and secondly, the impulse to do something is intentionally "bad": "I want to do something bad", whereas in the case of *anger* or *gniew* it does not have to be bad: "because of this I want to do something" (it is worth mentioning that the basic meaning of the adjective *zły* is "bad", so that *złość* means literally "badness".)

Do the four concepts explicated above ("anger", "liget", "song", and "złość") have an identifiable common core? *Anger*, *złość*, and *song* share the components "this person did something", and "because of this, this person feels something bad", but *liget* does not include them. *Anger*, *złość*, and *liget* share the component "I don't want this", but *song* does not appear to include it. It is possible, then, that all that these four concepts share (in addition to a general "feeling" component) is the volitional component "because of this, I want to do something". But this is not enough to distinguish *anger* from *enthusiasm*.

Of course, one could still claim that "something like *anger*" is a universal human emotion, recognisable through a universal set of facial expressions—but if we realise that *anger* is just an English word without exact equivalents in other languages (and sometimes even without any inexact equivalents), and that other languages have lexicalised other emotion concepts, it becomes clear that it is really imperative to define "something like anger" on the basis of some universal reference points. If we do not do that, the phrase "something like anger" explains very little.

IDENTIFYING EMOTIONS OR MATCHING PHOTOGRAPHS WITH NEAREST LABELS

Ekman (1989, p. 151) writes:

> The people in each culture are shown still photographs of facial expressions, and asked to select a single emotion word or category from a list of words or categories. Very high agreement was found in the specific emotions attributed to facial expressions across five literate cultures . . . and in the study of a non-Western literate culture . . . These studies have provided consistent evidence for the common recognition of at least six emotions (happiness, anger, fear, sadness, surprise, and disgust).

However, if people are provided with a set of photographs and with a list of words and are instructed to match one with the other, it can hardly be concluded that they "recognise" or "identify" certain emotions in those photographs. At the most, it can be claimed that people *prefer* to link a smiling face with one of the words provided (in English, *happiness*), and a non-smiling face with the eyes wide open with another word (in English, *fear*) than vice versa. Or, if the set of photographs includes two faces with bared teeth, one of which shows the corners of the lips raised, and the other, a squarish mouth (like that of a dog baring his teeth), with the upper and lower teeth close together, observers will consistently choose the word closer to *happiness* for the former and the word closer to *anger* for the latter (given that some words comparable to *happiness* and *anger* are included in their list of words to choose from); but this does not prove that the observers *recognise* "happiness" and "anger" in these two faces.

At the most, we can conclude that observers can distinguish those facial expressions which are associated with emotions based on the thought "something good is happening" from facial expressions which are associated with emotions based on the thought "something bad is happening (happened?)", or from facial expressions which are associated with emotions based on the thought "I want to do something bad to someone". But this is very different from saying that observers from different cultures can consistenly "recognise" or "identify" emotions such as "happiness", "sadness", or "anger".

Let us consider, from this point of view, Ekman's (1975, p. 36) data and comments on the recognition of facial expressions in five literate societies.

The comment "everyone agrees on what faces say" is very striking, in the light of the figures which show clearly that *not* everyone agrees on what these faces say. The agreement might be higher if the respondents were asked to link these faces, respectively, with thoughts such as "something good is happening", "something bad is happening", "something bad happened", "I want to do something", and "this is bad".

Reporting his new findings on smiling, and referring to his description of 18 different types of smiling, Ekman (1989, p. 156) writes:

These studies show that smiles should no longer be considered a single category of behavior. They can be usefully distinguished by measuring different facets of the smile. Cross-cultural studies of different forms of smiling need to be done. It also remains to be determined how many different smiles may provide different social signals, have different functions in social interaction, and relate to different aspects of subjective experience and concomitant physiology.

However, if "smile" is too crude a tool for analysing facial expressions, "happiness" or "anger" are too crude for analysing emotions. If we want to understand the relations between facial behaviour and emotions better we have to sharpen our analytical tools for both these areas (and not only for the first of them). A global label such as "happiness" is an obstacle, not a help, in the investigation of emotions, just as crude global labels such as "smile", "grimace", "frown", or "pout" would be an obstacle rather than a help in the investigation of expressive facial behaviour. More subtle categories are needed on both sides. And it would not do to say that there are 18, or whatever, different types of "happiness" or "anger", as there are 18 different types of smiles, because "happiness" and "anger" are English folk-concepts, not universal categories of human experience (cf. Lutz, 1985; the same can be said, of course, of "smile", "grin", or "grimace": these, too, are English folk-concepts, without exact equivalents in all the languages of the world). By contrast, categories such as "emotions based on the thought 'something good is happening'", or "emotions based on the thought 'something bad happened'", can indeed be thought of as universal categories of human experience. How such universal categories of human experience are correlated with different types of facial behaviour remains to be established.

One thing, however, seems certain: Given the complex and culture-specific nature of concepts such as "happiness", "sadness", or "anger", it is an illusion to think that concepts of this kind identify discrete and count-able phenomena which "objectively" exist as separate categories of experience (even in those societies whose lexicons imply a different cate-gorisation of emotions, cf. Russell, 1989). Consequently, it is an illusion to think that emotions can be divided in a non-arbitrary way into primary or simple ones, such as happiness, anger, or sadness, and "blends". For example, Ekman (1973, p. 198) writes:

> Many of the anatomically possible expressions depict blends of emotions rather than single emotions. . . . While the single emotions are universal, we contend that cultures do vary in the particular blends of emotion that frequently occur.

However, we have seen that the "scripts" for "happiness", "sadness", or "anger" are also complex. A concept such as "liget" may seem complex to English-speakers, as it combines elements of "anger", "passion", and "envy", whereas "anger" appears to them simple; but the same concept of "anger" is likely to appear quite complex to the Ilongots or the Ifaluks, because it combines elements of "liget" (or "song") and something else.

Can one recognise a *liget* face or a *song* face, as one allegedly can recognise an *angry* or a *sad* face? And is *anger* any more "simple" and "discrete", any less of a "blend" than *liget* or *song*? Perhaps all we can (sometimes) read off faces is conceptual components, such as "I feel something good" or "I feel something bad", "I want to do something" or

"I can't do anything"? Or perhaps there is a range of components compatible with a given facial expression rather than some definite components? Perhaps, for example, all we can say is that the "characteristic upturned mouth" of a sincere smile is compatible with a set of components including "something good happened", "something good is happening", "I want this", "I feel something good", and that any more specific readings are subject to variation and individual interpretation?

CAN THERE BE UNIVERSAL EMOTIONS?

In the literature on emotions, emotions are often confused with emotion concepts; in particular, the question of the "universality of emotions" is confused with the universality of emotion concepts. We know now that there are no universal emotion concepts: in particular, "anger", "happiness", "sadness", "fear", and "disgust" are English cultural artefacts, and as such they cannot identify any "universal human emotions".

Nor can they identify any "universal facial expressions". For example, Ekman's smiling faces do not show "happiness . . . to preliterate New Guinea tribesmen, Japanese, and American college students alike" (Ekman, 1975, p. 35). It is conceivable, however, that a range of smiling faces could be universally linked with the idea "this person feels something good". It is also conceivable that some other facial expressions could be universally linked with specific thoughts, such as "something good is happening", "something bad is happening", or "I want to do something bad to someone" (the squarish mouth and bared, clenched teeth). In any case, hypotheses of this kind would be free from ethnocentric bias and could be tested without the "language problem" which vitiates the study of facial expressions carried out in terms of English words such as *anger*, *happiness*, and so on.

Similarly, when Johnson-Laird and Oatley (1980, p. 90) speak of happiness, sadness, anger, fear, and disgust as universally "discriminable categories of direct experience", this cannot be correct, as the categories in question are language-specific. They could, however, reformulate their claim: There are five universally discriminable categories of direct experience. But then they would have to show *how* these categories can be discriminated, and to show it in terms of universal human concepts, not in terms of English cultural artefacts. Hypotheses along these lines *can* be formulated and, I presume, could be tested (for example, using the techniques developed by Ekman and his associates)—but they would have to be tested without the use of any ready-made emotion terms.

CONCLUSION

Russell and Bullock (1986, p. 338) wrote: " 'Happiness', 'anger', 'fear', and the rest are concepts we inherit from our culture to distinguish types of events." This is undoubtedly true. Other people, in other societies, inherit other concepts from *their* culture, and our concepts do not have any privileged status. It is, therefore, as inappropriate to talk about human emotions in general in terms of "happiness", "anger", and "fear" as it would be to talk about them in terms of "liget", "song", or "złość". However, this does not mean that we cannot penetrate into the emotional world of speakers of languages other than our own. Nor does it mean that there can be no universal (universally recognisable) human emotions. Universality of emotions and of the expression of emotions is an open issue which requires further investigation. But for this further investigation to be fully productive it has to be undertaken from a universal, language- and culture-independent perspective; and it has to be carried out in a universalist framework. The natural semantic metalanguage based on universal (or near-universal) semantic primitives (or near-primitives) facilitates such a perspective and offers such a framework.

Manuscript received 12 June 1990
Revised manuscript received 14 November 1990

REFERENCES

The American Heritage word frequency book (1971). John B. Carroll, Peter Davies, & Barry Richman (Eds). New York: Houghton Mifflin.

Conway, M.A. & Bekerian, D.A. (1987). Situational knowledge and emotions. *Cognition and Emotion, 1*, 145–191.

Ekman, P. (1973). Cross-cultural studies of facial expressions. In Paul Ekman (Ed), *Darwin and facial expression: a century of research in review*. New York: Academic Press, pp. 169–229.

Ekman, P. (1975). The universal smile: Face muscles talk every language. *Psychology Today, Sept.*, 35–39.

Ekman, P. (1989). The argument and evidence about universals in facial expressions of emotion. In H. Wagner & A. Manstead (Eds), *Handbook of social psychophysiology*. New York: John Wiley, pp. 143–164.

Fehr, B. (1988). Prototype analysis of the concepts of love and commitment. *Journal of Personality and Social Psychology, 55*, 557–579.

Fehr, B. & Russell, J.A. (1984). Concept of emotion viewed from a prototype perspective. *Journal of Experimental Psychology: General, 113*, 464–486.

Frijda, N.H. (1986). *The emotions*. Cambridge University Press.

Goddard, C. (1987). *A basic Pitjantjatjara/Yankunytjatjara to English dictionary*. Alice Springs: Institute for Aboriginal Development.

Goddard, C. (1989a). Issues in natural semantic metalanguage. *Quaderni di Semantica*. *10*(1), 51–64. (Round table on semantic primitives, 1.)

Goddard, C. (1989b). The goals and limits of semantic representation. *Quaderni di Semantica, 10*(2), 297–308. (Round table on semantic primitives, 2.)

Iordanskaja, L. (1974). Tentative lexicographic definitions for a group of Russian words denoting emotions. In J. Rozencvejg (Ed.), *Machine translation and applied linguistics*. Vol. 2. Frankfurt: Athenäum, pp. 88–117.

Izard, C. (1977). *Human emotions*. New York: Plenum Press.

Johnson-Laird, P.N. & Oatley, K. (1989). The language of emotions: an analysis of a semantic field. *Cognition and Emotion, 3*, 81-123.

Kučera, H. & Francis, W.N. (1967). *Computational analysis of present-day American English*. Providence, R.I.: Brown University Press.

Levy, R.I. (1973). *Tahitians: mind and experience in the Society Islands*. University of Chicago Press.

Lutz, C. (1982). The domain of emotion words on Ifaluk. *American Ethnologist, 9*(1), 113–128.

Lutz, C. (1983). Parental goals, ethnopsychology, and the development of emotional meaning. *Ethos 11*(4), 246–262.

Lutz, C. (1985). Ethnopsychology compared to what? Explaining behavior and consciousness among the Ifaluk. In Geoffrey M. White & John Kirkpatrick (Eds), *Person, self, and experience: exploring Pacific ethnopsychologies*. Berkeley: University of California Press, pp. 35–79.

Lutz, C. (1987). Goals, events and understanding in Ifaluk emotion theory. In Dorothy Holland & Naomi Quinn (Eds), *Cultural models in language and thought*. Cambridge University Press, pp. 290–312.

Medin, D.L. (1989). Concepts and conceptual structure. *American Psychologist, 44*, 1469–1481.

Morice, R.D. (1977). Know your speech community. *Aboriginal Health Worker, 1*(1), 4–91.

Myers, F.R. (1976). *'To have and to hold': a study of persistence and change in Pintupi social life*. Ph.D. Thesis, Bryn Mawr.

Myers, F.R. (1979). Emotions and the self: a theory of personhood and political order among Pintupi Aborigines. *Ethos, 7*, 343–370.

Ortony, A. & Clore, G.L. (1989). Emotions, moods, and conscious awareness. *Cognition and Emotion, 3*(2), 125–137.

Ortony, A., Clore, G.L. & Collins, A. (1988). *The cognitive structure of emotions*. Cambridge University Press.

Rosaldo, M. (1980). *Knowledge and passion: Ilongot notions of self and social life*. Cambridge University Press.

Rosaldo, M. (1984). Toward an anthropology of self and feeling. In R.A. Shweder & R.A. LeVine (Eds), *Culture theory: essays on mind, self, and emotion*. Cambridge University Press, pp. 137–157.

Russell, J.A. (1989). Culture, scripts, and children's understanding of emotion. In C. Saarni & P.L. Harris (Eds), *Children's understanding of emotion*. Cambridge: Cambridge University Press, pp. 293–318.

Russell, J.A. & Bullock, M. (1986). Fuzzy concepts and the perception of emotion in facial expressions. *Social Cognition, 4*, 309–341.

Spiro, M.E. (1984). Some reflections on cultural determinism and relativism with special reference to emotion and reason. In R.A. Schweder & R.A. LeVine (Eds), *Culture theory: essays on mind, self, and emotion*. Cambridge University Press, pp. 323–346.

Vértes, A.O. (1989). Language and affective behaviour: Their historical changes and psychosomatic diseases. *Annales Universitatis Scientiarum Budapestinensis. Sectio linguistica. Tomus XVIII*.

Wierzbicka, A. (1972). *Semantic primitives*. Frankfurt: Athenäum.

Wierzbicka, A. (1973). The semantic structure of words for emotions. In R. Jakobson, C.H. van Schooneveld, & D.S. Worth (Eds), *Slavic poetics: essays in honour of Kiril Taranovsky*. The Hague: Mouton, pp. 499–505.

Wierzbicka, A. (1980). *Lingua mentalis: the semantics of natural language*. Sydney/New York: Academic Press.

Wierzbicka, A. (1985). *Lexicography and conceptual analysis*. Ann Arbor: Karoma.

Wierzbicka, A. (1986). Human emotions: universal or culture-specific? *American Anthropologist, 88*(3), 584–594.

Wierzbicka, A. (1987). *English speech act verbs: a semantic dictionary*. Sydney: Academic Press.

Wierzbicka, A. (1988a). L'amour, la colère, la joie, l'ennui: la sémantique des émotions dans une perspective transculturelle. *Langages, 89*, 97–101.

Wierzbicka, A. (1988b). *The semantics of grammar*. Amsterdam: John Benjamins.

Wierzbicka, A. (1988c). Emotions across cultures: similarities and differences—a rejoinder to Konstantin Kolenda. *American Anthropologist, 90*(4), 982–983.

Wierzbicka, A. (1989a). Semantic primitives and lexical universals. *Quaderni di Semantica, 10*(1), 103–121. (Round table on semantic primitives, 1.)

Wierzbicka, A. (1989b). Semantic primitives: the expanding set. *Quaderni di Semantica, 10*(2) (Round table on semantic primitives, 2.)

Wierzbicka, A. (1989c). Soul and mind: linguistic evidence for ethnopsychology and cultural history. *American Anthropologist, 91*(1), 41–58.

Wierzbicka, A. (1990a). The meaning of color terms: semantics, culture and cognition. *Cognition Linguistics, 1*(1), 99–150.

Wierzbicka, A. (1990b). The semantics of emotions: fear and its relatives. *Australian Journal of Linguistics, 10*(2), 133–138.

Wierzbicka, A. (1991a). *Cross-cultural pragmatics: the semantics of human interaction*. Berlin: Mouton de Gruyter, pp. 383–415.

Wierzbicka, A. (1991b). Lexical universals and universals of grammar. In Michel Kefer & Johann van der Auwera (Eds), *Meaning and grammar*. Berlin: Mouton de Gruyter.

Wierzbicka, A. (1992). *Semantics, culture and cognition*. New York: Oxford University Press.

Zajonc, R.B. (1980). Feeling and thinking: preferences need no inferences. *American Psychologist, 35*, 151–175.

Postscript

It will probably be agreed that one useful way to approach the issue of "basic emotions" is to investigate the differences in emotional expression between adults and young children. From this point it is interesting to note that Camras' paper (this issue, p. 270) casts doubt on the assumption that there is "an underlying innate emotion or 'discrete set of neural processes' (Izard & Malatesta, 1987) for each basic or 'primary' emotion". As Camras (p. 272) points out: "The morphological differences between adult and infant expressions as well as the morphological commonalities among the Affex-specified infant negative affect expressions might be interpreted as evidence for less differentiated negative emotion experiences in infants."

Thus, contrary to the hypothesis that small children may have a fully differentiated emotional keyboard (Shweder, 1991, pp. 285–259), "with each key being a discrete emotion: disgust, interest, distress, anger, fear, contempt, shame, shyness, guilt, and so on". Camras' paper suggests that in the early stages of a baby's life there may be very little differentiation of expressive signals, and certainly nothing like a differentiated emotional keyboard of discrete emotions. It is true that Shweder is talking of 4-year-olds, and Camras of much younger babies, but the main issue is whether the "keyboard" is innate and universal or whether it is culturally constituted.

Camras' findings suggest that perhaps young infants may have at their disposal only one undifferentiated expressive signal of "negative affect". In terms of universal semantic primitives, this undifferentiated negative affect can be represented as follows:

I feel something bad

As Izard and Malatesta (1987, p. 506) put it, "the physical distress expression is . . . present at birth". One can wonder, however, why the newborn baby's screwed up and crying face has to be interpreted in terms of "physical distress" rather than a more general "ill-feeling" (I feel something bad)—including, perhaps, existential terror? (Compare William Blake: "My mother groan'd! My father wept./Into the dangerous world I leapt:/Helpless, naked, piping loud:/Like a fiend hid in a cloud".)

Camras' data suggest further that the earliest differentiation of the "negative affect states" is not one between "anger" and "distress-pain" (all complex and English-specific categories) but between two much simpler and much more universal states:

A. something bad is happening
   I feel something bad because of this

B. something bad is happening to me
   I feel something bad because of this

Camras (p. 272) writes: ". . . two infant expressions (the 'anger' and 'distress-pain' configurations) are morphologically indistinguishable save that the eyes are open for anger and closed for distress-pain". I suggest that the "closed eyes" face can perhaps be interpreted as an "introverted" signal: "Something bad is happening to me"; whereas the "open eyes" face can be interpreted as an "extroverted" or neutral signal: "Something bad is happening". Camras observes (pp. 272) that:

... the Affex-specified anger configuration is the most common discrete negative facial expression in all studies presenting any form of negative elicitor to infants over 2 months of age: e.g. DPT inoculation, arm restraint, cookie removal, separation from mother, contingency interruption, and mothers' facial and vocal expressions of sadness.

This wide range of situations is consistent not with the concept of "anger" but with the more general cognitive structure (A) posited here ("something bad is happening—I feel something bad because of this").

The fact that so-called "distress-pain expressions are the predominant response shown by 2-month-olds to clearly painful DPT inoculations" (p. 272) (although in older infants they have also been observed in face-to-face-interaction with mothers) is consistent with the proposed configuration (B) "something bad is happening TO ME—I feel something bad because of this"). Camras' observation (p. 273) that the "distress-pain" pattern was also seen "in response to elicitors that were not likely to be causing physical pain or discomfort (e.g. termination of physical contact with mother; bathing; being moved, lifted or leaned; pacifier removal)" points in the same direction.

It should be emphasised that components such as "(I think) something bad is happening" and "I feel something bad" are not meant to represent "read-outs" of the baby's actual thoughts. (I am not questioning here Izard and Malatesta's claim (p. 509) that "the emotion system can operate independently of cognition", and the view that a baby can have "feelings" before it can have "thoughts" seems to me rather plausible.) Rather, components of this kind are intended to capture the "meaning" of the baby's facial expression, as it would be normally interpreted by other people. The baby's face makes other people think:

> this baby feels something bad
> sometimes people think something like this:
> > something bad is happening to me
> because of this, they feel something bad
> this baby feels something like this

This does not commit us to the view that the baby actually "thinks" something, and at the same time it allows for the possibility of effective communication with the preverbal infant based on an "innate expression-feeling concordance", as posited by Izard and Malatesta (1987, p. 516). (Technical terms, such as "appraisal", which are often used in the literature about emotions, tend to obscure the difference between two different concepts: "thinking" and "knowing". In particular, it is easier to attribute to a newborn infant the capacity for "appraisal" than the capacity for "thought". The use of simple and intuitively intelligible words such as *think* and *know*, forces us, I think, to give a sharper focus to our questions.)

In addition to the potentially meaningful contrast between closed eyes and open eyes, Camras draws also attention to the potential significance of the contrast between the opening and the closing of the mouth. She writes (p. 273):

> ... the distress-pain, anger, and sadness patterns were frequently seen together in a single episode of crying. During these episodes, the three facial configurations appeared to be differentially associated with opening vs. closing the mouth and thus the waxing and waning of the crying response. Together, these observations suggest that the anger and distress-pain patterns are distress responses of increasing intensity while the sadness pattern may reflect a waning or relatively low level of distress.

(Camras appears to be using here the words *distress* in two different senses: In the expression *distress-pain* it is contrasted with *anger* and *sadness*, whereas when used on its own it appears to stand for a more general "negative affect".) I suggest that the semantic contrast between opening and not opening the mouth can be interpreted in terms of an "active" (C) and "passive", "helpless" attitude (D):

C. I want to do something
D. I can't do anything

In C, the act of opening the mouth can be interpreted as a signal of a desire to do something (for example, cry); in D, the closed mouth (which for a human being is an unmarked state) is interpreted not as an act of closing the mouth, but as an absence of an act of opening the mouth, that is, as a signal of a passive state. This passive state, in combination with the components "something bad is happening (to me)" and "I feel something bad because of this" is likely to be interpreted in terms of something like helplessness.

As component C is part of the meaning of the English words *anger* and *distress*, and D, part of the meaning of the English word *sadness* (cf. Wierzbicka, in press a), it is easy to see why the words *anger*, *distress*, and *sadness* may come to mind when the expressions in question are being analysed. In fact, however, the cognitive structures involved appear to be not those associated with the English words *anger*, *distress*, and *sadness* (in the normal sense of these words), but the following ones:

1. A+C. *"negative affect", open eyes, opening of the mouth*:
   something bad is happening
   I feel something bad because of this
   I want to do something

2. B+C. *"negative affect", closed eyes, opening of the mouth*:
   something bad is happening to me
   I feel something bad because of this
   I want to do something

3. A+D. *"negative affect", open eyes, closed mouth*:
   something bad is happening
   I feel something bad because of this
   (if I could, I would want to do something)
   (I can't do anything)

4. B+D. *"negative affect", closed eyes, closed mouth*:
   something bad is happening to me
   I feel something bad because of this
   (if I could, I would want to do something)
   (I can't do anything)

The two last lines in configurations 3 and 4 above are given in parentheses, because if the closed mouth is regarded as an unmarked state then perhaps no meaning needs to be attributed to it. At the same time, the combination of a closed mouth with the first two components of 3 and 4 (especially 4) may well invite the inference that the infant feels helpless and passive, and consequently, for an Anglo observer, bring to mind the word *sadness* rather than the word *anger*.

Finally, the differentiation of the negative affect expressions in terms of "intensity", repeatedly mentioned by Camras, can be portrayed in terms of the universal conceptual primitive "very":

E. something VERY bad is happening (to me)
F. I feel something VERY bad because of this

It should be noted that Camras' observations concerning the significance of elements of "facial behaviour" such as open eyes vs. closed eyes or open mouth vs. closed mouth appear to lend support to Ortony and Turner's (1990) ideas about "dissociable components of facial expressions" and "dissociable components of emotions". For example, wide open eyes (with the upper eyelids raised) can be associated with many different emotional states, including those which the English language identifies as *surprise*, *fear*, *horror*, and (some varieties of) *anger*, and a facial expression including this component can be interpreted in many different ways, depending on the other facial components with which this one is combined (as well as on the other bodily clues, and also situational clues). Nonetheless, the facial component: "raised upper eyelids" can be assigned a constant, invariant semantic component along the lines of "I want to know more about this". Recognising the importance of facial components in human expressive behaviour does not force us to reject the possibility that there may also be some innate full-face emotional expressions. Izard and Malatesta (1987, p. 515) say that "there is developmental change from reflex— or instinct-like full-face expressions—to more controlled and limited configurations of emotion signals"; perhaps the initial undifferentiated signal "I feel something bad" constitutes such a full-face expression. The "Duchenne smile", which combines the raising of the corners of the mouth with the contraction of the muscle that orbits the eye, may be regarded as another full-face expression, with an undifferentiated "positive" meaning: "I feel something good" (cf. Davidson et al., 1990; Ekman, 1982; Ekman, Davidson, & Friesen, 1990).

In conclusion, Camras' finding (p. 273) that "considerable overlap was observed among elicitors of the Affex-defined expressions of distress-pain, anger, sadness, and to some extent, disgust", seems inconsistent with the interpretation of infants' facial expressions in terms of the differential emotions theory, and it underscores the inadequacy of an analytical framework which operates with global labels such as *anger*, *distress* or *sadness*. By contrast, semantic components phrased in terms of lexical universals such as "good", "bad", "happen (to)", "do", and so on, allow us, I believe, to offer interpretations much more consistent with empirical findings such as those reported in Camras' illuminating and intriguing paper. They also open possibilities for greater precision in the "component" approach to the study of emotional expression, initiated by the important paper by Ortony and Turner (1990). (For further discussion, see Wierzbicka, in press b.) The use of semantic components allows us to interpret human subjective experience, human conceptualisation of experience, and the reflection of experience in the human face, in terms of a unitary and highly flexible framework, and helps us to reach for true cognitive constants, hidden behind variable, imprecise, and culturally determined labels.

Manuscript recieved 23 October 1991
Revised manuscript received 21 November 1991

REFERENCES

Davidson, R.J., Ekman, P. Saron, C.D., Senulis, J.A., & Friesen, W.V. (1990). Approach/withdrawal and cerebral asymmetry: Emotional expression and brain physiology. I. *Journal of Personality and Social Psychology, 58*, 330–341.

Ekman, P. (1982). *Emotion in the human face* (2nd edn). Cambridge University Press.

Ekman, P. Davidson, R.J., & Friesen, W.V. (1990). The Duchenne smile: Emotional expression and brain physiology. II. *Journal of Personality and Social Psychology, 58,* 342–353.

Izard, C.E. & Malatesta, C.Z. (1987). Perspectives on emotional development. I: Differential emotions, theory of early emotional development. In J.D. Osofsky (Ed.), *Handbook of infant development* (2nd edn). New York: Wiley, pp. 494–554.

Ortony, A. & Turner, T.J. (1990). What's basic about basic emotions? *Psychological Review, 97,* 314–331.

Shweder, R.A. (1991). *Thinking through cultures: Expeditions in cultural psychology.* Cambridge, MA.: Harvard University Press.

Wierzbicka, A. (In press a). Defining emotion concepts. *Cognitive Science.*

Wierzbicka, A. (In press b). Reading human faces: Emotion components and universal semantics. *Pragmatics and Cognition.*

Subject Index

Action plans, 182, 206–207
Action readiness, 181–182
Adaptation, 161, 170–171, 246–247, *see also Evolution*
Affex coding system, 271–275, 279
Anger, 174, 193, 226
  in animals, 179
  ANS activity, 179, 181
  approach and non-approach, 263–264
  children, 231, 264
  facial expression labelling, 308–309
  facial expressions, 175–176
  family of expressions, 172–173
  and goals, 209, 211–212, 231
  infants, 272–276, 279, 314–318
  and ("something like anger", 303–307
Animal studies, 162, *see also Primates; Rats*
Antecedent events, 183–184, 227–229
Appraisal theory, 163–164, 315–316
  categories or variants of basic emotions, 166, 173–174
  definitions of emotions, 166
  elicitation of emotion, 163–164, 167, 227–229
  and evolution, 171
  independence of components, 165–166, 210–213
  mechanisms, 187–189, 226, 228
Approach/withdrawal, 163, 182, 231, 247, 252, 259–265
  and CNS, 260–265
Argentina, facial expression labelling, 309
Attitudes, emotional, 194
Autonomic nervous system (ANS), 179–183
  action-specific changes, 253–254
  duration of response, 186
  and emotion, 167, 253
  emotion regulation, 255–259
  and expression, 184–185
Awe, 191, 193

Babies, *see Infants*
Basic emotions, 162–167
  in adults, 270

arguments against, 210–213, 232, 245–265, 269–281
arguments for, 169–196, 201–221, 225–242
characteristics distinguishing, 174–189, 192–193, 209–210
vs. components of emotions, 165–166, 202, 210–213, 221, 318
definition of, 170–171, 196–197, 202
in development, 271
expressive development, 269–281
and language, 286, 296–297
possible candidates, 193, 208–213
testability of, 218–220
Blends of emotions, 194–195
Brazil, facial expression labelling, 309

Central nervous system (CNS), 182–183
  and facial expressions, 185
  hemispheric specialisation and approach/withdrawal, 260–265
Characteristics of basic emotions, 174–189, 192–193, 209–210
  automatic appraisal mechanism, 187–189
  brief duration, 185–187
  coherence in response systems, 184–185
  comparable expressions in other animals, 178–179, 248
  distinctive universal signals, 175–178, 248, 251
  emotion-specific physiology, 179–183, 248, 251
  quick onset, 185
  unbidden occurrence, 189
  universal antecedent events, 183–184, 248
Children, 239
  anger, 264
  emotional lexicon, 241
  fear expressions, 250, 254
  goals and emotions, 229, 238
  happiness and approach, 252
  infants' facial expressions, 271–276, 313–318
  socialisation, 239–241
  thoughts and emotions, 315–316